Properly Defining Sin:

Defending the Biblical Definition

Properly Defining Sin
Defending the Biblical Definition

Copyright 2023 Brian Black

Heritage Publications
Middleburg, PA
drbriandblack@gmail.com

"... a book that exalts the power of God and the atonement of Christ to deal conclusively with sin, both in principle and in action."
~**Leonard L. Sankey**, former General Secretary of InterChurch Holiness Convention

I highly recommend this new book by Dr. Brian Black. In a day of confusion on the subject of sin, Dr. Black writes with clarity and certainty. The overview of various doctrinal camps' interpretation of sin is helpful to understanding our definition of sin. The historical review of the doctrine of sin is well documented. This is a needed book in our day.
~**Dr. John A. Whitaker**, Vice-President of Union Bible College; Conference President of the Pilgrim Holiness Church of New York

Dr. Black, you have supplied much needed material to help students and teachers who are attempting to defend the correct Wesleyan definition of sin. I like the way you have organized the material, and I am confident that it will be helpful. Thank you for your diligent research in putting this volume together. God Bless!
~**Dr. Paul. Kaufman**, Ph.D., Division of Bible & Theology Chair, Hobe Sound Bible College

When I got saved and was introduced into the Conservative Holiness Movement in 1978, there were some things that were just understood. One of those was the definition of sin. In Bible College, Dr. Leslie Wilcox's course on Theology of Holiness confirmed that. But today, teaching has infiltrated our movement that is causing many of our young people to question Biblical truth and our spiritual heritage. Dr. Black has taken the time to delineate for us the Biblical definition of sin and our defense of it. If the message of entire sanctification is going to be given with no uncertain sound, it begins right here in the pages of this book.
~**Daniel R. Hardy, Sr.**, President, Allegheny Wesleyan College

Brian Black is a man of God, husband, father, Christian scholar, whose children speak for him in the gates (Psalm 127:5). All four of his sons have pursued advanced studies in Bible and doctrine; they join him in publishing their findings. Dr. Black is highly knowledgeable in church history, and more particularly, the history and literature of the Holiness Movement. In this book, he shines the light from many Christian writers across the centuries to demonstrate the biblical position on sin. Through the array of Wesleyan holiness authors, he demonstrates the prominence in the Holiness Movement of defining sin as a willful transgression against a known law of God and how that relates to our understanding of entire sanctification. Faithfully, he declares there is victory over sin!

~**Timothy L. Cooley**, Sr., Ph D, Academic Dean, Penn View Bible Institute

In the 1700's, John Wesley acutely defined sin as "a willful transgression against a known law of God." We live in a day when there is much confusion about the definition of sin. Now, in this 21st century, Dr. Brian Black is especially gifted in writing this exceptional and essential book, *Properly Defining Sin.* As Rev. Black states, "Perhaps the clearest definition of sin in Scripture is found in 1 John 3:4." This verse states, "Whosoever committeth sin transgresseth also the law: for sin is the transgression of the law." I highly recommend the prayerful reading of this comprehensive book, knowing that any searching soul can come to the knowledge of a transformed, holy life without sin.

~**Michael D. Marshall,** former President of Allegheny Wesleyan Methodist Connection

It must be that one of Satan's top priorities is to cloud and misstate the Bible view of sin and salvation. Nothing gets closer to who we are and who God provided for us to be in the plan of redemption than this. The consequences of misstating this definition are never inconsequential. Every generation needs someone to rise up and state it clearly. The Biblical/Wesleyan concept of sin and salvation is obviously the passion of the author. To present his position, it is clear in these pages that Black appeals to 1) The Bible 2) Historical context and 3) Reason. I have been struck by the beautiful, victorious concept of sin and salvation presented in these pages that fare very well in all three arenas. The Bible/Wesleyan theology presented here is Biblical, historical, and reasonable. To reject his conclusions, we would be forced into the undesirable position of defending either 1) The right of a Christian to commit sin as a Christian or 2) The inability of a Christian to keep from sinning as a Christian. Dr. Brian Black presents the beautiful alternative to both of these undesirable possibilities. It is the Bible/Wesleyan position on sin and salvation. It is with great joy that I recommend *Properly Defining Sin*. This book is a clear presentation of Wesleyan theology that is desperately needed today.

~Darrell Stetler, pastor and church leader

Dedication

To my wife

Sharon

whose support and assistance made this work possible.

And to my sons

Nicholas Black and Caleb Black

whose research was invaluable in writing this book.

Table of Contents

1. Summary of the Doctrine 1
2. Overview and Importance of the Topic 15
3. Competing Evangelical Theories of Salvation 27
4. Understanding the Wesleyan Concept of Salvation 33
5. Reformed Views of Salvation 47
6. Defining Sin Biblically 62
7. Summarizing the Definition of Sin 75
8. The Calvinist Understanding of Sin 83
9. The Keswickian Understanding of Sin 93
10. The Relational Definition of Sin 102
11. Scriptural Evidences that Christians do not Sin 107
12. Historical Understanding of the Doctrine of Sin 127
13. The Concept of Sin from Wesley to the Present 140
14. Defining the Sin Nature 158
15. The Definition of Sin Affects all Theology 164
16. Philosophical and Theological Fallacies 171
Appendix A. Dealing with Sin in 1 John 3 183
Appendix B. Answering Calvinists Objections 197
Appendix C. Righteousness is Required for Heaven 211

Preface

The evangelical churches in America today teach two radically different and competing views of salvation. One view states that all Christians sin daily, while the other teaches that Christians can and must live without sinning. A person's eternal destiny is based upon believing and following the correct doctrine. The foundation of this doctrinal division is a proper definition of sin. This is why a study of the biblical definition of sin is of utmost importance. Reformed theology presented the idea that sin is a failure to be perfect like God. Methodist theology maintains that sin is a voluntary choice to disobey God. The Bible teaches that it is possible, through grace to live a consistent, obedient life; accordingly, it is possible to live a sinless life.

The Calvinistic definition of sin leads to the belief that one continues to be sinful throughout all of life, and that Christ's righteousness merely covers up for a person's continued sinfulness. Logically, this leads to the eternal security position that a one-time act of faith in being born again is sufficient for eternal salvation. From this misconception comes the teaching that it really does not matter for salvation how morally evil a person is.

The Wesleyan position teaches that one is actually made righteous and cleansed from sin through the grace of God and the power of the Holy Spirit. One must live a victorious, sinless life to be eligible for heaven. This doctrine is based upon the biblical principle that sin is a willful choice to rebel against God. If after being converted a person returns back to a life of rebellion against God, he has rejected salvation and is no longer eligible for heaven.

The doctrine of sin is the foundation for these competing views of the Christian life and eternal salvation. This doctrine needs to be studied to properly understand God's plan of salvation and to accurately understand those of differing theologies. This book is attempting to define these differences and bring a biblical, logical, and historical understanding of the issue into focus.

Chapter 1
Summary of the Doctrine

Is living a righteous life necessary for heaven? Does the born again experience transform a person into a new creature in Christ (2Co 5:17)? Does salvation enable one to live without sinning or does it merely cover up sin? Our eternal destiny may hang upon how these questions are answered. The core of Wesleyan theology is the understanding that God delivers from all sin, both in practice and in heart as John Wesley states, "The whole thing which I contend for [is] an entire deliverance from sin."[1] Understanding the correct definition of sin is a necessity for correct doctrinal beliefs. W.T. Purkiser notes, "One of the most important issues emerging in modern evangelical circles is concerned with the definition of sin. It is more than a theological argument over the proper usage of terms. It goes directly to the heart of Christian life and experience. It has a bearing on every branch of the doctrine of salvation. Our conception of the whole plan of redemption is radically affected thereby."[2]

James B. Chapman, a former Church of the Nazarene General Superintendent, recalled, "One day a man accused me of being an extremist because I preached that one can be saved from all sin in this life. I admitted the charge, but answered that there is no escape from being an extremist-either for Christ or for sin. For if we hold that Jesus Christ can save from all sin, we are extremists for Christ, but if we hold that Jesus cannot save from all sin, then we are extremists for sin.

> Sin is a moral issue in which a person voluntarily disobeys and rebels against God.

---

[1] John Wesley, *The Works of John Wesley*, 3rd ed, vol. 12 (London: Wesleyan Methodist Book room, 1872), 416.

[2] W.T. Purkiser, cited by Donald Metz: Donald Metz: *Studies in Biblical Holiness* (Kansas City: Beacon Hill Press, 1971), 72.

And I elect to be an extremist for Jesus."[3]

Properly understanding sin is at the core of doctrine regarding salvation. This is not merely a debate over terminology. Scripture is very clear that, at the Judgment, God will either condemn one to hell or allow one into heaven based upon the sinlessness of his life. The issue of dealing with sin has divided all of Christianity into theological groups. It has divided evangelicals into the Calvinistic and Wesleyan camps. Evangelicals are in agreement with the basic understanding of a corrupting sin nature which has been passed down to all humanity from Adam. They are in agreement that all people have chosen to commit sin and are accordingly guilty before God. Agreement includes the concept of human failure, infirmities, and ignorance which leads to wrong actions which one needs to confess both to God and to those who were wronged. The difference occurs in understanding which actions are correctly termed *sin*. Wesleyans believe that God can empower a person to live without sinning and to cleanse the heart from the sin nature. Actions that are the result of infirmity or ignorance would not be considered sins in the proper sense by Wesleyans.

In general, Wesleyans believe that sin is a moral issue in which a person voluntarily disobeys and rebels against God. Calvinists believe that sin is a failure to come up to an objective standard of righteousness. Both Calvinists and Wesleyans agree that, because of the Fall, human beings cannot meet that objective standard while in this life. Calvinists conclude, therefore, that all people sin continually and constantly even after being saved. Wesleyans, in contrast, focus upon the voluntary aspect of sin and do not feel that unavoidable human failures should properly be called sin. This terminological difference is critically significant because it lays the foundation for one's beliefs regarding salvation, and therefore, entrance into heaven!

If a Christian constantly sins because of his humanity, then he is never truly righteous. According to the Calvinist doctrine, a person would merely be considered righteous because he is clothed in the righteousness of Christ, although he is still sinful. In contrast, if sin is

---

[3] James Blaine Chapman, *Holiness Triumphant, and Other Sermons on Holiness* (Kansas City: Beacon Hill Press 1946), 16. https://a.co/2rZc2J1.

defined as a choice, a person can live without sinning and be truly righteousness. At issue is whether a Christian is allowed to sin or not in order to go to heaven. This becomes a heaven or hell issue. If Christ's righteousness is only imputed to us but not imparted and a person is still unrighteousness, does it really matter how many sins one commits? Is not the blood of Christ sufficient for all sins? Can a person become converted at a young age, live like the devil the rest of his life, and still go to heaven at death? Since Calvinists believe that all "Christians" sin, how much sin is acceptable? An Arminian concept of universal salvation followed by the eternal security doctrine is convincing millions of people that they are headed for heaven while, in fact, they are headed to hell. This has also hindered evangelism, since few believe that they are lost.

Some Calvinists would strongly disagree that a person could live a licentious lifestyle and still be a Christian. They would emphasize that being regenerated by God in the salvation experience changes the person who would thereafter live a transformed life. Works would then be the evidence of whether one had faith. Some Calvinists would hold that if a person did not live a changed life, he had never been saved. Yet, many an individual has been converted, lived a good life for many years with a testimony of being a Christian, then fallen away and lived a wicked life and died in that condition. How then can a person know that he is a Christian and not self-deceived? If works are the evidence of salvation, is he not then trusting in his works? Even if a person is still living a good life, how can he know that he is not deceived about his salvation? If given sufficient temptation, would he fall away? This is not eternal security; this is a very insecure position. Having a correct assurance of being right with God and making it to heaven is what truly counts.

> Truth will never contradict itself. If two passages of Scripture seem to disagree then the conflict must be resolved.

Wesleyans are in agreement that salvation is by faith, and there is nothing anyone can do to merit salvation. No works are acceptable which would undo the sins which have been committed. Once a person has been convicted by the Spirit and repents of sin, all one can do is to cast himself down at the foot of the cross and trust in the death of Christ for his salvation. It is the grace of God which works through the whole process, convicting of sin, enabling one to believe from the heart for salvation, and empowering one to live a righteous life. The Wesleyan/Holiness belief holds that the time of probation is throughout one's entire life, and after being saved, a person may choose to later reject God by denying the faith or by deliberate disobedience. Entrance to heaven is based upon enduring to the end and living a holy life. Warnings against losing the faith are one of the major themes of Hebrews, 2 Peter, Jude, and 2 Timothy. A majority of the Scriptures which give the guidelines for entrance to heaven emphasize the necessity of holiness of life (Mt 7:21-23, Ro 2:5-13, He 12:14, Re 20:13).

Truth will never contradict itself. If two passages of Scripture seem to disagree then the conflict must be resolved. Logic demands that contradicting concepts cannot both be correct. Likewise, only one set of theological truths are correct. Calvinistic theology and Arminian theology cannot both be accurate. One must be wrong. Postmodernism has challenged the concept of absolute truth by teaching that each person can have his own truth; however, truth is still truth if everyone or if no one believes it. The earth is either flat or round and that is independent of the conjectures of society. God's plan of salvation is true independently of whether it is approved by most scholars in religious society or whether it is not.

Issues relating to the means of salvation and qualification for entrance into heaven at the Judgment are of supreme importance. Many believe that their salvation is secure based upon the current presuppositions of the eternal security doctrine. This doctrine is a twisted form of what Calvinism originally taught and has little historical or biblical validity. Initially, Calvinism believed, that once a person was saved, he would persevere in living a holy life until death, and if a person started living wickedly, it was evidence he had never been saved. However, this new Calvinistic doctrine has led to a false security, and many evil people are confident that they are going to heaven; yet, if they have unforgiven sin in their lives, they will end up in hell. The Wesleyan/Arminian doctrine of backsliding addresses the issue by teaching that a person can choose to reject God after being saved; accordingly, God does not tolerate deliberate evil in the life of one who professes Christianity. Neither Calvinism nor Wesleyan doctrine originally believed anyone living in disobedience to God would be allowed into heaven.

Concepts regarding sin underlie the foundation of the major theological positions of the church world. Reformed theology, as developed by the Calvinists, taught that God predestined those who would be saved and the rest would be lost. Their concept of predestination was based upon the idea that it was impossible to live a sinless life or to have a heart purified of sin; therefore, God chose an elect group of people to whom He imputed the righteousness of Christ which would cover the continual sinning of the justified person. They believed that a person's spiritual state was sinful, but one's standing before God was righteous. In contrast, the Methodist message believed that the grace of God enabled a person to personally choose salvation; furthermore, it taught that one could be delivered from committing sin as well as obtain heart purity from the corruption of indwelling sin.

Reformed theology considered sin to be any failure to be perfect. Although it lacked a Scriptural or an ancient historical basis, this belief dominated the Protestant landscape until challenged by the Methodists. "Implicit in Holiness teachings was a redefinition of sin. . . . [From] the prevailing view in much colonial and 19th-century American Protestantism, . . . this imperfection was simply viewed as part of the human condition, and as a stark contrast to the perfection of God. However, the Holiness Movement viewed sin as a voluntary transgression of one of God's known laws."[4] John Wesley went back to the early church for his doctrine of sin. Saint Augustine reveals how thorough and widespread the later doctrine of the Wesleyan/Holiness movement was on sin in the Early Church. He said, "In fact, sin is so much a voluntary evil that it is not sin at all unless it is voluntary. This is so obvious that no one denies it, either of the handful of the learned or of the mass of the unlearned. We must either say that no sin has been

---

[4] Ralph W. Hood, Jr., Peter C. Hill, and W. Paul Williamson, *The Psychology of Religious Fundamentalism* (New York: The Guilford Press, 2005), 59.

committed or confess that it has been willingly committed."[5]

Calvinism and Arminianism are just two of the broad categories. In each of these categories is much variation. Sometimes attempts have been made to blend these two thoughts which came out of the Reformation into a synthesis, but they are contradictory in their foundational philosophy and do not mix well.

The doctrine of sin is perhaps the key foundational doctrine of Scripture. Richard S. Taylor stated that "the doctrines relating to sin form the center around which we build our entire theological system. . . . When our concept of sin is off-center our theology will become distorted."[6] The way in which a person reads and understands Scripture is commonly seen through a theological mindset. Doctrines of the atonement, predestination, the incarnation, salvation, sanctification, and eternal judgment all base their foundational understanding upon the definition of sin. Taylor is correct when he writes, "One who does not have correct views of sin is not apt to have correct views of any other fundamental question."[7]

Definitions of Sin

Sin is a personal choice to voluntarily disobey God. According to the Wesleyan or ethical (also called moral) definition, for an action to be considered sin, it must be done knowingly, intentionally, and willfully in disobedience to the commands of God. John Wesley defined sin saying, "Nothing is sin, strictly speaking, but a voluntary transgression of a known law of God. Therefore, every voluntary break of the law of love is sin: and nothing else if we speak properly. To strain the matter farther is only to make way for Calvinism."[8] This ethical definition has always been the understanding of the church throughout history. Thomas Aquinas, the leading Catholic scholar, quoted Augustine, the leading scholar from the Early Church,

---

[5] St. Augustine, *Of True Religion* (Chicago: Henry Regnery Company, 1964), 24-25.
[6] Richard S. Taylor, *A Right Conception of Sin*, rev. ed. (Salem, OH: Schmul Publishing Co., 2002) 12-13.
[7] Richard S. Taylor, *A Right Conception of Sin*, 13.
[8] John Wesley, *The Works of John Wesley*, 394.

defending this definition. He said, "Every sin is a voluntary act, because, as Augustine states, so true is it that every sin is voluntary, that unless it be voluntary, it is no sin at all."[9]

Wesley's study of the Early Church led him to agree with this concept, stating, "But is 'a voluntary transgression of a known law' a proper definition of sin? . . . It is a definition which has passed uncensored in the church for at least fifteen hundred years."[10] Wesley's definition has been commonly accepted among those whose heritage is from a Methodist background.

The New Testament teaches the same truth and ties knowledge together with sin in the definitions it gives of sin (Ja 4:17, Ro 14:22-23, and 1Jo 3:4). Certainly, every Christian should stand with the Bible and with the historical understanding of Scripture.

One of the best scriptural definitions of sin is from the *Manual of the Church of the Nazarene*. It says, "We believe that actual or personal sin is a voluntary violation of a known law of God by a morally responsible person. It is therefore not to be confused with involuntary and inescapable shortcomings, infirmities, faults, mistakes, failures, or other deviations from a standard of perfect conduct that are the residual effects of the Fall."[11]

> If Christ's death on the cross did not deliver from sin, then the redemptive plan is a stupendous failure.

In contrast to the ethical definition is the legal or absolute definition of sin. This is the definition commonly accepted among those of a Reformed doctrine developed from the teachings of John Calvin. This idea teaches that "sin is anything that falls short of God's moral nature . . . It is plain, then, that the ultimate objective standard is God's absolute moral perfection, and anything that falls short of it is sin."[12]

---

[9] Thomas Aquinas, *The Summa Theologica of Thomas Aquinas*. accessed April 7, 2023, https://www.ccel.org/ccel/aquinas/summa.FS_Q74_A2.html.
[10] John Wesley, *The Works of John Wesley*, 239.
[11] Dean G. Blevins et al., eds., *Church of the Nazarene: Manual, 2017–2021* (Kansas City, MO: Nazarene Publishing House, 2017), 28. https://2017.manual.nazarene.org/section/church-constitution/.
[12] Norman Geisler, *Systematic Theology*, vol. 3 (Minneapolis: Bethany House, 2004), 106.

This would include such things as mistakes or human limitations due to ignorance. According to this definition, all people sin in word, thought, and deed every day.

Scripture teaches that Christians do not sin (1Jn 3:5-10, Ro 6:16-22). The legal definition based upon Reformed theology would make it impossible for any person to meet God's ultimate standard. Any definition which calls improper actions due to ignorance 'sins' goes against the plain teaching of God's Word and logically forces one to accept the concept that saved people sin, cannot be delivered from sinning, but are not held guilty before God for that sin. As Daniel Steele said, "To assert that the Holy God has made sin necessary under the reign of grace is to slander the Father, and pronounce the redemptive plan a stupendous failure."[13] Furthermore, the New Testament does not have separate categories for sin. Sin is simply called sin.

Both the Wesleyan and the Calvinistic concepts of sin have dangers. The legal definition makes everything sin and makes it impossible to live a Christian life. It may make little distinction between human limitations and outright rebellion, to which God is especially opposed. The Wesleyan definition can easily devolve into nothing more than a subjective concept of sin which allows everyone to do that which is right in his own eyes; accordingly, every sin can be excused. The New Testament teaches both the absolute and the subjective aspects of sin. There is a clear code of ethics given in the New Testament for God's people to follow; yet, sin is identified subjectively as disobedience or rebellion to God's known law. Scripture also gives a number of absolute statements with the stern warning that those who commit *such things shall not inherit the kingdom of God* (Ga 5:19-21). A proper Wesleyan understanding is a middle position which recognizes both the absolute and the moral nature of sin. Everyone is under the absolute moral law of God, but this law is applied subjectively by the Spirit upon the hearts and minds of believers. This is the concept of Hebrews 8:8-13 where it states that

---

[13] Daniel Steele, *Love Enthroned* (digital edition) http://wesley.nnu.edu/wesleyctr/books/1801-1900/HDM1892.pdf.

God will write His laws on the minds and the hearts of His people. It is the laws of God, not a person's opinion, which is written upon the heart. Since it is written upon the minds and the heart, it has a subjective application based upon the will and knowledge of the individual.

Appropriately defining sin is a salvation issue. God demands an obedient life in order to enter heaven (Mt. 7:21-23). The doctrines which teach that a person can sin and still go to heaven are deceiving tens of millions into believing that they are going to heaven when they are actually headed for hell. The Apostle John says that anyone who says *I know him, [Christ] and keepeth not his commandments, is a liar, and the truth is not in him* (1Jo 2:4). While it is true that forgiveness is readily available for those who fall, Scripture teaches clearly that keeping God's commands are a necessity in order to know Christ (1Jn 2:1-4).

Another major problem with the idea that all people sin is the doctrine of the incarnation of Jesus Christ. Christ was fully human and was tempted like us, but did not sin (Heb. 4:15). To be fully human, Christ would have had the limitations of humanity. Any doctrine which teaches that humans cannot live above sin undermines the truth that God, as Christ, came in human form; thus, any definition of sin which links human failure with sin, in reality, is a denial of the incarnation. Sin is not a problem of being human, being tempted, being ignorant, or of human failure, but it is a moral issue of disobedience. Since Christ was truly human, He would have been tempted and had normal human limitations. However, since He was never disobedient, He was sinless.

Scriptural Definitions of Sin

The most common Greek word used in the New Testament to refer to sin is the verb *hamartano*. The original etymology of the word meant to miss the mark. But what mark does God want one to hit? Scripture teaches that the mark is to keep the law of God. Those who hold the legal definition simply assume without any biblical basis that the mark is the absolute perfection of God. After demanding righteousness, does God then make it impossible to obtain? Despair is, therefore, the logical outcome of their doctrine. Is hopeless despair God's goal?

Both the Old and the New Testaments define sin as failure to keep the law, but the New Covenant which we are under says that the law is now written upon our hearts and minds, making it impossible to ignorantly sin (He 8:8-13).This law is also the law of love lived out by a Spirit- possessed individual who has been transformed by the grace of God (Ga 5:18 & Ro 13:10). Ultimately, the promise that Jesus would "save his people from their sins" (Mt 1:21) becomes possible through the presence of the Holy Spirit in a person's heart (Ac 15:8-9).

Perhaps the clearest definition of sin in Scripture is found in 1 John 3:4. It literally means, *Sin is lawlessness.* The word *lawlessness* has the concept of one who is a criminal and lives in rebellion against the law. It indicates deliberate actions known to be wrong. It is specifically this definition of sin that is used when John asserts that Christians do not sin (1Jn 3:5-10 & 1Jn 5:18).

Jesus teaches the same idea in His dealings with the Pharisees. He said, *If ye were blind, ye should have no sin: but now ye say, We see; therefore your sin remaineth.* (Jo 9:41) These Pharisees had been ignorant of the truth and were not guilty for committing sin; however, when Christ came and was rejected by them, their willful action in rejecting Christ made them guilty of sinful actions. The wrong action itself was not considered sin until it was combined with the knowledge that the action was wrong.

Another New Testament passage that helps to define sin is James 4:17 which says, *Therefore to him that knoweth to do good, and doeth it not, to him it is sin.* Sin is not only doing something that is wrong, but also the failure to do what a person should. This verse teaches us that our responsibility to God is based upon our knowledge. James gives no hint that he is trying to set an impossible standard, but is simply expecting obedience to known truth.

Paul gives a corroborating definition for sin in Romans 14:23. His focus is upon an act which is believed to be done in disobedience to God. The Scripture states that to do something which one believes to be wrong is sin. Paul makes it clear that the action itself was not wrong, but if the person believed it to be wrong, it was a sin to go ahead and do it. Here is a clear-cut example of a choice between the legal definition and the moral/ethical definition. The legal concept says it is not a sin because it is not actually wrong while the moral definition says it is a sin because a person is doing something that he thinks is in disobedience to God. Scripture takes the position that sin is a moral failure.

Another passage Paul uses to describe sin is Romans 5:19. It states, *For as by one man's disobedience many were made sinners, so by the obedience of one shall many be made righteous.* This passage identifies that disobedience causes one to become a sinner. The Fall identifies sin with deliberate disobedience. It was not failure, infirmity, or human ignorance that made Adam a sinner; it was deliberate disobedience. According to Paul in this passage, sin is willful disobedience to God.

Christians Do Not Sin

Scripture is emphatic that Christians keep God's commands and do not sin. Any definition of sin must take into account this requirement. While some feel that the Old Testament teaches that a person cannot live a sinless life, this certainly is not the clear teaching of any New Testament passage. There is greater victory for the Christian since the Spirit came at Pentecost and now indwells the hearts of believers. The following are several passages which teach this truth.

1. *In him [Christ] is no sin. Whosoever abideth in him sinneth not: Whosoever sinneth hath not seen him, neither known him* (1Jo 3:5-6). Our sinlessness comes from abiding in Christ, Who is sinless. The Greek tense is used in this passage as a present statement of fact. Some misunderstand the use of the present indicative Greek tense and accept some sin but not a continual practice of sin; however, if sins of ignorance exist, then sin is constantly practiced.[14] Some other places where this tense is used as a statement of fact are for Christ's birth (Mt 2:4) and the second coming (1Th 5:2). These events clearly are not continual, but one-time occurrences.

2. 1 John 3:9 says, *His [Christ's] seed remaineth in him: and he cannot sin, because he is born of God.* As long as Christ is in a person,

---

[14] More information on the correct meaning of the passage in 1 John 3 is given in the appendix.

it is impossible to sin. If a person chooses to sin, Christ leaves.
3. 1 John 5:18 records, *We know that whosoever is born of God sinneth not.* Anyone who has the life of God inside of him does not sin.
4. In the book of Romans, Paul teaches total victory over sin. Three times in Romans chapter six the Bible states that Christians are *free from sin (6:7, 18, and 24)*. If Christians are free from sin, then they do not sin.
5. If a person sins, it identifies that individual with the devil. In 1John 3:8 it says, *He that committeth sin is of the devil.*
6. Exodus 32:33 says, *And the LORD said unto Moses, Whosoever hath sinned against me, him will I blot out of my book.* God does erase names out of the book of life, and it is on the basis of intentional, deliberate sin.

The Consequences of Sin - Missing Heaven and Going to Eternal Hell

Even small sins separate a person from God, just as it did Adam and Eve in the garden. The person who sins shall die eternally (Eze 18:20). Two synonyms for sin are unrighteousness and iniquity (1Jn 5:10, Mt 7:23). Iniquity means to violate the law. God promises that the righteous go into life eternal, and those who are unrighteous will go away into everlasting punishment (Mt 25:46). At the judgment, Christ will say, *Depart from me, ye that work iniquity* (Mt. 7:21-23).

1Corinthians 6:9-10 states, *The unrighteous shall not inherit the kingdom of God. Be not deceived: neither fornicators,* [committing sex before or outside of marriage] *. . . nor abusers of themselves with mankind,* [homosexuals] *nor thieves, nor covetous . . . shall inherit the kingdom of God.* Some other passages which teach this concept that entrance to heaven depends upon a holy life are Hebrews 10:26-27, Matthew 13:41-42, Matthew 19:16-17, Romans 2:6-9, 2Thessalonians 1:8, Hebrews 12:14, Galatians 5:19-21, Ephesians 5:5, Hebrews 5:9, and Revelation 21:8.

Testing the Two Definitions

The best way to test the accuracy of the meaning of sin is to compare Scriptures using the two definitions. The legal definition

(God-like perfection) often makes no sense at all while the Wesleyan definition (intentional disobedience to God) always fits perfectly. Here are a few Scriptures which show the legal definition for sin does not make sense. I have made a comparison in each of the following verses. The word *sin* is replaced with the contrasting definitions.
Examples:

1. Timothy 5:20: *Them that sin rebuke before all, that others also may fear.*
   Legal definition: Them that fail to be perfect like God rebuke before all, that others also may fear.
   Wesleyan definition: Them that willfully disobey God rebuke before all, that others also may fear.
2. John 8:11: *Jesus said unto her . . . Go, and sin no more.*
   Legal definition: Go, and do not make mistakes and then be perfect like God.
   Wesleyan definition: Go, and willfully disobey God no more.
3. 1 John 3:8: *He that committeth sin is of the devil.*
   Legal definition: He that falls short of being perfect like God is of the devil.
   Wesleyan definition: He that willfully disobeys God is of the devil.
4. 1 John 5:18: *We know that whosoever is born of God sinneth not.*
   Legal definition: We know that whosoever is born of God does not make any mistakes and is absolutely perfect.
   Wesleyan definition: We know that whosoever is born of God does not willfully disobey God.
5. Romans 6:18: *Being then made free from sin.*
   Legal definition: Being then made free from mistakes and any imperfections.
   Wesleyan definition: Being then made free from willful disobedience.

This is an overview of some of the reasons for the historical and biblical definition of sin followed by Wesley. There can be victory over sin here and now in this life. In His death on the cross, Christ not only forgave sin, He also empowered the regenerated person to live a life of victory over all sin. Salvation does not make one perfect in overcoming mistakes, ignorance, infirmity, or human limitations, but it sets one's heart right with God. Salvation enables a person to grow spiritually and develop into the perfect likeness of Christ. As John Wesley said, "True Christianity implies a destruction of the kingdom of sin."[15]

---

[15] John Wesley, *The Works of John Wesley*, 451.

Chapter 2
Overview and Importance of the Topic

Underlying the differences between the Wesleyan/Holiness concept of salvation and the Calvinistic/neo-Calvinistic concepts of salvation is what could be called the winning attitude. Do we expect to live a victorious life and be an overcomer or is our expectation constant defeat by sin? Do we believe that it is impossible to overcome sin in this life? Is our picture of salvation one of personal despair, hopelessness, and defeat? Is this the best the grace of God has to offer? Do we strive to overcome sin and hope that next year our defeats will be fewer? Did the second member of the Trinity, Jesus Christ, die to produce failures? Will He who spoke the world into existence give us more personal victory in this life than continual defeat? The Wesleyan message is one of victory through the overcoming grace and power of the blood of Christ. Any theology that teaches a powerless gospel to give victory over sin is a religion of hopeless despair. In this sense, the incarnation of Christ in identifying with humanity and taking our sin to the cross has empowered believers to victorious Christian living.

> Any theology that teaches a gospel which is powerless to give victory over sin is a religion of hopeless despair.

This principle has always been true in warfare. When hope of successful victory disappears and defeat becomes certain, men will no longer choose to fight. One example of this occurred in World War I. It became a war of attrition with both sides digging trenches and unable to effectively attack. As the war dragged on, it became evident that the side that ran out of soldiers or war supplies first would lose. By the spring of 1917, the French army was reeling. Soldiers refused to attack, mutinied, and their army began to disintegrate. One push by the Germans at this time would have ended the war with a German victory. The French army was collapsing because of continual losses in battle, and the men believed defeat was inevitable. Why fight and die for a lost cause? Psychologically, the army was beaten, and it was over. Morale had to be restored, and French leadership desperately worked to save the day. Their successful argument was that the United States had just entered the war. Given time, American troops would make the difference, and the French and their allies would win the war. It was this hope that kept the French fighting for another year. The following year, French troops, along with the arriving American soldiers, stopped a final German advance. Now the Germans recognized inevitable defeat. Their lines collapsed and were sent reeling in retreat. The German high command then offered to surrender even before any Allied soldiers had invaded German territory.

Do we have a defeatist theology or a victorious theology? Do we expect to be overcomers through Christ, or do we expect failure? If you expect to fail, you will probably not be disappointed. You will be content to continue in sin. However, if you expect the grace and power of God to deliver you from all sin, you will find His power is sufficient. The attitude will make the difference. Yes, you must lay the groundwork and the battles will seem enormous, but overcoming power is given to the believer who trusts Christ for victory. A Calvinist will fail to have victory over sin, even over what is called willful sin because he does not believe it is possible. A losing mentality will destroy a person. The goal is victory, not how to become a better loser. God has better things than defeat for the Christian if one relies upon the power of God rather than his own strength. Read the Scriptures; it is the constant story of victory and overcoming through grace.

Scriptures that Teach Victory

The Bible is all about victory and overcoming power; it is not about a limited salvation with Christians unable to cope with the battles of this life. Note the resounding words of victory in the following verses:

1. *Greater is he that is in you, than he that is in the world* (1Jo 4:4).
2. *For whatsoever is born of God overcometh the world: and this is the victory that overcometh the world, even our faith* (1Jo 5:4).
3. *But thanks be to God, which giveth us the victory through our*

Lord Jesus Christ (1Co 15:57).
4. *Nay, in all these things we are more than conquerors through him that loved us* (Ro 8:37).
5. *He that is begotten of God keepeth himself, and that wicked one toucheth him not* (1Jo 5:18).
6. *Give diligence to make your calling and election sure: for if ye do these things, ye shall never fall* (2Pe 1:10).
7. *I write unto you, young men, because ye have overcome the wicked one* (1Jo 2:13).
8. *He that overcometh, the same shall be clothed in white raiment; and I will not blot out his name out of the book of life* (Re 3:5).

Scripture Teaches Deliverance from all Sin

The very purpose of the coming of Jesus Christ was to *save his people from their sins* (Mt 1:21). The very reason He died on the cross was to make a holy or sanctified group of people (Heb 13:12). Christ came to *destroy the works of the devil* (1Jo 3:8). From the context in 1 John, the major works of the devil that Christ came to destroy was sin in the lives of God's people. The final goal of Jesus was to present *to himself a glorious church, not having spot, or wrinkle, or any such thing; but that it should be holy and without blemish* (Eph 5:27). The perfection of the church in this passage has to do with the moral condition of people in the church. The Christ that shed His blood on the cross according to the divine plan of God certainly did not fail. He overcame and destroyed sin. Daniel Steele stated, "To assert that the Holy God has made a sin necessary under the reign of grace is to slander the Father, and pronounce the redemptive plan a stupendous failure."[1]

> The idea that wicked people are proclaimed as saints by God makes a mockery of God. He is not self-deceived.

Salvation radically transforms an individual; life and Scripture says,

---

[1] Daniel Steele, *Love Enthroned* (digital edition) accessed July 10, 2023, http://wesley.nnu.edu/wesleyctr/books/1801-1900/HDM1892.pdf.

"Therefore if any man be in Christ, he is a new creature: old things are passed away; behold, all things are become new" (2Co 5:17). At salvation, the aid of the Holy Spirit and the grace of God will enable a person to live a life that does not commit sin. A life without sin is even more fully realized when one is given the Holy Spirit and the heart is purified by faith in a second work by the grace of God (Ac 15:8-9). Scripture is very clear that this transformation means a sinless life. In our own strength it is impossible to live a holy life. If a person cannot live as a Christian, it is because he lacks sufficient grace and power of God to have victory. John Wesley stated in his sermon on Christian Perfection, "We may safely affirm with St. John, that since the gospel was given, *'He that is born of God sinneth not.'*"[2] Notice the emphatic teaching of the following Scriptures:

1. *We know that whosoever is born of God sinneth not; but he that is begotten of God keepeth himself* (1Jo 5:18).
2. *Whosoever is born of God doth not commit sin; for his seed remaineth in him: and he cannot sin, because he is born of God* (1Jo 3:9).
3. *Whosoever abideth in him sinneth not: whosoever sinneth hath not seen him, neither known him* (1Jo 3:6).
4. *Being then made free from sin, ye became the servants of righteousness* (Ro 6:18).
5. *But now being made free from sin, and become servants to God, ye have your fruit unto holiness* (Ro 6:22).
6. *Behold, thou art made whole: sin no more, lest a worse thing come unto thee* (Joh 5:14).
7. *And Jesus said unto her, Neither do I condemn thee: go, and sin no more* (Joh 8:11).
8. *Now unto him that is able to keep you from falling, and to present you faultless before the presence of his glory with exceeding joy* (Jude 1:24).

---

[2]John Wesley, *Wesley's Standard Sermons* (Salem, OH: Schmul Publishing Co., repr, 1982), 400.

9. *According as his divine power hath given unto us all things that pertain unto life and godliness* (2Pe 1:3).
10. *For he that hath suffered in the flesh hath ceased from sin* (1Pe 4:1).

Scripture has no concept of a double standard for life. Calvinistic theology, however, teaches a double standard: God only sees a person through the righteous blood of Christ and cannot see the sins which the person continues to commit. This is their concept of imputed righteousness which is just a covering for sin rather than genuine cleansing. It is nothing more than just a way to deceive God. However, God will not be tricked! If God who knows all things proclaims one as righteous, he is righteous. If God says one is just, he is truly just. Ed Parish Sanders, one of the most influential New Testament scholars of the last fifty years says, "Mere imputation is not Paul's view of Christian Righteousness. He believed that those who died with Christ were really changed . . . at the same time justified and a sinner? That was not Paul's view: He believed in transformation."[3] The idea that wicked people are proclaimed as saints by God makes a mockery of God. He is not self-deceived. God only declares what is true and cannot lie (Heb 6:18). Jesus said that He is truth, and the Spirit is called the Spirit of truth (Joh 14:6 and 14:17). The promise of God is that a person can be morally blameless in the sight of God. The following Scriptures show that to live a life of sin while being a Christian is impossible:

1. *A good tree cannot bring forth evil fruit, neither can a corrupt tree bring forth good fruit* (Mt 7:18).
2. *Doth a fountain send forth at the same place sweet water and bitter* (Jas 3:11)?
3. *That the righteousness of the law might be fulfilled in us, who walk not after the flesh, but after the Spirit* (Ro 8:4).
4. *Ye might be partakers of the divine nature, having escaped the corruption that is in the world through lust* (2Pe 1:4).

---

[3] Ed Parish Sanders, *Paul: The Apostle's Life, Letters, and Thought* (Minneapolis: Fortress Press, 2015), 457.

5. *And they were both righteous before God, walking in all the commandments and ordinances of the Lord blameless* (Lu 1:6).
6. *Who shall also confirm you unto the end, that ye may be blameless in the day of our Lord Jesus Christ* (1Co 1:8).
7. *That ye may be blameless and harmless, the sons of God, without rebuke, in the midst of a crooked and perverse nation, among whom ye shine as lights in the world* (Php 2:15).
8. *And the very God of peace sanctify you wholly; and I pray God your whole spirit and soul and body be preserved blameless unto the coming of our Lord Jesus Christ* (1Th 5:23).
9. *Wherefore, beloved, seeing that ye look for such things, be diligent that ye may be found of him in peace, without spot, and blameless* (2Pe 3:14).

Those Who Struggle

God has the power to keep anyone who is converted from sinning, but sometimes there are many struggles and ups and downs in the young life of a Christian. This is especially true if one has little self-discipline, is living where there are a lot of temptations, or is struggling in his commitment to serve God. In many ways, this is similar to a young child learning to walk. It is a continual process for a time of taking a baby step, falling, and then getting back up again. For some, this is how their Christian lives began. This is not God's plan, but it sometimes happens. If one does fall after becoming a Christian, the Scripture says, *These things write I unto you, that ye sin not. And if any man sin, we have an advocate with the Father, Jesus Christ the righteous: And he is the propitiation for our sins* (1Jo 2:1-2). For anyone who struggles, there is a Savior waiting with open arms ready to forgive and to help establish them in the Christian faith. One should never give up! Immediately confess the problem and restore the relationship with God. Christ will not give up on any honest seeker!

> As he victoriously overcame sin, we, too, through His grace can overcome.

This is exemplified in the story of Peter walking on the Sea of Galilee. When he saw Jesus walking on the water, he asked to be allowed to walk on the water to Him. Christ encouraged him to come, but after walking some distance, Peter took his eyes off of Christ and saw that the wind and waves were fearful. His faith collapsed, and he began to sink; but then he cried out, *"Lord, save me"* (Mt 14:30). Jesus immediately reached out and rescued him. In the battles of life, especially for a new convert, it is easy to get one's eyes off of Christ and sink back into sin. Jesus died to give victory, and He will continue to reach out to establish anyone who is struggling in the faith. This is not to excuse anyone who sins. It is clear from 1John 2:3-4 that anyone who disobeys the commands of God is not a Christian, but restoration and help are immediately possible. Christ is right there, waiting to rescue the needy soul.

Other passages teach this same principle that through the love and aid of Christ, there is victory. Hebrews 4:15-16 discusses how Jesus Christ as a human suffered through the same infirmities that we experience and empathizes with our difficulties and struggles. As He victoriously overcame sin, we, too, through His grace can overcome. Those who struggle or fail should boldly take their needs to the throne of grace where they can find mercy and help. While holiness and justice are at the core of the nature of God, so are love and compassion. While He does not excuse sin, God's love will go to any degree possible in accordance with His nature to forgive and deliver those who come to Him. He will not break a bruised reed or quench a smoking flax. He works to strengthen those who are bruised and set aflame those whose fire has turned into only smoke (Mt 12:20).The answer for those who struggle is more of the grace, power, and presence of God in their lives. A self-focus concentrating on our personal failures will always lead toward disaster. The self-focus in our world today upon personal feelings and emotional battles rather than trusting God is destructive. We are broken people who live in a fallen world. We must lift our eyes heavenward to the God who has the power to transform. The biblical solution is not to excuse sin, but to gain the victory over sin through the atoning blood of Jesus.

Temptation

Temptation is not sin. Christ *was tempted in all points as we are, yet without sin* (Heb 4:15). James teaches that "every man is tempted, when he is drawn away of his own lust, [desires] and enticed" (Jas 1:14). Temptation is normal. It is only when a person decides that he would commit an evil act, if it were possible, that it should be considered sin. As James says, *"When lust hath conceived, it bringeth forth sin: and sin, when it is finished, bringeth forth death"* (Jas 1:15). For example: most people would desire to have more money. If one happened to have a serious financial need and while walking across a parking lot discovered a $100.00 bill lying on the pavement, the normal natural desire would be to consider it as an answer to prayer and pocket the money. Yet, it is not actually one's money if it is reasonably possible to find the owner. Perhaps he notices a seedy looking couple walking around looking down at the ground. It seems obvious that they are looking for something. One could reason that he has better uses for the money than wasting it on alcohol or drugs as it seems like some would. However, it is still stealing if it is not his money. There is no excuse for sin, and to commit one sin makes one guilty of breaking all the law (Jas 2:10). James also teaches that an act of sin causes one to die spiritually; accordingly, anyone who is overcome by evil desires has no claim to be a Christian until he or she has gone to Christ for forgiveness (Jas 1:15). Paul also teaches that temptation is common to all people and that God will not allow a person to be tempted above what one can endure. God has also promised that in temptation, He will provide a means of escape and that it will be possible to bear the temptation (1Co 10:13). Temptation can be overcome; one does not have to sin, but a misunderstanding which confuses sin with temptation can lead to hopeless despair.

Not only will a Christian face temptation, he may also be persecuted. Scripture does not teach that God will give the Christian an easy life. In fact, it seems that Scripture teaches that when one becomes a Christian, persecution will come, and some aspects of life may be far more difficult. Christians will be tempted and will struggle with difficulty in this life. What God has promised, though, is peace in the storm and victory over temptation and persecution.

Human Faults

When failure occurs even by mistake, anyone who truly knows God will humbly confess it, apologize to those who have been hurt, and will turn to God for His grace and help. Let it also be clear that human limitations and mistakes are not considered sin according to the Wesleyan/Holiness or Scriptural understanding of sin. Every saved and sanctified individual will have numerous faults and failures due to the limited knowledge and abilities of being human. The third work of grace, glorification, will deal with these aspects of the Fall in the resurrection. God will continue perfecting these shortcomings throughout this life in Christian maturity. These shortcomings should not be considered acceptable behavior. When mistakes occur, even though unintentional, anyone who truly knows God will humbly confess it, apologize to any who may have been hurt, and turn to God for His grace and help. As Richard S. Taylor says, "The damaging effects of even inadvertent and impulsive offenses are so potentially devastating and far-reaching that a cavalier attitude toward them is extremely incompatible with the Christian life."[4] While the action itself may have devastating consequences, if the motive was right, it should not be considered sin. Yet, it could become sin if, after becoming aware that it is wrong, one fails to apologize, humbly admit one's mistake, and take action to undo the damage. Genuine Christianity is often better displayed by how one reacts to awareness of personal shortcomings than to one's successes.

Sensitive Consciences

Those with an overly sensitive conscience may also struggle with the idea that it is possible to live victoriously without sin. They view any failure to be absolutely perfect as a personal, moral failure. The devil constantly hounds these people by accusing them of sin. They feel that they can never measure up to the expectations demanded by God. A mixture of the Calvinistic definition of sin, which demands human perfection, along with the Wesleyan/Arminian concept of the requirement of a sinless life will lead one with an overly sensitive conscience to despair. One direction that some have turned in their hopelessness is to a theology that teaches that one cannot lose his salvation for committing evil behavior. The eternal security belief teaches that a one-time confession of

---

[4] Richard S. Taylor, *A Right Conception of Sin: Revised and Enlarged* (Salem, OH: Schmul Publishing Co., 2002), 115.

faith eternally secures one's salvation, no matter how evil and continuous the subsequent wickedness of the individual. The impetus for their acceptance of this theology is their personal experience of failure. They have effectively replaced biblical theology with a theology based upon their personal experience and struggle.

To some degree the Lutheran portion of the Protestant Reformation was based upon a morbidly, overly sensitive conscience. It is well-known that, as a monk, Martin Luther lived with a terror of God, and accordingly, feared and hated God. Luther believed that the "divinely righteous standard was unattainable."[5] In his despair, he was constantly going to confession and doing penance to a degree that it was severely damaging to his health. He could find no spiritual peace or rest. Somehow in his despair, through the teaching of the book of Romans, he grasped the concept of faith for salvation and the fact that Christ alone had paid the price for our sins. He now pictured the Christian message as good news and bringing peace and "a sure confidence to those who believed."[6] However, Luther's personal psychological struggles regarding forgiveness for sin stamped the Reformation with a distorted theology of predestination based solely upon the grace of God choosing those to be saved. Most Protestants today would disagree with Luther and would hold that salvation occurs from a synergistic combination of both God and man. God provides salvation and prevenient grace; man then chooses to participate or reject the proffered grace.

A far better answer to an overly sensitive conscience is to seek out a proper definition of sin. Sin is only what Scripture calls sin: a behavior for which God will send a person to hell, or deliberate disobedience to God. Liberalism sees almost nothing as sin, and Calvinism sees every shortcoming as sin. Both end up excusing sin. The evil and destructive power of sin must never be excused in one's life. Sin must be defined according to the way God, through Scripture, defined it. God does demand that a person must live righteously and must obey Him, but He does not demand absolute perfection. Only God is capable of that. One must always

---

[5] James R. Dayton, Jr., *Getting the Reformation Wrong* (Downers Grove, IL: IVP Academic, 2010), 77.
[6] James R. Dayton, Jr., *Getting the Reformation Wrong* 77.

do good according to what a person knows (Jas 4:17), and a person should continue to improve doing the best he can for God. The Parable of the Ten Talents teaches that the lazy and slothful servant was condemned for doing nothing rather than succeeding as the other two servants did (Mt 25:24-30). One must always strive to do his utmost for God out of love for Him; but in order to maintain salvation, a person must not willfully disobey God.

All Christians must firmly keep in mind that none will have their sins forgiven by any efforts of their own. We are totally saved by grace through faith in Christ. Yet, we must never forget that one who is *just shall live by faith* (Ro 1:17). It is not a single act of faith but a continual life of faith that leads to final salvation (Ro 11:19-22). The word translated *faith* can also be translated *faithfulness*.[7] To have faith in Christ also means to be faithful to Christ. Faithfulness to Christ involves keeping the commands of Christ. At the judgment, Christ will tell those who commit iniquity to depart from Him (Mt 7:23). Genuine faith will produce a life which is evidenced by righteous living. Without the evidence of righteousness, it is evident that one does not have genuine faith. As the Sermon on the Mount says, *A good tree cannot bring forth evil fruit, neither can a corrupt tree bring forth good fruit* (Mt 7:18).

Historical Impact of Those Who Believed in Victory

Those who believe in overcoming victory are the ones who have taken the world for God. These are the ones who get their prayers through, and God always makes their lives count. Even when their theology may not have been exactly correct in every detail, God honored their holy life and changed their world. The only answer for our world today is a renewed dedication to holiness within the people of the church. Somehow the philosophy of evangelism is often based upon compromising our lifestyle to fit in with the world. Yet, our cheapened theology on the doctrine of sin has left us with a powerless and godless church that is collapsing before a secular world. Let the church be what God wants the church to be, then

---

[7] Matthew W. Bates, "The external-relational shift in faith (pistis) in New Testament research: Romans 1 as Gospel-allegiance test case." *Currents in Biblical Research* 18, no. 2 (2020): 176-202.

take that message of transformation to our world, and God will work.

The principle of the Church being holy as the means of impacting the world for Christ has been proven again and again throughout history. In the first three centuries of church history, the church took on the Roman Empire and came out victoriously. With the constant threat of death, they lived exemplary lives. Throughout the Middle Ages, it was those monks and nuns who were dedicated to God that empowered the church to keep expanding throughout Europe. The first Great Awakening in America was caused by revivalistic preaching that confronted sin and demanded repentance. It was the dedication and message of the Methodist movement that turned England and then America into the powerhouses for God that they became. The Keswick movement in England that preached victory over all willful sin led England in some of the great revivals of its day. It was also one of the greatest factors in driving the worldwide missions movement of that day. When the Methodist and the Holiness people in America preached an unyielding message of deliverance from sin, they grew. When the message of holiness of life began to falter, growth declined. Victory over sin is the message. It must be preached loud and long till all people hear. It is the message of the holiness people and, in reality, the message of all Christians everywhere.

As Christians, we are engaged in the great war of the ages against the powers of sin and the devil. Our attitude makes the difference. We must recognize the inevitability of final victory. Jesus Christ has won the battle over sin, hell, and Satan. Sin has been totally defeated at the cross. That is why the Scripture says, "Our old man is crucified with him, that the body of sin might be destroyed, that henceforth we should not serve sin." (Ro 6:6) Because of this, a person is freed from not only the guilt and the penalty of sin, but also from the power of sin itself. It is time for all Christians everywhere to recognize that we serve a victorious conquering Savior who has the power to give victory in this life for all of His people.

Chapter 3
Competing Evangelical Theories of Salvation

The question over the definition of sin is not merely a semantic debate over wording; it is the foundation for salvation. What are the requirements for entrance into heaven? This is ultimately the most important theological question that exists. Wesleyans believe people are saved by the grace of God, and not by any human merit. Wesleyan/Holiness people also teach that, in order for this grace to become effective in lives and for people ultimately to go to heaven, they must repent of their sins and trust in Christ's death for salvation. This would be followed by a life of obedience to God.

Any religion that excuses sin is a false religion, and false religions always twist their theology to excuse sin. This is how a person can determine what is the true religion and what religions teach false

> Any religion that excuses sin is a false religion, and false religions always twist their theology to excuse sin.

doctrine. Some religions excuse sin by calling so many things sin that it is impossible to live holy. Others go to the opposite extreme and call almost nothing sin and, accordingly, excuse that which is truly sinful. Another direction some have gone is to allow sin, provided it is confessed to the priest who forgives them. Some groups have also taught that there is little penalty for sin by teaching that there is no eternal punishment. There have been holy people in almost all of the Christian denominations who have lived higher than the weaknesses in their theology. However, over time excuses have been made for sin or doctrines have been changed to match a sinful lifestyle. The Calvinist doctrine originally emphasized that those who were saved lived holy lives, or they had never been saved. Now many of them are teaching that it does not matter how people live; they will still go to heaven. Some Wesleyans have had the same problem and in the last generation have reworked their doctrine of sin to excuse sinful behavior. The original Wesleyan doctrine expected their people to live a holy life of obedience to God.

Ultimately, any doctrine regarding how a person gains acceptance into heaven is heavily based upon its definition of sin. Since Wesleyans hold that obedience to God's law as given in the New Covenant is required for entrance to heaven, the question over the definition of sin is critically important. Scripture teaches a person must meet the requirements of God (Ro 2:1-13, Mt 7:21-23). Doctrines about sin, salvation, and the law are at the core of understanding God's plan of salvation. Will a Christian backslide and not go to heaven if he commits sin? Do proponents of eternal security trust in a false security? Are sins of ignorance acceptable while willful sin is not? Does God allow some willful sin as long as it is not too much? Salvation depends upon finding the correct answers to these questions.

One of the key differences among all of the theological groups common among American evangelicals is their theology regarding salvation. This includes both initial salvation in forgiveness of sins and the requirements for entrance into heaven or, as it could be called, final salvation. Underlying the doctrine of soteriology (salvation) is the concept of sin. Calvinistic soteriology is based upon the idea that it is impossible to keep the law of God; accordingly, a person must continue to commit sin throughout his Christian life. In addition, sin is also defined as any failure to be perfect like God. The doctrinal groups which have historically descended from Calvinism have developed their theology based upon this idea that it is impossible for people to be righteous; therefore, salvation must be based upon their concept of imputed righteousness in which God sees people as righteous even though they are still sinful. The Wesleyan view of imputation rejects the concept that while one is unrighteous "Christ's righteousness is substituted for theirs in such a way as to render them as legally righteous as if they had themselves rendered perfect obedience."[1] The Wesleyan position holds that, not only is righteousness imputed, it is also imparted so that "we ourselves are actually made

---

[1] Richard S. Taylor, ed., *Beacon Dictionary of Theology* (Kansas City: Beacon Hill Press of Kansas City, 1983), 277.

righteous by God's grace."[2] Holding a different definition of sin forces one to hold a different view of salvation.

In contrast, Wesleyan/Holiness theology believes that sin is a moral issue and is limited to known and willful violations of God's law. This theology also teaches that keeping the law is a necessity for entrance to heaven (Mt 7:23); however, God's grace enables a person to keep the law of Christ as given in the New Testament and live without sinning. Properly defining sin is at the center of the issue of salvation. Holding a different definition of sin forces one to hold a different view of salvation. Wesleyan/Holiness proponents believe that it is impossible for people to intentionally disobey God without losing their salvation. It is also an evidence of a loss of faith in God. Since the word for faith also includes the concept of faithfulness, deliberate disobedience is an act of being unfaithful to God. No one who lacks faith along with faithfulness to God or is living in disobedience to the commands of God can validly claim to be a Christian (1Jn 2:3-4, Ro 11:20-22).

Wesleyans strongly hold to the traditional Reformation emphasis that man is saved by God's grace and that there is nothing a person can do to merit his own salvation outside of realizing his helplessness and casting himself at the foot of the cross pleading for mercy. It is then faith in Christ that saves a person, and there is nothing which one can do to merit salvation (Eph 2:8-9). Scripture does teach the necessity of confession of sins (1Jn 1:9), repentance (Lu 13:3,5, Ac 2:38, Ac 3:19, 2 Co 7:10, 2 Pe 3:9), and a testimony that one has chosen to follow Christ (Ro 10:9-10). Outside of those who believe in predestination, this is traditional Protestant theology. In general, there is agreement that, in order for a person to become saved, there are some requirements—namely repentance and faith. Christianity, however, is facing a new challenge from those who have abandoned traditional Protestant theology and do not believe repentance or a life change is necessary for salvation.

Differing Evangelical Theologies

Modern evangelicalism can be identified by the beliefs that all spiritual truth is to be found in the Bible, the necessity of a born-again

---

[2] Richard S. Taylor, *Beacon Dictionary of Theology*, 276.

experience, the need to evangelize others with the good news of the gospel, and the belief that the death of Christ provided atonement for sin.[3] Evangelicals in America could be divided into five major sets of beliefs regarding sin and salvation. All of these church groups hold that salvation is by faith through the grace of God, but exactly what this means is the area of disagreement. This breakdown is just a generalization, and there are wide variations within each doctrinal position. They also overlap and do not have a distinct line separating one group from another; yet, in the larger picture there are sharp differences in their beliefs regarding the doctrines of sin and salvation. The following is a list of these five doctrines:

1. Wesleyan/Holiness Theology - This follows the teachings of John Wesley and the original Methodist doctrinal position on salvation and sin. The major distinction between Wesleyans and other evangelicals is their position that God both enables and requires a Christian to refrain from sin; however, sin is narrowly defined as a willful act of disobedience to God. They view that the time of probation is one's entire life. Thus, one could choose to serve God, but later change his mind. Accordingly, obedience to the commands of God is a necessity following the born-again experience.

2. Calvinist or Reformed Theology - This is the historic theology of John Calvin and those who followed him at the time of the Reformation. Their major distinctive belief is predestination, which is that God alone in His sovereignty chooses some (the elect) for salvation, and makes no provision for those who are not elect to be saved. Holiness of life is evidence that one is part of the elect. Those who do not live holy are not part of those chosen by God to salvation.

3. Neo-Calvinistic Theology - This would be the best term to use for the doctrinal position of many of the churches which had a historic background in Reformed theology but have made a number of substantial changes. Modified Calvinists deny the Calvinist view of a limited

---

[3] Mark Noll, *The Rise of Evangelicalism* (Downers Grove, IL: InterVarsity Press, 2003), 19.

atonement and predestination, and they teach that everyone has the freedom to choose salvation. However, they hold with the Calvinist view that saints will persevere to the end by living a transformed life, or they were never truly converted.

4. Free-grace Theology – This is similar to neo-Calvinism but sufficiently large and distinct enough to have its own category. Its major distinction is the insistence that all law has been replaced by a one-time act of faith. This is sufficient for eternal salvation even if a person later apostatizes and lives an evil life. According to this doctrine, a person should live a good life, but is under no law whatsoever. No matter how wicked one is, he is still saved and assured of heaven. Other Reformed groups hold that one's holy life is evidence of salvation, but the free-grace group denies the necessity of any obedience to the law or the necessity of any holiness of life by a Christian.

5. Evangelical Arminian Theology- This is a general grouping of several church traditions which are characterized by many variations which are part Wesleyan Arminian and part Calvinistic. Some of these groups have a Wesleyan concept of salvation with a Calvinistic definition of sin. Many hold that it is possible for a person to backslide, but also that it is impossible to live without committing sins of infirmity or ignorance. Some also hold that a person may commit willful sin and still remain a Christian, but that it cannot be the practice of life. These would emphasize that a person would backslide when he commits habitual sin or does not show repentance for the sins which are committed. This grouping would include newer groups that teach process and relational theologies.

These are general groupings for those who are identified with the evangelicals. Outside of these categories are the mainline or liberal churches which do not hold to the necessity of a born-again experience. They generally accept that all people will go to heaven with each person having his own way to God. Those of the Catholic tradition believe salvation is obtained through the church and the church's sacraments. In addition, a number of denominations do not follow orthodox Christianity and would generally be identified as cults.

Among Evangelicals there are five different positions held in regard to the concept of salvation in evangelical Christianity in America. The distinguishing point between them is the question of sin. Wesleyan-Holiness theology holds that while one is saved by grace, one must also through grace obey God by keeping the New Covenant law for entrance to heaven. Thus, the question regarding the definition of sin and its relationship to the Christian life is not a question of misunderstood wording. It is, instead, a foundational question of one's salvation theology. Wesleyan-Holiness theology holds that, by grace, one must be keeping the New Covenant law of Christ (i.e., not committing sin) for entrance to heaven. A different definition of sin, therefore, is a different theology of salvation. Thus it is vitally important to define the terms carefully and from God's point of view.

Chapter 4
Understanding the Wesleyan Concept of Salvation

John Wesley was one of the greatest theologians of all time. His focus was not on writing theology or dealing with abstract questions, but upon building a practical religion that would change lives. He took the ideas of Reformed scholars, the Anglican Church, James Arminius's theology, and the writing of the Early Church to develop a practical, experiential theology that worked in real life. Undergirding all of Wesley's theology was, first and foremost, Scripture. As a secondary source to verify truth, Wesley would also use historical tradition, logic, and experience. The theology of Wesley, along with the church he founded, transformed England, America, and much of the rest of the world. A common, simple way to define the Wesleyan doctrine of salvation includes the following four points:

All People Need to be Saved from Sin

Wesley held with the traditional Reformation view that one was born with a sin nature: that the heart was polluted by sin. He held that all men have no desire to serve God and have chosen to disobey Him and are lost without any hope of salvation. However, Wesley held that the prevenient grace of God overcame the total corruption in enabling people with a free-will to choose their eternal destiny. Wesley's doctrine contrasts strongly with the liberal relational theology of today or the rationalism of the enlightenment that denies total corruption. Likewise, in no way should Wesley be identified with the ancient Pelagian doctrine which did not believe that man's will was corrupted.

All People Can be Saved from Sin

Wesleyan theologians hold traditional doctrines regarding how a person obtains salvation. They teach the necessity of repentance and faith in Christ for salvation, as do most evangelicals today. John Wesley developed his doctrine when traditional Reformed theology was the dominant belief among conservative scholars in England; however, he rejected predestination and taught that all people could be saved. This would have been the major issue of controversy Wesley had with the Calvinists. He adopted the aspects of James Arminius' theological position on free-will. Wesley believed that the grace of God through Christ's atonement provided salvation to all people if they would respond to the gospel.

All People Can Know They Are Saved from Sin

During the time of John Wesley many people were insecure regarding their personal salvation. Wesley himself sought God for assurance for years before receiving that confidence at Aldersgate. From that time he preached a clear experience of a new birth with assurance that one was prepared for heaven. Calvinists were quite insecure regarding their personal salvation. They knew God had predestined an elect for heaven, but they had no definite assurance that they were one of the elect. Some Calvinists did teach a personal experience which helped to identify them as one of the elect, and also believed a holy life gave further evidence of being chosen by God. However, they also knew many people who had lived a holy life for many years later fell away. They believed these people were self-deceived and had never truly been saved. According to their belief, only those who persevered in a holy life until death were genuinely converted. Therefore, the question in their minds remained - were they genuinely converted or just self-deceived? Wesley's preaching that one could know he was saved brought great opposition from the Calvinists of his day.

All People Can be Saved from all Sin

Another issue of controversy was Wesley's teaching about sin. He believed that the sin nature could be removed and replaced by the love of God. Wesley also taught that a Christian could and must live a life of complete victory over sin through the empowering grace of God. However, he defined sin only as a willful transgression of the known law of Christ. Neither Wesley nor his followers believed that human faults, failures, or ignorance should be considered sin. From the human perspective, a failure may seem to be sinful because man can only look upon the outward appearance; however, from God's perspective, only a deliberate choice of disobedience is sin since God looketh upon the heart. A failure to understand the difference between the human and divine points of view regarding sin is at the core of the theological difference. The eradication of the sin nature and complete victory over willful sin were two of the key beliefs of the Methodist Church. This is not a fringe doctrine of some small sect; the Methodist Episcopal Church was the largest Protestant denomination in the United States until the mid-twentieth century. About the same time as the Methodist Church began accepting liberal theology, the Holiness and the Pentecostal movements left the Methodist Church. Many Holiness proponents and Pentecostals have continued teaching this same concept of victory to the present.

Final Salvation and the Possibility of Backsliding

Those of the Methodist tradition accept the ideas of John Wesley that final salvation is dependent upon living a grace enabled holy life after conversion. Wesleyan/Holiness theologians insisted that the necessity of continued faith and obedience is not a salvation by works. These works are not done in any way to merit heaven, which is purely a gift from God. It is simply choosing throughout one's life to accept God's gift. They would phrase it differently, but would agree with St. Augustine who stated, "The faithful . . . would endanger the salvation of their souls if they acted on the false assurance that faith alone is sufficient for salvation or that they need not perform good works in order to be saved."[1] The "works" Wesleyans insist upon would be repentance, faith, and continued obedience. These concepts are clearly in line with much Reformation thought regarding

---

[1] Augustine, *On Faith and Works*, quoted by Michael Allen, ed. Matthew Barrett, *Reformation Theology* (Wheaton, IL: Crossway, 2017), p. 570.

salvation.² The reformers insisted that repentance worked together with faith in salvation and is followed by an obedient life. As Martin Luther stated in his first point of the 95 Thesis which began the Protestant Reformation, "When our Lord and Master Jesus Christ said, 'Repent' (Mt 4:17), he willed the entire life of believers to be one of repentance."³ The major distinction is that Wesley defined sin as a moral choice rather than as an absolute, legal concept. Almost all evangelicals agree that there are actions (or works) a sinner must do to become saved. A person must repent, believe in Christ, and testify to being a Christian. (Ac 2:38 and Ro 10:9-10) Repentance is a change of direction in life from following sin to obedience in following the Savior. A person is then saved as he trusts in Christ as his Savior and Lord. A continuation of what was necessary to become saved, namely obedience and continued faith, is a necessity to remain saved. One must continue to obey Christ as one began in repentance and continue to trust Him for salvation. The Apostle Paul teaches, *For not the hearers of the law are just before God, but the doers of the law shall be justified.* (Ro 2:13) Obedience in a person's life is a necessity for final salvation. This should not be considered "works" which merit salvation any more than repentance and obedience necessary to surrender one's life to Christ in the new birth is "works."

It is critically important to understand the difference between conversion (also called initial salvation) and entrance into heaven (Also called final salvation). In initial salvation a person's sins are forgiven; he is justified before God and is prepared to go to heaven. All evangelicals, including Wesleyans, would agree that there is nothing a person can do to merit the forgiveness of sins. Redemption is totally by grace through repenting of one's sins and trusting in the sacrifice of Christ. Final

---

[2] The Reformation was much more than the Lutheran and Reformed doctrine. It would also include Anglican and Anabaptist theology. John Wesley felt that he was clearly in line with the Anglican Church. Luther and Calvin also insisted upon repentance, faith, and the necessity of a holy life following regeneration. Luther has made some contradictory remarks; yet many scholars feel that this is a proper representation of Luther.

[3] Martin Luther, *The 95 Thesis*, 1517, no. 1. Https://www.luther.de/en/95/thesen.html.

salvation occurs at the end of life when a person dies. Scripture says, "But he that shall endure unto the end, the same shall be saved." (Mt 24:13) Initial salvation justifies a person from the sins which have been committed. Final salvation means that the initial steps taken to become saved are continued to the end. Some theologies teach that initial salvation ensures final salvation. They believe that, once a person is saved, he will inescapably persevere to the end or that God will preserve him. Others, including Wesleyan theologians, hold that it is possible to *fall from grace* (Ga 5:4) and ultimately miss heaven. As Adam Clarke stated, "Unless a believer live[s] and walk[s] in the spirit of obedience, he will fall from the grace of God, and forfeit all his Christian privileges and rights . . . and, if so, perish everlastingly."[4] H. Orton Wiley viewed sin as incompatible with entering heaven, and he explains, "Nothing unholy ever enters that city—no sin, whether of act or condition."[5]

> "But he that shall endure unto the end, the same shall be saved." (Mt 24:13)

The Greek word for faith is *pistis,* which not only conveys the idea of trust, but also carries the concept of faithfulness.[6] The New Testament understanding of faith is placing trust in Christ and being faithful to Him. The noun form of *pistis* is almost always currently translated either *faith* or *believe* in modern translations. However, the adjective form of the same word *pistos* is almost always translated faithful. These two concepts cannot be separated in the Greek and should not be in the English, either. In Romans chapter 4 Paul makes his case that Abraham was saved by faith and not by works. Scripture states, *Abraham believed God, and it was counted unto him for righteousness* (Ro 4:3, Ge 15:6). In Nehemiah 9:8 there is another account of Abraham using the same passage from Genesis 15:6. This account in Nehemiah states that God chose Abraham because

---

[4] Adam Clarke and Samuel Dunn, *Christian Theology*, 2nd ed. (London; Glasgow; Dublin: Thomas Tegg & Son; R. Griffin & Co.; Tegg, Wise, & Co., 1835), 439.
[5] H. Orton Wiley, *God has the Answer* (digital edition) accessed July 10, 2023, http://wesley.nnu.edu/holiness-classics-library/?rows=30&search=author&search_value=wiley.
[6] Bates, Matthew W. "The external-relational shift in faith (pistis) in New Testament research: Romans 1 as Gospel-allegiance test case." *Currents in Biblical Research* 18, no. 2 (2020): 176-202.

He found *his heart faithful*. Paul, who would have been familiar with both passages, was emphasizing that a person was not saved by his own merit or by the works of the Old Testament Law, but by having faith in and being faithful to Jesus Christ. Any doctrine that allows for continued sin in the life of a Christian undermines the concept that faithfulness to the commands of Christ is a necessity; accordingly, it undermines the doctrine of salvation as taught in the New Testament.

Historic Christian doctrine always expected its people to live according to Scripture. The separation of faith from obedience in modern America means that few of those who profess Christianity today actually live as the Bible demands! All Christian faiths at one time taught the necessity of an experience of salvation which transformed a person from a sinner to a saint. Evidence of this experience was exemplified by a holy life. This has changed. Today, it is a commonly known fact that among those called "Christians," only a minority professes to even keep the Ten Commandments. Studies show that there is no difference in the lifestyle of the average "Christian" and that of society. Some "Christian" churches today have lost all sense of biblical morality and are even ordaining lesbians and homosexuals into the ministry.

Outside of Reformed theology, almost all Christian groups teach that it is possible to backslide and lose one's salvation after one is justified. This includes the teaching of the Early Church and the teaching of the church during the Middle Ages. Even at the time of the Reformation, many of the Protestants groups did not accept the idea that one could not backslide. Among those who identified with Calvinists, there was diversity on this doctrine. One example is the Calvinistic Puritan, John Bunyan, who wrote *Pilgrim's Progress*. This book is the story of Pilgrim traveling to the celestial city. It gives all of the temptations and dangers he faced that tried to prevent him from making it through. The book's main teaching is that to fail or turn back at any point along the way will cause one to miss making it to heaven.

The source of all spiritual truth is the teaching of the Bible, and Wesleyan theology is thoroughly biblical. Repeatedly, Scripture warns against backsliding. The danger of falling away from God and missing heaven is the major theme of Hebrews, 2 Peter, and Jude, and is a key message of several other books. Here are a few Scriptures that teach this doctrine:

Scriptures Which Teach the Possibility of Losing Salvation

Galatians 5:2-4 *Christ shall profit you nothing . . . [and] is become of no effect unto you . . . ye are fallen from grace.* This passage teaches that people are saved by faith in Christ, but if they turn back to the Old Testament Law for their salvation, then they will fall from grace. The consequence is that the saving blood of Christ will no longer have the effect of forgiving them of their sins and that their former faith in Christ would profit them nothing.

Romans 11:20-22 *Because of unbelief they were broken off, and thou standest by faith. Be not highminded, but fear: . . . otherwise thou also shalt be cut off.* Paul is expounding that God had rejected the Jewish people who did not believe and had accepted the Gentiles who did believe. While this passage is also discussing God's acceptance of the Gentiles, it is very clear from the context that the individuals within each group were accepted or rejected on the basis of their continuation of faith. Thus, to lose one's faith is to lose one's salvation. This verse is not contrasting faith and works, but the contrast is between a single act of faith or a continuing faith.

Re 22:19, Re 20:22-15, Ex 32:33, and Re 3:5 *And if any man shall take away from the words of the book of this prophecy, God shall take away his part out of the book of life, and out of the holy city.* At the Judgment, anyone whose name was *not found written in the book of life was cast into the lake of fire.* God said, *whosoever hath sinned against me, him will I blot out of my book.* God does erase names out of the book of life.

Hebrews 6:4-8 *Those who were once enlightened, and have tasted of the heavenly gift, and were made partakers of the Holy Ghost, and have tasted the good word of God, and the powers of the world to come, If they shall fall away . . . whose end is to be burned.* These people clearly were once saved and the apostle is warning them against falling away and becoming like thorns and briars that would be burned.

2 Pe 2:20 *For if after they have escaped the pollutions of the world through the knowledge of the Lord and Saviour Jesus Christ, they are again entangled therein, and overcome, the latter end is worse with them than the beginning.* The final end of everyone is eternal life in heaven or eternal death in hell. If a person cannot lose his salvation, his latter end would still be heaven and would be far better, but this is not what the Bible teaches. It teaches even more severe punishment for those who again get entangled in sin than if they had never been saved. To go back to the world means missing heaven.

It is also very clear that God requires people to keep His commandments, or they do not know Christ. The Bible is very clear that only those who keep the commands of God go to heaven; those who do not obey go to hell. Here are a few of the dozens of verses that teach this principle:

Scriptures Which Show That Those Who Do Not Keep God's Commands Are Not Saved

1 Jo 2:3 *And hereby we do know that we know him, if we keep his commandments.*
This passage very clearly teaches that, in order to know Christ, one must be keeping Christ's commands. Anyone who says he is a Christian but is not living in obedience to Christ is a liar.

Mt 7:21, 23 *Not every one that saith unto me, Lord, Lord, shall enter into the kingdom of heaven; but he that doeth the will of my Father which is in heaven. . . depart from me, ye that work iniquity.* It is obvious that the criteria for entrance to heaven according to this passage is obedience to doing the will of God and not committing iniquity which means not breaking God's law.

Mt 13:41-42 *The Son of man shall send forth his angels, and they shall gather out of his kingdom all things that offend, and them which do iniquity; And shall cast them into a furnace of fire: there shall be wailing and gnashing of teeth.* Clearly, this is a statement giving the criteria used at the judgment. This shows the necessity of a life that is not offensive to God and one which does not break the law.

Mt 19:16-17 *What good thing shall I do, that I may have eternal life?* [Christ said] *if thou wilt enter into life, keep the commandments.* When the rich, young ruler asked the question of what it took to have eternal life, Christ's immediate answer was obedience to the commandments. Our theology can go no higher or be more accurate than the words of Christ Himself.

Ro 2:6-10 At the Judgment, God *will render to every man according to his deeds.* The context then continues to show that a person's eternal judgment is based upon his behavior, and those who live godly receive eternal life while those who do not obey the truth are punished. God demands holy living for entrance to heaven, and genuine Christians keep all of His commands.

Ac 10:34-35 *Then Peter opened his mouth, and said, Of a truth I perceive that God is no respecter of persons: But in every nation he that feareth him, and worketh righteousness, is accepted with him.* The key to being accepted by God is a proper reverence for God and working righteousness. The guideline used by God at the final judgment to determine if one qualifies for entrance to heaven is righteousness. Being justified by faith is the means by which one becomes personally righteous.

Heb 5:9 *And being made perfect, he [Jesus Christ] became the author of eternal salvation unto all them that obey him.* Obedience is the criteria given here for final salvation.

The Law of Christ Given in the New Covenant

Sin is the transgression of the law. Biblically there is no debate, but this leads to the question, what is the law which a Christian must obey? Is it the law given to Adam? Is it the Law given to Moses? Or is it the natural law given to all mankind? If a person is a citizen of the United States, then he is not under the laws of England when he is in America. Likewise in the spiritual realm, a Christian is under the laws of the kingdom of Christ. Christians are not Jews living in the Old Testament context; Christians live under the New Testament kingdom of God.

The New Covenant is based upon fulfilling "the law of Christ." (Ga 6:2) Christ summarized its principles as loving God *with all thy heart* [and] *loving thy neighbor as thyself. . . . On these two commandments hang all the law and the prophets.* (Mt 22:37-40) Paul also stated that *love is the fulfilling of the law.* (Ro 13:10) The Old Testament law was fulfilled in the death and resurrection of Jesus Christ and the coming of the Holy Spirit at Pentecost. Accordingly, the legalistic system of the Mosaic law was abolished, along with the Old Testament law, and has been replaced by a new and better covenant.

> The Old Testament Law has been replaced by a new and better covenant.

This certainly does not mean that Christians are not under law at all, nor does it mean that the moral principles of the Old Testament such as the Ten Commandments have not been appropriated into the New Covenant. The same God who gave the Jews the old Law is the same God who has given Christians the new law. Almost all of the same moral truth is written into the New Testament, but its application is through the Spirit living within his people. It is also objectively given in the written New Testament code. "The New Covenant has as its central genius the change, not of the commandments but of the human heart. God proposes through Christ to internalize His law."[7] The Old Testament legalistically gave the moral commands but did not change the heart. In the New Testament, God transforms the person so there is a new knowledge, a new heart, and the proper desires and attitudes. His grace changes the desires of the heart. Sin is no longer defined in terms of violation of a written code, but by rejection of God's will. Violation of the law is based upon intention rather than a legalistic morality. Richard S. Taylor states, "The standards of right and wrong are not changed to fit man's nature, but man's nature is changed to fit those standards . . . That is, if we are led of the Spirit, we will practice by joyous, divine impulse the principles of righteousness indicated in the law."[8]

The concept of the two covenants is promised in Jeremiah 31:33, and then it is fulfilled in the covenant given by Christ. One of the major purposes for the book of Hebrews was to help the Jewish people

---

[7] Richard S. Taylor, *Exploring Christian Holiness* (Kansas City: Beacon Hill Press of Kansas City, 1985), 112.
[8] Richard S. Taylor, *A Right Conception of Sin* (Kansas City: Beacon Hill Press of Kansas City, 1945), 96.

understand how Christ was the fulfillment of the Old Testament Mosaic Law. Accordingly, the book explains how the priesthood of Christ replaced the Aaronic priesthood, how the sacrifice of Christ on the cross replaced the sacrificial system, and how heaven itself replaced the altar and the Holy Place. Hebrews explains that the covenant with Israel given at Mount Sinai has been replaced by a New Covenant established by God through the death of Christ at Mount Calvary. In Galatians 3:29 and Romans 4:11-13, Paul makes it clear that Christians now fully participate in the salvation given not just to the Jews but to all people and that there is now no difference between the Jew and the Gentile. Christians no longer look to the Aaronic priesthood, offer animal sacrifices, or pour blood on the altar in the holy place. Yet, some still look to the old covenant rather than accepting its replacement with the New Covenant. Just as ceremonial law was a physical revelation of God's ultimate plan in salvation, the written code of ethics in the Mosaic Law was an external example of what God would one day do in changing the heart of the believer.

The book of Hebrews states that the Lord has made *a new covenant with the house of Israel and with the house of Judah.* (Heb 8:8) This covenant would be based not upon an external written code; instead God said, *I will put my laws into their mind, and write them in their hearts.* (Heb 8:10) Furthermore, when God established the New Covenant, He cancelled the covenant given at Sinai. The book of Hebrews states, *In that he saith, A new covenant, he hath made the first old. Now that which decayeth and waxeth old is ready to vanish away.* (Heb 8:8-13, Heb 10:16) Thus it happened, just as predicted, within a few years the Romans destroyed Jerusalem and the Temple. The Jewish system of worship given under the Law disappeared and has never been reinstated.

The legal code of the Mosaic Law has been replaced by the personal infilling and leadership of the Spirit as Galatians 5:18 says, *But if ye be led of the Spirit, ye are not under the law.* Certainly a person cannot be committing sin when he is walking according to the Spirit and fulfilling the law of love. (Ro 13:8) It is impossible for one to be violating the law and fulfilling the law at the same time. When one's motives are right but through ignorance his actions are wrong, those actions are not sin. That would be impossible if one understands the New Testament law of Christ;

however, under the Old Testament Mosaic Law, wrong actions are sin regardless of motive.

The concept of law has not disappeared in the dispensation of grace, but it has been changed in its format. By a constant repetition of the use of the term *law*, it shows that there is a continuity of the concept of law. Salvation under the New Testament does include law, but it is not simply a repetition of the Old Testament Mosaic Law. Paul stated that he was *not without law to God, but under the law to Christ.* (1 Co 9:21, Ga 6:2) James used the terms *royal law* and *law of liberty* to identify the new covenant law. (Jas 2:8 and 2:12)

John Wesley, likewise, understood that the change in the covenant ended the concept of sinning in ignorance. In his sermon on *Christian Perfection,* John Wesley stated, "Yea, thus it was from Adam . . . to Christ. There was then no man that sinneth not." But "we may safely affirm with St. John, that since the gospel was given, 'He that is born of God sinneth not.'"[9] Wesley believed, "that every command in holy writ is only a covered promise. For by that solemn declaration, *'This is the covenant I will make after those days saith the Lord: I will put my laws in your minds, and write them in your hearts.'* God hath engaged to give whatsoever he commands."[10] Under the old covenant, Israelites failed, through ignorance, to perfectly keep the ceremonial laws of uncleanness; however, the ceremonial laws were fulfilled and ended under the New Covenant. It is impossible to ignorantly violate a law which is written on the mind. Wesley understood the power of the gospel when he declared, "'*The righteousness of the law is fulfilled in us,*' through faith which is in Christ Jesus."[11]

Those who hold to sins of ignorance and infirmity have never theologically advanced to the promises of the New Testament. This distinction between the law in the Old Covenant, which could be broken

---

[9] John Wesley, *Wesley's Standard Sermons*, (Salem, OH: Schmul Publishing Co., repr., 1982), 400.
[10] John Wesley, *Wesley's Standard Sermons,* 249. Wesley is quoting Hebrews 8:10 to show the change between the Old and New Covenants.
[11] John Wesley, *Wesley's Standard Sermons,* 249. Wesley is quoting Romans 8:4 to prove his concept.

ignorantly, and that of the New Covenant is of vital importance. God has provided a better salvation in this dispensation that enables one to completely overcome sin. Thus, Jesus has the power through grace to make one free from all sin, and whom the son sets free *shall be free indeed.* (Jn 8:36) In his commentary on Hebrews, W.B. Godbey pointed out that we are no longer under the old covenant where one may not have known the law and thus could have sinned ignorantly; we now have the law in the New Covenant which is the law of Christ written on our hearts and minds. He comments, "Here God clearly defines and lucidly expounds the differential of the New Covenant. It is peculiarized by his putting his laws in our minds and writing them in our hearts, so we have nothing to do, but read them, the Holy Spirit giving us all the help we need to discern and understand them."[12]

In many places the New Testament expounds that a Christian is not under law but under grace. Paul uses the illustration of a woman whose first husband has died, stating, *Ye also are become dead to the law by the body of Christ; that ye should be married to another.* He stated that *now we are delivered from the law.* (Ro 7:4-6) In another example Paul shows the law as a schoolmaster and says, *After that faith is come, we are no longer under a schoolmaster.* (Ga 3:24-25) The external law has been replaced by the inner workings of the Spirit as Paul states, *But if ye be led of the Spirit, ye are not under the law.* (Ga 5:18) Most scholars are in agreement that the term *law* used by Paul does not mean all rules or all morality, but is specifically referring to the Old Testament Law no longer being in effect.

It is not that law no longer exists or is now completely subjective or destroyed. If this were true, God would be accepting either the antinomianism (lawlessness) of the type found in free grace theology or the rank subjectivism of every man doing that which is *right in his own eyes* (Jg 17:6). Instead, it is the objective moral law of God which is written upon the heart and mind under the leadership of the Spirit. This is why Scripture says, *If ye be led of the Spirit, ye are not under the law.* (Ga 5:18) Under His control, one will fulfill the morality and the spirit of the

---

[12] W. B. Godbey, *Commentary on the New Testament*, vol. II (Cincinnati, OH: Revivalist Office, 1897), 102.

law. However, if a person is not led of the Spirit, the verse strongly implies that he is still under the law and will be found guilty of any violation.

It must be recognized that the Old Testament is the inspired Word of God and the law given in it is still of great value. While a Christian is not directly under the Mosaic commands, they still give the principles of morality based upon the unchanging character of God. Christians today would still follow those principles. The moral component of the Law has been repeated and written into the code of the New Covenant and Christians must keep the commands of the New Testament. These are the same eternal moral laws which are written upon the mind and heart.

The following is a good summary of the Wesleyan/Holiness concept of the law. When God has given a person the law, then that person has been given enabling grace through the Spirit to keep that law. If God has not yet given a person a certain law, then that person cannot disobey a command that has not been given; he cannot break a law that does not exist. Herein lays the simplicity of the relationship between sin and the law. A command from God must be given for a person to be able to rebel against it. One cannot rebel against that which, for them, does not exist. If a law has been given, then any breaking of that command is a voluntary known violation of the law that he has been given. If he has not been given the law, then he cannot break what does not exist. This principle is taught by Paul in Romans. He said, *Where no law is, there is no transgression*, and *sin is not imputed when there is no law*. (Ro 4:15 and 5:13) God does not excuse poor behavior, but holds humans accountable for their disobedience to him.

Chapter 5:
Reformed Views of Salvation

Reformation theology should be a somewhat nebulous term since there are five major Protestant groups which came out of the Reformation: Lutherans, Calvinists, Anabaptists, Anglicans, and Arminians. Although other theological traditions from that time could equally claim their roots in the Reformation, Reformed theology exclusively refers to the theological tradition based upon the Calvinistic doctrine. Many groups in America have a background in Reformed doctrine but have made major changes to their theology. Few evangelicals today would be comfortable with the Reformed doctrines of infant baptism, a limited atonement, predestination, and the concept of an enforced state church. The Reformed belief of salvation is based upon the concept of predestination as well as the idea that sin is any failure to be perfect like God. This is the historical doctrine of the Presbyterians, Puritans, the Dutch Reformed and Swiss Reformed Churches. Lutherans and most American Baptists, although they had other differences in theology, originally accepted the Calvinistic definition of sin and that salvation was determined by God's predestination of the elect.

The foundation for Reformed theology is that God has given mankind a law. God holds him accountable to that law and condemns him for not following that law. Man is, therefore, guilty for not keeping the law, and God demands that man be punished for failure to obey the law. However, this theology maintains that man is incapable of keeping the law and does not even know all of what God requires. They believe that salvation is, therefore, purely based upon God imposing His own righteousness upon a sinful man which remains sinful. In contrast, Wesleyan theology is based upon the transforming power of God's grace, which makes one righteous. Thus, people are able to know and keep the law of Christ, which is based upon the guidance of the Spirit of God.

There is much agreement over the means and the impact of the experience of salvation between traditional Calvinists and modern evangelicals. Reformed theology, as well as Lutheran theology, accepted the concept of John Calvin, "It is therefore faith alone which justifies, and yet the faith which justifies is not alone."[1] Both Calvin and Luther would have agreed, "It is difficult and dangerous to teach that we are justified by faith without works and yet to require works at the same time."[2] Both Reformed and Lutheran theology affirm that faith alone brings salvation, but this new birth is evidenced by being a new creature in Christ Jesus and living a holy life. Most of the modern evangelical groups would agree that repentance is a necessary part of saving faith. Repentance is then followed by faith in Christ, which provides salvation, and this new birth is followed by living out our salvation in a transformed life. The Reformers insisted that while a person was saved by faith alone, it was a faith that is not alone. The contradiction in this terminology of salvation has led some to accept only faith as a necessity of the Christian life. This has led to the development of a lawless, licentious religion which is neither biblical nor founded upon a correct understanding of the Protestant Reformers.

The five basic tenets of Calvinistic doctrine about salvation are commonly summarized in the following acrostic.

T **Total Depravity** means that man is so corrupted and sinful that he is not capable of choosing salvation.

U - Unconditional Election means that God sovereignly elects some to salvation.

L **Limited Atonement** means that Christ only died for those who are elected to salvation

I - Irresistible Grace means that those elected to salvation are sovereignly drawn to salvation.

P - Perseverance of the Saints means that those elected to salvation will persevere in holiness of life. Thus, a person cannot lose his salvation

---

[1] John Calvin, *Reformation Theology*, Matthew Barrett, ed., quoted by Korey D. Maas (Wheaton, IL: Crossway, 2017), p. 529-30. See also Paul A. Rainbow, *The Way of Salvation* (Eugene, Oregon: Wipf &Stock, 2005), p. 39.

[2] Martin Luther, *Reformation Theology*, Matthew Barrett ed., quoted by Korey D. Maas (Wheaton, IL: Crossway, 2017), p. 531.

but will also live a holy life. If he does not live holy, it means that he has never been genuinely converted.

Traditional Calvinism, along with Martin Luther, emphasized the sovereignty of God and believed man was so corrupted that he was incapable of choosing to serve God. One good description of this belief comes from Luther, who believed that "man is justified passively, as if he were a stone; he takes no part in his own justification, which is totally the work of God. . . . Man is passive, and God active, in justification. God operates upon man, and man contributes nothing to the process except the inert material upon which God operates."[3] Accordingly, he believed that Christ only died for a select group that was then elected to salvation. All others would be lost. It was purely the mercy and grace of God that provided salvation for the elect. Those who were saved could do nothing to become part of the chosen. In reality, it was not their own faith that saved them; it was a faith that was sovereignly imposed upon them by God. Salvation came only through the grace of God, and a person was chosen by God to believe in Christ for salvation. They had no choice. God elected them, gave them faith for salvation, and caused them to persevere to the end. Calvinists would affirm that the grace and faith that saves, as given in Ephesians 2:8, was not one's own faith but a faith which was a gift given to him by God.

The evidence of salvation for a Calvinist was perseverance in living a holy life. John Calvin wrote, "Those who fall away have never been thoroughly imbued with the knowledge of Christ but only had a slight and passing taste of it."[4] "Falling away" was considered evidence that the individual had never been saved. Calvin also believed that those who fell away perished. He said, "In the elect alone he implants the living root of faith, so that they persevere even to the end. Thus we dispose of the objection, that if God truly displays his grace, it must endure forever.

---

[3] Alister E. McGrath, "John Henry Newman's Lectures on Justification: The High Church Misrepresentation of Luther." *Churchman* 97, no. 2 (1983): 112-122.
[4] David Wishart Torrance, ed., *John 11-21 and I John*, (Grand Rapids: Eerdmans, 1994) 258.

There is nothing inconsistent in this with the fact of his enlightening some with a present sense of grace, which afterward proves evanescent."[5] This emphasis in Calvinism upon holiness of life has produced some of the Godliest saints who have ever lived. Traditional Calvinism, though, produced a very insecure religion, since one could only hope one had been chosen to be one of the elect who would persevere. However, this insecurity did lead to a careful lifestyle.

In spite of the emphasis upon a holy life, the faulty definition of sin is one of the reasons Calvinism has often struggled with the rise of antinomianism (lawlessness) among their theological circles. The Calvinistic theological system holds that all Christians constantly sin. The difference in the definition of sin is at the core of the debate. Calvinists hold to an absolute, objective definition that any failure, even through ignorance or human inability, is a sin. For example, to tell something that is not true is considered to be a lie even if a person had good reason to believe what he was saying was accurate and had carefully checked the facts. This teaching promotes an impossible standard for a human to live up to, and, accordingly, all people must sin because they are human. Wesleyan theology views sin as a moral issue involving the intent of disobedience to God's law. Through God's grace, Christians have the power to obey God. This is a standard which is achievable. An improper understanding of sin makes it difficult for Calvinists to distinguish between sins that are acceptable and those not acceptable. It becomes a logical inconsistency. For the Calvinist, "sins of ignorance" are still sin. The acceptance of any sin in the life of a Christian will often lead to the acceptance of all sin. Degrees of sin are impossible to distinguish both biblically and logically. This is one of the reasons why Calvinism has often struggled with the rise of antinomianism (lawlessness) among their theological circles.

---

[5] John Calvin, *Institutes of the Christian Religion*, 1559 ed., Trans, Henry Beverage, Book 3, Chap. 2, Sec. 11. 362. https://ccel.org/ccel/calvin/institutes/institutes.v.iii.html.

Modified Reformed Theology - Neo-Calvinism

Neo-Calvinism has changed the traditional understanding of Reformed theology in a number of ways by retaining only one of the original five basic points of Calvinism. However, there would be wide variation among their theologians as to whether a person would accept one point, two points, or three points of Calvinist doctrine. Logically and practically, it seems that if the concept of predestination is dropped, then all of the following points except perseverance of the saints must be either modified or rejected. The following is the Calvinistic acrostic with the modifications below each statement which would fit a modified Reformed theology.

T - Total Depravity means that mankind is so corrupted and sinful that he is not capable of choosing salvation.
Neo-Calvinist - They believe that God's grace gives all mankind the privilege of choosing salvation.

U - Unconditional Election means that God sovereignly elects some to salvation.
Neo-Calvinist - They believe that salvation can be accepted or rejected by all.

L - Limited Atonement means that Christ only died for those who are elected to salvation.
Neo-Calvinist - They believe that Christ died for the whole world.

I - Irresistible Grace means that those elected to salvation are sovereignly drawn to salvation.
Neo-Calvinist - They believe it is possible to accept or reject the grace of God.

P - Perseverance of the Saints means that those elected to salvation will persevere in holiness of life. If they do not live holy, it means that they are not saved.
Neo-Calvinist - This is the only one of the core beliefs which is still held. They hold that a person cannot lose his salvation, but will also live a holy life or he has never been genuinely saved.

Traditional Calvinistic theology has been replaced by many or most of those denominations which historically held to predestination. Those groups now hold that through the death of Christ, all of "the world through him might be saved;" (Jo 3:17) accordingly, salvation is available for all people. Anyone may choose to accept or reject this gift of salvation. Neo-Calvinists do believe that a genuinely saved individual lives a life that reflects what God has done. If a person knows God, he would have the fruit of the Spirit in his life. They would also teach that a person who completely abandons God has never been saved. At one time neo-Calvinists were strong in their belief in the necessity of perseverance for the saints, and there may have been little practical distinction in everyday life between traditional Calvinists and the new Calvinism or between a Wesleyan and a Calvinist. A Calvinist who lived a sinful life would have been informed that he had never been saved and needed to be converted. A Wesleyan who lived a sinful life would have been considered backslidden and accordingly needed to be saved. The concept that a person can live a life of deliberate disobedience in defiance of righteousness and still go to heaven is a recent change of doctrine. In 1913 the Sunday School Board of the Southern Baptist Convention published a book entitled, *What Baptists Believe*. In the section on "Perseverance of the Saints" it states, "We believe that such only are real believers as endure unto the end; that their persevering attachment to Christ is the grand mark which distinguishes them from superficial professors."[6] The book also states,

> Traditional Calvinism, which demanded a holy life as evidence of salvation, has been replaced by a religion that excuses sin.

> A man may be self-deceived. He may have refused the complete surrender of his heart which the gospel demanded, believing that he could obtain eternal life at smaller cost. He may have persuaded himself that he has indeed obtained life. In that hope he may have entered into the discharge of the duties of the Christian life, and long

---

[6] O. C. S. Wallace, *What Baptists Believe* (1913 repr., Piqua, OH: Calvary Baptist Church, 2000), 118.

have met no test which he did not appear to sustain with fair credit. Self-deceived, he has been lulled into a false security. The awakening comes with some unexpected test, some temptation for which he was not prepared. Then it is revealed that the life of the past was an outer conformity and not the result of an inner change. As long as life lasts there is the possibility of such failure. If it comes even at the last of life, it is as sure proof as if it had come earlier that the soul has not passed from death unto life.[7]

Free-Grace Theology

Free-grace theology would, in reality, be the most extreme form of neo-Calvinism, and it accepts all of the changes made to Reformed doctrine by neo-Calvinists. In addition, there is a modification of the final point of Calvinism, as well. The following is a summary of the free-grace theological position on the Calvinistic five points. The free-grace position cannot accurately claim to be grounded in Reformed theology at all, since it either rejects or modifies all of its essential doctrinal beliefs regarding salvation, but it does have a background in the Calvinistic theological tradition.

> **T Total Depravity** - Free-grace partially rejects this doctrine. Adherents believe that God's grace gives all mankind the privilege of choosing salvation.
> **U Unconditional Election** - Free-grace rejects this doctrine. Adherents believe that salvation can be accepted or rejected by all
> **L Limited Atonement** - Free-grace rejects this doctrine. Adherents believe that Christ died for the whole world.
> **I - Irresistible Grace** - Free-grace rejects this doctrine. Adherents believe it is possible to reject the grace of God.
> **P - Perseverance of the Saints** - Free-grace has modified

---
[7] O. C. S. Wallace, *What Baptists Believe*, 121-122.

this doctrine to **Preservation by God**. Adherents have shifted from what man does as evidence of salvation to the idea that God keeps His people, even if they are totally sinful.

In reality, the logical outcome of this Calvinistic doctrine of sin ends up allowing any and all sin in the life of a believer. After all, if God only sees one through the righteousness of Jesus Christ, it does not matter what a person does. God still sees him as righteous no matter how wicked he is. When this theology teaches only a simplistic, intellectual belief in Christ without repentance or a transformational conversion, it undermines and destroys all true Christianity. This is commonly called free-grace theology. It is similar to the neo-Calvinistic position, but takes the ideas much further. Various forms of this position are rapidly becoming the major belief of all the denominations which at one time held to John Calvin's doctrine of election. In all of these variations of Calvinist doctrine there is a wide gray area where one belief system gradually merges into the next.

The free-grace doctrine has spread quite widely throughout evangelical circles. The idea that behavior of life has little or nothing to do with salvation is not just an abstract theory; it has become perhaps the dominant belief and practice of the modern American church. Even some of the leading theologians and preachers are spreading this ideology. Martyn Lloyd-Jones said, "If your presentation of the gospel does not expose it to the charge of antinomianism you are not putting it correctly."[8] Kevin DeYoung declared, "If people hear us talking about justification and don't almost think that we are giving them a license to sin, we aren't preaching grace strong enough."[9] Charles Stanley wrote, "It is not lying, cheating, stealing, raping, murdering, or being unfaithful that sends people to hell. . . . Neither do we become unsaved by acting unsaved. . . . Even if a believer for all practical purposes becomes an unbeliever, his salvation is

---

[8] Martin Lloyd Jones, *Righteous Judgment of God*, 186-187, quoted by Vic Reasoner, *Fundamental Wesleyan Systematic Theology* (Evansville:IN, 2021), 732.

[9] Kevin DeYoung, The Justification Debate, 36, quoted by Vic Reasoner, *Fundamental Wesleyan Systematic Theology* (Evansville:IN, 2021), 732.

not in jeopardy."[10] This free-grace doctrine has spread throughout the pulpits and media ministries of America. This doctrine was not the original beliefs of the Calvinists and a shrinking minority still emphasizes the necessity of a holy life.

The free-grace position is a major theological shift which has undermined the lifestyle of those in the Christian church. Traditional Calvinists abhor this antinomianism. They hold that salvation makes a difference in the life of the saved individual; it is the evidence of genuine salvation. This new doctrine is simply a repetition of a struggle with excusing sin which the church has faced down through the ages. One problem is the change of emphasis from having faith that comes from the heart to a head acceptance of an objective set of beliefs. Genuine faith is knowing God in your heart rather than only having a theological understanding. (Ro 10:9) Free-grace doctrine is completely undermining the lifestyle as well as the existence of the church. Those in the church live little different from those in the world, and it is loudly proclaimed that it does not matter. This belief has destroyed much of the spiritual motivation people have for regular church attendance, forcing the church to turn into an entertainment complex rather than a spiritual center. It also has undermined evangelism, since it seems that most people in American society claim to have been born again without regard to the way they live or whether they attend church. Systematic worship of God and fellowship with other believers has become optional.

> Many followers of free-grace doctrine blithely march straight onward feeling secure, not knowing their real destination is hell.

Many followers of this doctrine blithely and confidently march straight onward feeling spiritually secure, not knowing their real destination is hell. The tragedy is that Scripture teaches that these people are not Christians, no matter what they think or profess. Paul preached justification by faith (Rom. 3:28) and a final judgment according to deeds. (Rom. 2:7-16)"[11]

---

[10] Charles Stanley, *Eternal Security*, 70-71, quoted by Vic Reasoner, *Fundamental Wesleyan Systematic Theology* (Evansville:IN, 2021), 750.
[11] Paul A. Rainbow, *The Way of Salvation* (Eugene, Oregon: Wipf &Stock, 2005), 16.

First John 2:3-4 says, *And hereby we do know that we know him, if we keep his commandments. He that saith, I know him, and keepeth not his commandments, is a liar, and the truth is not in him."* Neither do people go to heaven that do not do the will of God. Matthew 7:21-23 says, *"Not every one that saith unto me, Lord, Lord, shall enter into the kingdom of heaven; but he that doeth the will of my Father which is in heaven. Many will say to me in that day, Lord, Lord, have we not prophesied in thy name? And in thy name have cast out devils? And in thy name done many wonderful works? And then will I profess unto them, I never knew you: depart from me, ye that work iniquity.*[12] A person's entrance into heaven is dependent not only upon faith in Christ, but also upon living out that faith in an obedient holy life. A person who deliberately and intentionally rebels against God in defying Him is certainly not going to heaven; yet this false doctrine is sweeping throughout America.

The extreme free-grace position teaches that only a belief in Christ is necessary for salvation. No other actions of any type matter. It does not demand repentance as a condition of salvation, nor does a person have to accept Jesus Christ as Lord as well as his Savior. A person can accept salvation by believing in Christ, but is never required to repent of sin or even stop sinful behavior. It also teaches that since a person is saved by a single act of faith, it does not matter how one lives. People are confidently assured that heaven is guaranteed, no matter their behavior. However, this is not the teaching of Scripture. The validity of their eternal security position is only as solid as the biblical accuracy of their beliefs. Scripture warns that there are two ways: the road to destruction and the road to life. (Mt 7:13-14) This doctrine has placed millions on the road to destruction. The structural soundness of a bridge over a chasm is not based upon one's feelings of confidence, but upon objective construction principles. As we travel the road of life, we will approach the bridge to the celestial city at the end of life. Immense confidence in a faulty theological structure will be a horrific reality for those who have misplaced trust.

While proponents of this theology emphasize that a person should

---

[12] Some of the other verses which teach this same truth are 1Co 6:9, 2Th 1:8, He 12:14, 1Jo 2:17, Re 22:14.

obey God, they do not believe it is necessary. This has led to many who live licentious lives still professing to be Christians. It has also encouraged the idea that practically all people in society are saved, even if they do not go to church or live morally. They teach that a person should obey God for the purpose of obtaining rewards for their good deeds. They also hold that God will punish sin in this life, or if one is exceptionally evil, God may immediately take him to heaven by causing him to die prematurely. Thus, the punishment for total wickedness is paradoxically, immediate entrance to heaven! It is a strange contradiction to teach that when a "Christian" is no longer fit to live on this earth, he is taken to heaven, where, apparently, he is fit to live.

Calvinists would explain that once a person has chosen salvation, he can never be lost since they believe a person is given eternal life. They strongly emphasize the security of the believer being kept by the power of God. Once one has been born into the family of God, they would insist a person can never be unborn. They maintain that a person may be a disobedient or willful child, but still a child of God. When confronted with the possibility that this allows for people living an evil life to still go to heaven, some accept that idea while others suggest that perhaps those people were never truly saved.

There are some real problems with the free-grace position. Those from the traditional Reformed perspective would note that it is obvious that a person has never been saved if not living right. The promise of eternal life is only to those who follow Christ. (Jo 10:27-28 and Mt 7:23) They would assert that a blatant sinner had never been born again and had never been a new creature in Christ. (2Co 5:17) A Wesleyan would consider one backslidden if he reverted to committing sin. Wesleyans note that the example of being born into God's family is not a good illustration. All of us were born a child of the devil and were part of his family before becoming part of the family of God. Were we unborn from the devil's family? Another argument is that the opposite of birth is death, not to be unborn. Scripture teaches that sin causes spiritual death. (Eph 2:1 and Co 2:13) Wesleyans certainly believe that a person is kept by God's power, but believe that salvation is also a volitional choice. Certainly, God promises the power to keep His people, but Scripture does not state that a person cannot change his mind about serving God. The promises of Scripture that discuss the keeping power of God all refer to outside forces over which God will give victory to those choosing to obey Him.

The misuse of a few Scriptures is the basis for free-grace theology. The use of John 10:28-29 to say that if a person is ever in the hand of God, nothing could ever remove him from God's hand does not read the context! According to the previous verse, the promise is only given to those who follow Christ. The free- grace position also misunderstands or ignores the meaning of the word *pluck*. It means to remove by force. It would not apply to a person who chooses to remove himself from the hand of God since no one is removing him by force.

Similar misconceptions apply to other passages used by Calvinists such as Romans 8:39 which says that no creature can separate one from the love of God. Sin is not a creature nor does this passage state that a person cannot choose to reject God. While there is no outside power or creature that can separate one from God, sin in the life of an individual does remove one from God. Isaiah 59:2 says, *But your iniquities have separated between you and your God, and your sins have hid his face from you.*

Evangelical Arminian - Blending Calvinist and Wesleyan/Arminian Theology

Religion in America is exemplified by freedom. Any and every theology is competing for members and attempting to build churches. Accordingly, there is a large theological mix, with many evangelicals not falling clearly into any distinct doctrinal camp. The mix of Wesleyan and Reformed theology has taken many forms. The traditional Reformed theology of election was overtaken in America by the freewill doctrine; however, most Reformed leaders held on to their doctrine defining sin. Men with a Calvinistic background such as Charles Finney, Dwight L. Moody, and R. A. Torrey accepted the Wesleyan doctrine of a second experience of the filling of the Spirit. Their theological blending was neither Calvinistic nor Wesleyan. Wesleyans who have attended Reformed theological schools have been influenced by the Calvinistic definition of sin and have tried to impose Wesleyan theology over a Reformed definition of sin. Jacob Arminius was a Calvinist, but he disagreed with the five points of Calvinistic theology relating to predestination. His followers at one time dominated the Baptist movement in England, but it was the Calvinistic doctrine of election that was accepted by most American Baptists. However, there are a number of General Baptists and Free-will Baptists in the United States. Pentecostals and Charismatics, in general, focus more on experience than theology. Most of these have a historical background in Wesleyan theology or in the Keswickian doctrine of the late 1800s. Some would follow Methodist doctrine on sin, but others have a blend of Wesleyan and Reformed theology. The tendency for all these groups would be to teach the possibility of backsliding and losing one's salvation, but also hold a Reformed concept of sin. Thus, they feel a person constantly and continually commits sins of infirmity and ignorance and sometimes might choose to disobey God, though willful sin would not be the practice of life.

One important change for the Wesleyan theological denominations was the rise of relational theology. This was a shift away from an objective standard of a holiness lifestyle to an emphasis upon a subjective, post-modern relational model of salvation. Holiness people have always understood sin as a moral choice to disobey God. Relational theology took the concept of sin in a different direction. Instead of defining sin as disobedience to the moral law written upon the heart, sin was viewed as the rejection of the love of God and was defined as "the absence of this relationship."[13] "Sin is whatever violates that relationship and causes a separation between God and mankind."[14] The failure of many to live the life demanded by their doctrine has led to this theological change. This was described as a "credibility gap" according to Mildred Wynkoop. She said, "The absolute of holiness theology may satisfy the mind but the imperfection of the human self seems to deny all that the perfection of

---

[13] Mildred Bangs Wynkoop, *A Theology of Love* (Kansas City: Beacon Hill Press of Kansas City, 1972), 154.
[14] H. Ray Dunning, *Grace, Faith, and Holiness: A Wesleyan Systematic Theology* (Kansas City: Beacon Hill Press of Kansas City, 1972), 286.

Christian doctrine affirms."[15] The purpose of the redefinition of sin was to make allowances for moral failures and unacceptable carnal actions and reactions. While relational theology is stated in Wesleyan terminology, it is a new theological system at its core. Relational theology is foundationally a rejection of Wesleyan/Holiness doctrine and is a new, post-modern theology. Those who follow this neo-Wesleyan relational theological system would readily admit that "repentance is essential to the Christian life because Christians sin."[16] They would agree, however, that "sin as a pattern can indeed be broken."[17] This concept shifts their doctrine from a life of complete victory to a limited concept of victory. According to them, sin may not be the practice or habit of life, but there would be occasional times in which deliberate disobedience or rebellion to God would occur while a person is still maintaining his Christian life and relationship with Christ. This doctrine clashes with the doctrine of John Wesley in his sermon on "The Marks of the New Birth." He contrasted the children of God and the children of the devil saying, "By this plain mark (the committing or not committing sin) are they distinguished from each other."[18]

> If a person is wrong about salvation, he may end up missing heaven.

A number of other major differences have arisen between traditional Wesleyan theology and many modern neo-Wesleyan relational theologians. The doctrine of sanctification has been changed. "Any underlying sinfulness of birth nature"[19] has been repudiated. Accordingly, the doctrine of eradication or cleansing of the sin nature from the heart is no longer believed. In addition, the baptism and filling of the Spirit as a second, instantaneous work of grace is no longer taught. The lifestyle has also radically changed with the denomination moving to accept many

---

[15] Mildred Bangs Wynkoop, *A Theology of Love*, 39.
[16] Diane Leclerc, *Discovering Christian Holiness* (Kansas City: Beacon Hill Press of Kansas City, 2010), 208.
[17] Diane Leclerc, *Discovering Christian Holiness*, 210.
[18] John Wesley, ed, by Nick Black, *The Basics of the Theology of John Wesley*, (Middleburg, PA):, Parenthesis given by Wesley.
[19] Richard S. Taylor, *Counterpoint: Dialogue with Drury on the Holiness Movement* (Schmul Publishing Co., 2005), 51.

behaviors which were formerly condemned, such as social drinking of alcoholic beverages. While homosexual behavior is still opposed there are many (particularly the relational theologians) in those denominations who argue that the acceptance of homosexuality is consistent with relational theology. While these changes relate to the concept of sin, salvation, and sanctification, the theory of evolution has also been accepted, and inerrancy, as understood by fundamentalists, evangelicals, and classic Wesleyan theologians, is no longer accepted. It is quite clear that the modern relational theologian is no longer the traditional follower of the Methodists, of Wesley, or of the Holiness movement of the nineteenth and twentieth centuries.

Summary

What a person believes about sin is critical for salvation. It lays the foundation for all of our soteriology. (Beliefs about salvation) If a person is wrong about salvation, he may end up missing heaven and going to hell. Catholics believe that salvation is through the sacraments of the church, and liberal Christianity accepts a universalist view that all religions have their own way to heaven and all will be eventually saved. Among evangelicals, there are five major concepts regarding sin and salvation. All of these groups believe in salvation by grace through faith. Listed below are the five groups with how they could be distinguished from other groups. They are:

1. Wesleyan/Holiness - A person can and must live a life without sin. Sin is defined as willful disobedience to God.
2. Calvinist/Reformed - God predestines those whom He chooses.
3. Neo-Calvinist - People have free-will, and God will cause one to persevere in a holy life as evidence of saving faith, they but will still commit sin.
4. Free-grace - People have free-will and are eternally secure once saved no matter their behavior.
5. Evangelical Arminian - Arminian theology with a Calvinistic definition of sin.

Chapter 6
Defining Sin Biblically

Sin in Scripture is used in a twofold sense. "Original sin may be defined as the sinful state and condition in which men are born."[1] Personal sin is choosing to disobey God, doing that which God has forbidden or refusing to do what God demands. All people have willfully and knowingly sinned in this way and are guilty before God. Personal sin is forgiven when a person is justified, but original sin is cleansed by God in the work of sanctification. Care must be taken to keep these two concepts of sin separated. Otherwise, confusion will result. Often in Scripture the singular term is used for the sin nature, but this is not always true; accordingly, sometimes passages have been interpreted either way.

One example which shows the difficulty of interpretation is the passage in 1Jn. 1:7-8. It states, *But if we walk in the light, as he is in the light, we have fellowship one with another, and the blood of Jesus Christ his Son cleanseth us from all sin. If we say that we have no sin, we deceive ourselves, and the truth is not in us.* Is this passage teaching that the sin nature will be cleansed if one walks in the light? Does the following verse mean that anyone who claims to have no need of that cleansing because he has no sin nature is self-deceived? Or does the passage mean that one who walks in the light is forgiven for committed sins, and the following verse teaches that anyone who thinks that he has not committed sin is self-deceived? The weight of evidence tends toward this passage dealing with original sin. This example shows how some of the most important verses theologically can be misinterpreted by a failure to understand to which type of sin the passage is referring.

The Old Testament does make a distinction between sins of ignorance and willful breaking of the law. It also makes a distinction between high-

---

[1] Paul Enns, *The Moody Handbook of Theology* (Chicago: Moody Publishers, 2008), 322.

handed sin and other sins. However, even in the Old Testament, outside of the Pentateuch, these distinctions are rarely, if ever, made. In the New Testament sin is seldom mentioned with any modifying statements. In both Testaments the basic meaning is to disobey God's law. The meaning of sin is the same, but the concept of the law is changed between the Old and New Testaments. Scripture does not teach that to miss an unobtainable mark of God's perfection is sin. The mark God expects is obedience to the law and this is possible; however, one must understand that the Old Testament Law was fulfilled in Christ's death, and the covenantal law of the New Testament is based upon faith and love and is written upon the heart. (He 8:7-13) The New Testament does not teach that deliberate disobedience and wrongs done in ignorance or due to human limitations are two separate types of sins. It simply states that a person who is born of God does not sin. (1Jn 3:9 and 1Jn 5:18)

In defining sin it must be firmly kept in mind that the Christian can live a sinless life and, furthermore, is required to do so for entrance to heaven since *the wages of sin is death.* (Ro 6:15-23, Mt 7:23) We must hold with the Apostle Paul when he stated, *What shall we say then? Shall we continue in sin, that grace may abound? God forbid. How shall we, that are dead to sin, live any longer therein?* (Ro 6:1-2) If Paul anathematized sinning religion, why should we defend it? Instead, our focus should be on finding complete victory in Christ over all sin. Any definition of sin which teaches that Christians must sin is a false definition and is not biblical. Scripture teaches complete victory over all sin in this present life. "If sin involves ignorant transgression or involuntary lack of conformity, then we cannot live without sin."[2] A legal definition of sin, which demands perfection of life, cannot be correct, since it would make a sinless life impossible, thus, making the biblical commands not to sin a complete farce. The moral definition, which demands that the intent of the heart be right, is not an easy standard, but is obtainable through the grace and power of God. Freedom from sin through grace is the core of the Wesleyan belief system while constant defeat regarding sin is one of the central tenets of Calvinism. Scripture teaches total defeat of the devil here

---

[2] Harold J. Ockenga, *The Church of God* (Westwood, N.J.: Fleming H. Revell Co., 1956), 226.

in this life. (1 Jn 3:8)

God's plan has never been to legalistically demand perfect obedience through the imposition of an external law. The Mosiac law *was added because of transgressions till the seed [Christ] should come.* (Ga 3:19) The law only served as a schoolmaster until the coming of faith in Christ. Christians are then *"no longer under a schoolmaster."* (Ga 3:25) God's purpose has always been for love to be the dominant, ruling force in the relationship between God and man. God uses the illustration of marriage to portray the relationship He wishes to have with mankind. What would a husband or wife want, a perfect spouse who lacked love or one who loved but made mistakes? What type of child would a father and mother desire, a perfect child or one who responded with love but sometimes unintentionally failed in his actions? God is far more concerned about our love for Him than our being perfect in action. However, it is also clear in Scripture that obedience to God is evidence of our love for Him. (Jn 14:15)

Greek Words

The major Greek word used for sin in the New Testament is the verb, *hamartano. The Concise New International Dictionary of New Testament Theology and Exegesis* states this regarding its definition: "It occurs exclusively in a moral sense. . . . The NT writers never use the term with a concrete/physical meaning ("fail to hit a target") or even with the sense "error, failure in judgment.". . . Instead, the actual images associated with the concept of sin incl. rebellion, corruption, violation, trespassing, disobedience, etc."[3] The original etymology of the word meant to miss the mark. But what is the target God wants one to hit? Biblically, the mark is to knowingly and willfully keep the law of God. In the translation of the Old Testament into Greek about 200 B.C., *hamartano* was used once to mean miss the mark. (Jg 20:16) However, the word was used hundreds of times in the moral sense of an offense against God. Those who hold the legal definition just assume without any scriptural basis that the mark is

---

[3] Christopher A. Beetham, ed., *The Concise New International Dictionary of New Testament Theology and Exegesis* (Grand Rapids: Zondervan Academic, 2021), 64.

the perfection of God. Does God demand an impossible perfection? Is hopeless despair God's goal? Does God demand the impossible? Are people guilty for failure to reach an impossible standard? This is the logical outcome of the legal definition.

The legal concept totally ignores another basic question. What is the law a Christian must obey? Is it the law of absolute perfection? Is it all the moral commandments of the Bible? Is it the law of love? Or is it the law of God written on the heart and mind? The definition of sin must ultimately be derived from the way Scripture defines it and from the way it is used in Scripture. Clearly the Mosaic Covenant has been superseded by the New Testament, and it presents a new concept of law which is in effect. Holiness people would hold that it is the law of love written upon the heart which is lived out by a Spirit-possessed individual who has been transformed by the grace of God. Accordingly, the promise that Jesus would *save his people from their sins* (Mt 1:21) becomes possible through the presence of the Holy Spirit in a person's life.

The word *adikia* which means unrighteousness indicates injustice or doing that which is morally wrong. John teaches that *all unrighteousness (adikia) is sin*, (1Jn 5:17) and that a person can be cleansed from all *adikia*. (1Jn 1:9) Luke states that the workers of *adikia* will be thrust out of the kingdom of God. (Lu 13:27-28) In his letter to the Corinthian Church, Paul says, *the unrighteous shall not inherit the kingdom of God?* (1Co 6:9) Unrighteousness can be used as the equivalent of sin. Scripture clearly teaches that a person may be completely delivered from unrighteousness and that righteousness is a necessity for heaven. Since it is possible to be genuinely righteous, the term must not refer to impossible standards. Righteousness must be applied only in the moral sense of knowingly doing that which is wrong. While sin and unrighteousness are equivalent terms, what unrighteousness means is perhaps less definitively defined in Scripture than the term *sin*.

The word *anomia* has the connotation of lawlessness or of breaking the law. John defines sin as *anomia* or lawlessness. (1Jn 3:4) *Anomia* is not inadvertent disobedience to the law, but the action of one who refuses to come under the authority of the law. "It is not that they lack law or do not know the law, but that they choose to operate outside of law. Thus sin is described in terms of a conscious rejection of God's revealed will."[4] This word then identifies that the willful violation of God's law is sin. God will not tolerate a person breaking His law and states at the judgment, *depart from me, ye that work anomia*. (Mt 7:23) Scripture also teaches that those which commit iniquity (anomia) shall be cast into the fire. (Mt 13:41-42)

There are other words that are sometimes used for the concept of sin. *Parabasis* is the word that is used for transgression and also is used for breaking of the law. *Paraptoma* means trespass or offence and refers to sin when it would be a willful trespass or an offence against God. It is a broader term than *hamartano* and can include both unintentional errors and willful transgressions.[5]

Sin has serious consequences. Those who sin will not go to heaven. To go down the road of excusing sin allows multitudes to think they are headed for heaven while in reality they are headed to hell. If sin is erroneously defined in such a way that makes it impossible to live without committing sin, it will undermine every warning in the Bible against sin and will deceive people into excusing behavior which is unacceptable to God. It is also easy to go to the other extreme and refuse to call actions sinful which are, and this also deceives multitudes. Our society is now questioning many things which were once clearly considered sin and taking the position that those actions are not wrong. We must get this doctrine right. Salvation depends on it. While a person may not be perfect in all ways, a person can always choose to obey God. In *The Biblical Illustrator,* D. N. Sheldon stated, "Sin always implies knowledge–knowledge of the law of which it is a transgression. It is the moral law, which is always made known, first of all, in the conscience . . . Sin always implies voluntariness, or that the action to which it is ascribed is the free action of its author. We may search among the Divine commandments in the Bible as long as we please, we shall not find one addressed to man

---

[4] Gary W. Derickson, *First, Second, and Third John*, ed. H. Wayne House, W. Hall Harris III, and Andrew W. Pitts, *Evangelical Exegetical Commentary* (Bellingham, WA: Lexham Press, 2012), 298.

[5] James Strong, *Strong's Exhasustive Concordance of the Bible and A Concise Dictionary of the Words in The Greek New Testament* (McLean, VA: MacDonald Publishing Company, n.d.), #3900, 55.

which it is not in his power to obey, if rightly disposed."[6]

Scriptural Definitions of Sin

Perhaps the best New Testament definition for sin is found in 1 John 3:4 which states, *Whosoever committeth sin transgresseth also the law: for sin is the transgression of the law.* This is sometimes translated, *sin is lawlessness.* To be lawless is to deliberately and intentionally refuse to come under the authority of the law; thus this passage forms the backbone of the Wesleyan definition of sin. Wesleyans state that sin is the willful transgression of the known law of God.

Jesus teaches the same concept in His dealings with the Pharisees. He said, *If ye were blind, ye should have no sin: but now ye say, We see; therefore your sin remaineth.* **(Jn 9:41)** These Pharisees had been of the truth and had not committed sin; however, when Christ came and was rejected, then they became guilty of committing sin. The behavior itself was not considered sin until it was combined with the knowledge that the action was wrong.

Another New Testament passage that helps to define sin is **James 4:17** which says, *Therefore to him that knoweth to do good, and doeth it not, to him it is sin.* Often we think about sin being doing something that is wrong, but this verse clearly states that sin is also the failure to do what a person should. "It is also universally true that if a man knows what is right, and does not do it, he is guilty of sin."[7] "This verse teaches us that our responsibility to God is commensurate with our knowledge."[8]

The Apostle Paul also gives a definition of sin in his writings in **Romans 6:16** when he uses disobedience to identify one as a servant of sin. The context of the chapter further helps explain Paul's definition. The chapter opens with vehement demand that a person should not continue in sin. Paul exclaims, *God forbid* even to the idea that one should sin.

---

[6] Joseph S. Exell, ed. *The Biblical Illustrator, John - Jude* (Grand Rapids: Baker Book House, 1958) 226-227.
[7] Albert Barnes, *Barnes Notes on the New Testament* (Grand Rapids: Kregel Publications, 1962), 1381.
[8] William Baxter Godbey, *Commentary on the New Testament*, vol. II (Cincinnati: Revivalist Office, 1897), 247.

Obviously, from this statement Paul does not consider sin to be identified with human infirmity or ignorance. Paul did not believe that a person sinned in "word, thought and deed every day." If human limitations are considered sin, then this admonition becomes a practical impossibility. In the last half of the chapter, Paul then expands beyond his repulsion to living a sinful life to emphasizing in strong language the concept that Christians do not sin at all and states, *His servants ye are to whom ye obey; whether of sin unto death, or of obedience unto righteousness.* (Ro 6:16) Paul clearly defined sin as disobedience in this passage. Paul then gives an absolute contrast between the Christian and the servants of sin. The servant of God is free from sin while the servant of sin is free from righteousness. Romans six teaches that a person can be delivered both from the sin nature as well as from committing personal sin. The passages which state that a person is *free from sin* in verse 18 and verse 22 are both referring to the behavior of the individual. In reality Paul is stating that a person is free from committing any act of sin because he has been freed from the source of sin in the nature that causes one to disobey and rebel against God. To summarize a few of the concepts of sin which Paul is teaching in this passage:

1. Christians are not to continue in sin meaning sin is something which is not practiced. (Ro 6:1)
2. Christians can and must be free from committing any act of sin. (Ro 6:15-18)
3. Sin is defined as disobedience to God. (Ro 6:16-17)
4. Sin and unrighteousness are used interchangeably. To sin is to be unrighteous and to be free from sin is to be righteous. (Ro 13, 18, and 20)
5. Christians can be freed not only from committing sin but also free from the sin nature. (Ro 6:6-8, 11, 18, and 22)

Another passage Paul uses to describe this concept of sin is **Romans 5:19.** It reads, *For as by one man's disobedience many were made sinners, so by the obedience of one shall many be made righteous.* This passage helps to identify that disobedience is what causes one to become a sinner. Earlier in the chapter in verse twelve Paul notes that sin entered the world through Adam. The Fall once again identifies sin with deliberate disobedience. It is not a failure, infirmity, or human ignorance that makes one a sinner; it is disobedience. According to Paul, sin is willful disobedience to God.

Paul gives another illustration of sin in **Romans 14:23.** Once again, he is focusing upon an act which is believed to be disobedience to God. The Scripture states that to do something which is believed to be wrong is sin. Paul says, *Happy is he that condemneth not himself in that thing which he alloweth. And he that doubteth is damned if he eat, because he eateth not of faith: for whatsoever is not of faith is sin.* (Ro 14:22-23) Paul is dealing with the dietary practices of the Jews and relating them to the gospel. He believed that it was morally acceptable to eat whatever meat a person wished. Nevertheless, if a person believed it was wrong, it was a sin to go ahead and eat. Here is a clear-cut example of a choice between the legal definition and the moral definition. The legal concept says it is not a sin because it is not actually wrong while the moral definition says it is a sin because a person is doing something he believes is in disobedience to God. Scripture takes the side of the ethical/moral position.

> Nowhere does the New Testament teach that sin is a failure to be perfect.

Scripture states that *all unrighteousness is sin* **(1Jo 5:17)** Sin and unrighteousness are equated together as synonyms, and both words teach the concept that God demands a person to live a life without sin. Scripture clearly teaches that a person can and should live a life of righteousness, and that this is the evidence of being born of God. (1Jo 2:29, and 1Jo 3:7-10) Righteousness is also a necessity for heaven as Scripture clearly states that *the unrighteous shall not inherit the kingdom of God?* (1Co 6:9 and Mt 13:40-43)

Romans identifies what sin is in **Romans 5:13** along with **4:15**. Here it states, *For until the law sin was in the world: but sin is not imputed when there is no law,* [And] *where no law is, there is no transgression.* Once again, Scripture defines sin objectively as breaking or transgressing the law. God does not consider a person to have sinned unless there is a violation of the law. In the context of Romans, it was referencing the natural law given to the Gentiles and the Law of Moses given to the Jewish people. Paul is using this concept to show that all people sinned in that they violated the law God had given them. (Ro 5:12) Yet, Christians are accountable to a new law in the dispensation of grace. How has the concept of sin for the Christian changed? Since sin is a violation of the law, the question arises, what is the law? Repeatedly, Scripture states that Christians are not under the Old Testament law. (Ro 6:14, Ro 6:15, and Ga 5:18) Yet the Bible also teaches that Christians are *under the law to Christ* (1Co 9:21), under the law of love (Ro 13:8), and that God's law is written upon the heart (He 8:10). The law to which Christians are accountable today is the absolute law of God which is subjectively written upon the mind and the heart of each believer. The Holy Spirit is then given in order to guide into all truth. (Jn 16:13) These passages clearly destroy the idea that God's requirement is absolute perfection.

A further study into the passages indicates that before the Old Testament Law, sin existed. Before the law was given *sin was in the world: but sin is not imputed when there is no law* (Ro 5:13). To understand this passage, it is necessary to analyze whether it is talking about the sin principle or the action of committing sin. We must also understand what the law is. Is it just the Old Testament Law or is it any commandment of God? This passage states that *sin is not imputed when there is no law*. This means that God did not even consider it sin for them when an improper action occurred in ignorance. Even before the Mosiac Law, people could have been in violation of the natural law and the law of God given to them through their conscience. From creation, the requirements of the law would have been also passed down from generation to generation. In other instances, God spoke directly to communicate His will. Certainly, people such as Adam, Noah, Abraham, Joseph, and Job all give indications that the law of God existed, and that it was possible to violate God's law before it was written in the Pentateuch. Since the existence of the law is necessary for sin to exist, God's law existed before the Law of Moses and the violation of this is the cause of sin.

Wesleyans agree that there is an absolute standard of morality based upon the character of God; however, God does not consider (reckon or impute) a failure as sin if it is done by a person who is in ignorance that such action is forbidden. The legal definition necessitates considering babies guilty of sin and headed for hell. Children below the age of accountability are not only guiltless, but also are not counted by God as having committed sin. New converts, likewise, are not regarded as sinners by God for unlawful behavior if it is done in ignorance. The action may be horrifically unacceptable to society, but God does not consider it sin. God writes His law upon our hearts, and Scripture does explain the morality of God that should be kept. God will quickly deal with any person whose behavior violates those things in Scripture which will keep one out of the kingdom of God. (1Co 6:9-10, Ga 5:19-21, Eph 5:5, and Re 21:8) There are also many admonitions in Scripture which have to do with carefulness or developing a godly lifestyle. Disobedience to God or a choice to refuse to do what is taught in the Scripture is sin and would keep one out of heaven; however, there are many admonitions which have to do with growth in grace and developing a better and more consistent Christian life. These should not be called sin unless they involve disobedience or the action is called sin in Scripture.

Testing the Two Definitions

How does Scripture use the term *sin*? Does its usage for personal sin match the moral definition used by the Wesleyan/Holiness people or does it match the absolute Calvinistic definition? The ethical or moral definition of sin used by the Wesleyan/Holiness people considers sin to be willful disobedience to the known law of God. The New Testament clearly uses the ethical/moral definition of those who follow John Wesley. This was also the conception of sin in the Early Church, as well as almost all other denominations outside the Reformed tradition.

A good way to test the correctness of the definitions of sin is to use them in verses and compare results. Any person can easily use a search engine of the Bible and replace the word sin with each definition. It is quite revealing. The Calvinistic definition often makes no sense at all while the Wesleyan definition always fits perfectly. W. T. Purkiser stated that there were forty-one instances of the verb *hamartano*. He said, "The ethical definition will fit and make good sense in all forty-one instances. There are no exceptions. The legal definition will fit and make good sense in only four of this number."[9]

Here are some examples of this test. The following passages from the New Testament contain the word *sin*. In the first copy of the verse, the word *sin* or one of its forms is replaced with the Wesleyan/Holiness definition (Sin is willful disobedience). In the second copy of the verse, sin is replaced with the Calvinist definition (Sin is coming short of the perfection of God). Read what it says and see for yourselves. A number of other verses are listed in the footnote for anyone who wishes to study it further.[10]

1. Jn 5:14   **Moral**: Afterward Jesus findeth him in the temple, and said unto him, Behold, thou art made whole: willfully disobey God no more, lest a worse thing come unto thee.

   Legal: Afterward Jesus findeth him in the temple, and said unto him, Behold, thou art made whole: do not fall short of the absolute perfection of God, lest a worse thing come unto thee.

2. Jn 8:11   **Moral**: And Jesus said unto her, Neither do I condemn thee: go, and willfully disobey God no more.

   Legal: And Jesus said unto her, Neither do I condemn thee: go, and be perfect like God.

3. Jn 9:2   **Moral**: And his disciples asked him, saying, Master, who committed willful disobedience to God, this man, or his parents,

---

[9] Westlake Taylor Purkiser, *Conflicting Concepts of Holiness* (Kansas City: Beacon Hill Press, 1964), 49-50.

[10] Here are the verses in which the verb form of sin is used in the New Testament. Mt 18:15, Mt 18:2, Mt 27:4, Lu 15:18, Lu 15:21, Lu 17:3 Lu 17:4, Joh 5:14, Joh 8:11, Joh 9:2, Joh 9:3, Ac 25:8, Ro 2:12, Ro 3:23, Ro 5:12, Ro 5:14, Ro 5:16, Ro 6:15, 1Co 6:18, 1Co 7:28, 1Co 7:36, 1Co 8:12, 1Co 15:24, Eph 4:26, 1Ti 5:20, Tit 3:11, He 3:17, He 10:26, 1Pe 2:20, 2Pe 2:4, 1Jn 1:10, 1Jn 2:1, 1Jn 3:6, 1Jn 3:8, 1Jn 3:9, 1Jn 5:16, 1Jn 5:18.

Defending the Biblical Definition 73

that he was born blind?
Legal: And his disciples asked him, saying, Master, who was not perfect like God, this man, or his parents, that he was born blind?

4. Ro 6:15   **Moral**: What then? shall we willfully disobey God, because we are not under the law, but under grace? God forbid.
Legal: What then? shall we fail to be perfect like God, because we are not under the law, but under grace? God forbid.

5. 1 Co 15:34 **Moral**: Awake to righteousness, and do not wilfully disobey God.
Legal: Awake to righteousness, and do not fail to be perfect like God.

6. 1 Ti 5:20 **Moral**: Them that wilfully disobey God rebuke before all, that others also may fear.
Legal: Them that fail to be perfect like God rebuke before all, that others also may fear.

7. He 10:26 **Moral**: For if we wilfully disobey God after that we have received the knowledge of the truth, there remaineth no more sacrifice for sins.
Legal: For if we wilfully fail to be perfect like God after that we have received the knowledge of the truth, there remaineth no more sacrifice for sins.

8. 1 Jn 2:1 **Moral**: My little children, these things write I unto you, that ye do not wilfully disobey God.
Legal: My little children, these things write I unto you, that ye be perfect like God.

9. 1 Jn 3:6 **Moral**: Whosoever abideth in him does not wilfully disobey God: whosoever wilfully disobeys God hath not seen him, neither known him.

>   **Legal**: Whosoever abideth in him does not fail to be perfect like God: whosoever fails to be perfect like God hath not seen him, neither known him.

10. 1 Jn 3:8   **Moral**: He that committeth wilful disobedience to God is of the devil.

>   **Legal**: He that falls short of being perfect like God is of the devil.

11. 1 Jn 3:9   **Moral**: Whosoever is born of God doth not commit wilful disobedience to God; for his seed remaineth in him: and he cannot wilfully disobey God, because he is born of God.

>   **Legal**: Whosoever is born of God doth not fail to be perfect like God; for his seed remaineth in him: and he cannot fall short of being absolutely perfect like God, because he is born of God.

12. 1 Jn 5:18   **Moral**: We know that whosoever is born of God does not wilfully disobey God.

>   **Legal**: We know that whosoever is born of God does not fall short of being perfect like God.

This chapter delineates the biblical basis for the Wesleyan/Holiness definition of sin. It comprises victory over sin here and now in this life. By His death on the cross, Christ not only forgave sin, He also empowered the regenerated person to live without sin in this life. Salvation does not make one perfect in the sense of overcoming mistakes, ignorance, infirmity, or other human limitations, but it does make one's heart right with God. This enables a person to grow spiritually and develop as God desires toward the perfect likeness of Christ.

Chapter 7
Summarizing the Definition of Sin

In defining personal sin, also called an act of sin, there are two major theological positions among Protestants: the legal concept and the ethical/moral concept.[1] The legal concept, also called the absolute concept, is based upon an absolute or legal definition of sin demanding conformity to the perfect law of God. It is impossible for finite beings to meet this requirement; thus, according to this definition, people sin in word, thought, and deed every day. In his *Systematic Theology,* Norman Geisler expounds this definition and says, "Sin is anything that falls short of God's moral nature . . . It is plain, then, that the ultimate objective standard is God's absolute moral perfection, and anything that falls short of it is sin."[2] According to Charles Hodge, "There is not a believer on earth who does not feel and acknowledge himself to be personally unrighteous, ill-deserving, meriting the wrath of God."[3]

In contrast, the ethical concept, also called the moral concept, focuses upon the knowledge and intention of the action. According to the moral definition, sin is a willful violation of the known law of God. It carries with it the moral responsibility of disobedience and rebellion against the law. The ethical/moral concept holds that a person is not accounted guilty by God for that which he did not know, could not have known, or could not have done differently. St. Augustine gives as an illustration of this principle that a woman who is raped is not guilty of adultery since it was beyond her power to prevent what happened. The volitional action would have been wrong, but it was beyond her control. Augustine writes extensively about this in his book, *The City of God.* He was offering

---
[1] Westlake Taylor Purkiser, *Conflicting Concepts of Holiness* (Kansas City: Beacon Hill Press, 1964) 45.
[2] Norman Geisler, *Systematic Theology,* vol. 3 (Minneapolis: Bethany House, 2004), 106.
[3] Charles Hodge as quoted in Irwin L. Brown, *Further Insights into Holiness,* ed. Kenneth Geiger (Salem, OH: Schmul Publishing Co. Inc., 1990), p. 168.

comfort to the multitudes of women who were raped in the sack of Rome.[4] This illustrates the twisted logic of sins of infirmity, namely sins which a person is powerless to prevent: Sex outside of marriage is a sin; rape is sex outside of marriage; therefore, the victim has sinned. This logic would also apply to child sexual abuse. If breaking the absolute law of God because of an inability to keep it is sin, then being abused is also sin. The idea that a victim of sexual abuse has sinned or is guilty should be absolutely rejected, as it was by both Wesley and Augustine who maintained that sin is a voluntary choice.[5]

The moral concept of sin harmonizes with Scripture and logic unlike the legal concept. This is not to deny the existence of an absolute law. "Both schools agree that both men and angels were placed under the universal moral law of God. Man intentionally transgressed this law and as a result, humanity has inherited a nature which renders the individual incapable of conforming to universal moral law."[6] It is agreed that the destruction of man's capabilities to perform perfectly in every way were destroyed in the Fall; so what does God demand from man now in the redemptive process? God has superimposed "a new law, the law of love, or the law of liberty . . . It is fulfilled, not in the perfection of intelligence, but in the perfection of loving obedience to the Lord Jesus Christ."[7]

To properly define acts of personal sin, these sample quotes accurately represent the greater holiness movement. Personal sin as defined in the Bible Methodist Discipline reads,

> We believe that acts of sin are committed by morally responsible persons choosing to do what they know is

---

[4] Jared Ortiz, *Catholic World Report* (November 25, 2019): https://www.catholicworldreport.com/2019/11/25/Augustine-consolation-after-rape-and –the-reshaping-of-society/.

[5] Augustine makes some of the strongest statements regarding sin being a voluntary action, but when Augustine later in life began emphasizing predestination, he becomes less clear in his statements.

[6] Irwin L. Brown, *Further Insights into Holiness*, ed. Kenneth Geiger (Salem, OH: Schmul Publishing Co. Inc., 1990), 167.

[7] Irwin L. Brown, *Further Insights into Holiness*, 168.

wrong or choosing not to do what they know is required. These acts of sin are therefore not to be confused with short-comings, infirmities, faults, mistakes, failures, or other such deviations from a standard of perfect conduct which are the residual effects of the Fall.[8]

The InterChurch Holiness Convention website says, "What is sin? John Wesley defined sin as 'a willful transgression against a known law of God.' This means that there must be knowledge of wrongdoing, or of refusing to obey God, before sin is committed. Mistakes are not sin."[9]

The Church of the Nazarene states,

> We believe that actual or personal sin is a voluntary violation of a known law of God by a morally responsible person. It is, therefore, not to be confused with involuntary and inescapable shortcomings, infirmities, faults, mistakes, failures, or other deviations from a standard of perfect conduct that are the residual effects of the Fall. However, such innocent effects do not include attitudes or responses contrary to the spirit of Christ, which may properly be called sins of the spirit. We believe that personal sin is primarily and essentially a violation of the law of love; and that in relation to Christ, sin may be defined as unbelief.[10]

This book is a defense of these definitions. John Wesley was correct in his understanding of what constituted sin. He acquired his concepts from the Early Church and other Reformation scholars such as Philip

---

[8] *Discipline of the Bible Methodist Connection of Churches*, (The General Conference, 2018), 15, https://www.biblemethodist.org/wp-content/uploads/2019/06/2018-Bible-Methodist-Discipline-rev.-2.pdf. 15.
[9] "Questions & Answers:," InterChurch Holiness Convention, accessed April 25, 2023, https://ihconvention.com/build-your-faith/questions-answers/salvation/ .
[10] Dean G. Blevins, ed., *Church of the Nazarene: Manual, 2017–2021* (Kansas City, MO: Nazarene Publishing House, 2017), 28. https://2017.manual.nazarene.org/section/church-constitution/.

Melanchthon, the author of the Lutheran Augsburg Confession, and James Arminius. This understanding of sin has historically been believed across the centuries.

Those who hold the moral concept believe sin is a personal, moral failure done in disobedience to God. Sin is intent to break God's law. One does not sin because of human limitations due to ignorance or mistakes. Sin is almost always recorded in the Bible as a deliberate action to rebel against God. Even the natural law has given all mankind through a person's conscience an understanding of right and wrong. Clearly, chapters 1 and 2 of Romans teach that the heathen are condemned for their failure to do what they knew to be right. Under the Old Testament Covenant, the Israelites had definite, specific laws which they were required to keep. Ignorantly breaking one of the laws required a sacrifice for sin in the Old Testament. However, the church today is no longer subject to the Old Testament Mosaic Covenant. God has provided another covenant through the dispensation of grace and has ended the Old Covenant of the Law. This New Testament Covenant writes God's law on the mind and the heart (Heb 8:6-13). Accordingly, it is impossible to ignorantly break the law of God written upon the mind, and it is likewise impossible to break God's law on the heart without the will choosing to defy God.

> Those who commit evil will not inherit the kingdom of God.

One danger of overemphasizing the subjective nature of the law is that a person might mistakenly believe he or she can do whatever one wishes if one does not see any wrong in that action. The ethical/moral concept does not accept the idea that everyone can do that which is right in his own eyes. Galatians 5:18 says, *If ye be led of the Spirit, ye are not under the law.* This passage shows that the believer is free to serve God through the Spirit. It also strongly implies that those who are not led of the Spirit are still under the law and facing the wrath of God. It is the absolute law of God written upon the mind that is subjectively applied to each believer. Galatians 5 continues, however, to describe the works of the flesh and then the fruit of the Spirit. It makes a definitive statement that those who do the works of the flesh *shall not inherit the kingdom of God* (Ga 5:21). This passage also lists out seventeen sins as examples, but clarifies that this is not a complete list. This is an excellent example of both the subjective aspect—a person is not under the law if he is led by the Spirit, and the absolute aspect—the sins which are listed will prevent a person from going to heaven. By no means does the ethical position allow for wild subjectivism. The ethical/moral definition is far more demanding of a moral life than the legal concept, which in one way or another excuses sin. Paul also teaches this same concept when he states, *For until the law sin was in the world: but sin is not imputed when there is no law.* (Ro 5:13) An absolute concept of sin does exist according to this passage, but it is not counted against one as sin when one does not yet have the law of God written on the heart.

Foundational Understanding of the Wesleyan/Holiness Concept of Sin

In order to fairly interpret and discuss the historic Methodist and holiness beliefs, it is necessary to understand the fundamental arguments behind their position. Here are some of the underlying biblical and philosophical foundations for the traditional Methodist/Holiness understanding of sin.

1. An act of personal sin is a moral act of disobedience rather than human failure. Sin is not understood in the absolute sense of failure to do what is right. Instead, sin is a choice to do that which is wrong. Daniel Steele exemplified this in his statement, "There is no sin where perfect love reigns. This may consist with innumerable defects, infirmities, and theoretical and practical errors . . . [but] lack the essential characteristic, namely, the voluntary element."[11] Thomas Oden also effectively summarized the concept, stating, "Such finitude is not properly viewed as sin if sin is willful disobedience to recognizable moral truth. The Manichaeanism that asserts that finitude is sin has long been consensually regarded as a heresy."[12]

---

[11] Daniel Steele, *Milestone Papers* (Holiness Data Ministry, 1995) original publication,1878, http://wesley.nnu.edu/wesleyctr/books/0101-0200/HDM0161.pdf.

[12] Thomas C. Oden, *Life in the Spirit: Systematic Theology, vol. III* (San

2. **Christians do not commit sin and are delivered from all sin.** In his sermon on the *Marks of the New Birth,* John Wesley says, "Whosoever is born of God doth not commit sin; for his seed remaineth in him: And he cannot sin, because he is born of God. [1Jn 3:9] But some men will say, True: Whosoever is born of God doth not commit sin *habitually. Habitually!* Whence is that? I read it not. It is not written in the Book. God plainly saith, 'He doth not commit sin'; and thou addest, *habitually!*"[13] In reality, even adding the word *habitually* or *practice* adds little credibility for those who believe Christians do sin. If failures due to ignorance or infirmity are sins, then these failures are committed daily, continually, habitually, and are practiced.[14] William Burt Pope concurs, "Scripture presents a sinless state as actually attained in this life."[15] Holiness proponents believe that this doctrine of a life without sinning is upheld in multiple other scriptural verses as well.[16]

3. **If the grace of God does not provide deliverance from all sin, it makes God the author of sin.** This is the fundamental difference between Arminianism and traditional Calvinism. Calvinists emphasize the sovereignty of God in predetermining every event, and accordingly, God would have had to predetermine man's fall and subsequent sin. In refuting

---

Francisco, CA: HarperSanFrancisco, 1992), 231–236.

[13] John Wesley, *Wesley's 52* Standard *Sermons,* (Schmul Publishing Co., 1982), 175.

[14] A number of leading scholars have challenged the use of the customary present tense, instead favoring the gnomic present tense such as Daniel Wallace, *Greek Grammar: Beyond the Basics* (Grand Rapids: Zondervan, 1996), 522-525. Bill Mounce, perhaps the primary translator of the ESV, on this passage stated, "I think if I had to do it over again, I would change my vote on 1 John 3:6." Comment from a youtube video at https://www.youtube.com/watch?v=7Ib4UxY7G8w. Some other Calvinistic scholars who question the use of the customary present are Sakae Kubo, Zane Hodges, and Thomas Constable.

[15] William Burt Pope, *A Compendium of Christian Theology: Being Analytical Outlines of a Course of Theological Study,* vol. 3 (London: Beveridge and Co., 1879), 49.

[16] Some of the other verses would be Mt. 1:21, 7:23, Jn. 5:14, 8:11, Rom. 6:7,18, 22, 8:2, I Pet. 4:1, and I Jn. 5:18.

predestination, James Arminius stated, "Of all blasphemies which can be uttered against God, the most grievous is that by which he is set down as the author of sin."[17] Mildred Bangs Wynkoop stated, "This would make God the only real sinner in the universe. No one taught such an extreme view, but Arminias pointed out the fact that . . . [logic] would ultimately force this conclusion."[18] "It follows from their doctrine that God is the author of sin . . . God ordained that man should sin and become corrupt."[19] Followers of Wesley believe that the grace of God includes complete freedom from sin here in this life. Roy Nicholson said, "The religion of Jesus Christ is supernatural. Since it is supernatural, it saves from all sin. . . . Thus to deny that one can be saved from all sin is to attack the holiness of God."[20] "To teach that one cannot live without sin is to teach that a just God has made a law one cannot obey."[21] Daniel Steele stated, "To assert that the Holy God has made sin necessary under the reign of grace is to slander the Father, and pronounce the redemptive plan a stupendous failure."[22]

4. The scriptural definition of sin is failing to keep God's law instead of falling short or a failure to be perfect. (Lev. 4:2, 14, 37; I Jn. 3:4) Some have used the Greek definition of *hamartia,* which means missing the mark, to conclude that everyone sins. But what is the mark? Calvinists assume that it would mean to miss the mark of perfection, yet give no Scripture to prove their assumption. Traditional holiness scholars would challenge that idea. As Adam Clarke said, "Where is this, in unequivocal words, written in the New Testament? Where, in that Book, is it intimated that sin is never wholly destroyed till death takes place, and the soul and

---

[17] James Arminius, quoted in Mildred Bangs Wynkoop, *Foundations of Wesleyan Arminian Theology* (Kansas City: Beacon Hill Press, 1967), 52.
[18] Mildred Bangs Wynkoop, *Foundations of Wesleyan Arminian Theology* (Kansas City: Beacon Hill Press, 1967), 52.
[19] James Arminius, *The Works of James Arminius*, 1550 – 1609, (Library of Alexandria), Kindle, https://a.co/gJELp7Y.
[20] Roy S. Nicholson, *True Holiness: The Wesleyan Emphasis* (Salem, OH: Schmul Publishing Co., repr., 2012), 14.
[21] Roy S. Nicholson, *True Holiness: The Wesleyan Emphasis,* 54.
[22] Daniel Steele, *Love Enthroned* (Holiness Data Ministries: digital ed. 2001), http://wesley.nnu.edu/wesleyctr/books/1801-1900/HDM1892.pdf.

the body are separated? No where."²³ Sin is not depicted in Scripture as an impossible perfection; it is simply obedience to the law.

5. The New Testament fundamentally changes the concept of the law from a legal code to a moral comprehension which is written in a person's mind and heart. Both the Old and the New Testaments define sin as failure to keep the law, but at issue is whether there is a change in the meaning of sin or law in the dispensation of grace. In his sermon on *Christian Perfection,* John Wesley said, "Yea, thus it was from Adam . . . to Christ. There was then no man that sinneth not. But we may safely affirm with St. John, that since the gospel was given, He that is born of God sinneth not. The privileges of Christians are in nowise to be measured by what the Old Testament records concerning those who were under the Jewish dispensation; seeing the fullness of time is now come, the Holy Ghost is now given."²⁴ The New Covenant has written the Law of God upon the hearts and minds. (Heb. 8:8-13) This New Covenant has superseded the Old Testament Covenant which has then vanished away. (Heb. 8:8-13) Therefore, John gives the definition of sin as lawlessness which carries the concept of rebellion rather than ignorance. (1 Jn. 3:4)

6. Those who commit sin will not go to heaven. As Adam Clarke stated, "Unless a believer live and walk in the spirit of obedience, he will fall from the grace of God, and forfeit all his Christian privileges and rights . . . and, if so, perish everlastingly."²⁵ H. Orton Wiley viewed sin as incompatible with entering heaven, and he explains, "Nothing unholy ever enters that city—no sin, whether of act or condition."²⁶

---

[23] Adam Clarke and Samuel Dunn, *Christian Theology*, Second Edition. (London; Glasgow; Dublin: Thomas Tegg & Son; R. Griffin & Co.; Tegg, Wise, & Co., 1835), 208–209.
[24] John Wesley, *The Works of John Wesley*, Third Edition., vol. 11 (London: Wesleyan Methodist Book Room, 1872), 375.
[25] Adam Clarke and Samuel Dunn, *Christian Theology*, 439.
[26] H. Orton Wiley, *God has the Answer* (Kansas City: Beacon Hill Press, 1956 digital edition 2006): http://wesley.nnu.edu/holiness-classics-library/?rows=30&search=author&search_value=wiley.

Chapter 8
The Calvinist Understanding of Sin

Calvinistic Theology alleges that people continuously and constantly sin. The premise is based upon the legal definition of sin, which makes it impossible to live a sinless life. Certainly, all people make mistakes, are limited in knowledge, have human failures, and struggle with human emotions. If God considered these things to be sin, then it would be impossible to live a sinless life. Their definition of sin is based upon the Calvinistic legal understanding of the Greek word, *hamartia*, which means "to miss the mark." Yet, this definition is almost meaningless unless a person knows to what mark God was referring. A person may repeatedly hit a bull's-eye, but if he is aiming for the wrong target, he has still missed. Calvinists have assumed that the target is the perfection of God but seem to base their conclusions on philosophical understandings rather than Scripture. Truly, God is the perfect standard which exemplifies what is right, but is this the standard which God set for mankind to achieve.

As a way to illustrate the Calvinistic principle of sin, one teacher suggested taking elementary school pupils to the gym, giving them a basketball, and telling them to make a basket from across the gym. Since they were young, it was impossible for them to even hit the rim much less to make a basket. This was to illustrate that the goal of the perfect righteousness of God is a human impossibility. The teacher then suggested lining up the students on one side of the court and telling them to jump completely across the court in one leap. This was to illustrate how man falls short of the requirements no matter how hard he tries. This doctrine teaches that God demands us to perform that which we cannot accomplish. Our failures are allegedly to show the utter worthlessness of our own attempts to meet the unreachable standard in order to show us the need for faith in the blood as our only hope. Calvinists teach that the righteousness of Christ is imputed to us to cover our continued unrighteousness. Therefore, they see salvation as not necessarily a change in who we are, but merely a change in the way we are viewed by God. However, this is not the doctrine portrayed in Scripture. While the Bible shows the impossibility of meeting God's requirements in carnal, human strength, Scripture constantly teaches that through the grace of God and the empowerment of the Holy Spirit, a regenerated person can meet the mark which God has set (Ge 6:9, Job 1:1, Lu 1:6, Php 2:15, Jude 1:24, etc.).

Another way to illustrate this principle is to consider a teacher's method for grading memorized Scripture. If the teacher's goal is for a student to accurately quote Scripture verbally, the teacher would not grade spelling, punctuation, or capitalization. If written upon paper, the verse might contain mistakes in spelling or punctuation but could completely meet the goal demanded by the teacher and receive a perfect grade. On the other hand, if a teacher demanded absolute, God–like perfection, it would always be possible to find a mistake somewhere. If the words were all correct, there might be a mistake in capitalization or spelling. If all the grammar were correct, it is doubtful that every letter was shaped perfectly in the handwriting. Perhaps there was even a flaw in the ink or in the paper itself. What kind of a God do we serve? One who carefully gives the achievable requirements and then gives grace to completely meet the goal, or do we have a God who is arbitrary, unreasonable, and impossible in His demands? We have a loving heavenly Father who gives clear direction through His Spirit and then aids us to achieve the guidelines He requires. If we fail, He does not excuse the failure or change the requirements, but is always there to forgive and provide the grace to live victoriously.

The Wesleyan doctrine teaches that the righteousness of Christ is imparted to the regenerated soul enabling a person to truly become righteous (Ro 5:19). When forgiveness of sins occurs, a person's sins are not held against him anymore. He or she becomes genuinely righteous; accordingly, a person may have a sinful past, but a sinless present. When a person is imputed to be righteous by forgiveness of past sins, impartation of righteousness also occurs. This means that when God declares us to be righteous, He transforms us to be righteous at the same time. When people are declared righteous by God, this righteousness is not some fictional abstraction in the mind of God. The God who cannot lie does not deceive

Himself into thinking a person who is sinful is instead righteous. The blood of Christ does neither deceive God nor blinds Him to a corrupted condition. God does not lie to Himself. All Christians have truly become righteous through the transforming power of God that produces new creatures in Christ Jesus (2Co 5:17).

The Legal Definition of Sin

Those who follow the teachings of John Calvin view sin as a failure to perfectly conform to the standard of God's righteousness. They emphasize the absolute nature of sin and even if done without evil intent, missteps are always considered wrong, and wrong actions are always sin. It does not matter if the actions are done in ignorance or through human failure, they believe that sin is objective and is any action or attitude that is not in alignment with the perfect character of God or His law. Those who hold this position believe that it is impossible for human beings to perfectly conform to God's standard of absolute perfection, and thus all people, even Christians, sin daily, constantly and habitually. In his *Systematic Theology,* Norman Geisler says "sin is anything that falls short of God's moral nature . . . It is plain, then, that the ultimate objective standard is God's absolute moral perfection, and anything that falls short of it is sin."[27] In the *Moody Handbook of Theology,* sin is defined as "a failure to conform to the standard of God . . . Hence, it means that all people have missed the mark of God's standard and continue to fall short of that standard."[28]

Their justification for the absolute concept of sin is the idea that wrong actions are always wrong no matter who does it or what the circumstances are. If their concept of the law is broken, to them it is sin. Their view of law ultimately is based upon the perfection of God, and they feel coming short of that absolute perfection must be sin. Those who emphasize the legal definition point out the principle of sins of ignorance found in the Old Testament (Le 4-5, Nu 15). However, sins of ignorance are not taught

---

[27] Norman Geisler, S*ystematic Theology*, vol. 3 (Minneapolis: Bethany House, 2004), 106.
[28] Paul Enns, *Moody Handbook of Theology* (Chicago: Moody Publishers, 2008), 322.

in the New Testament and are explicitly rejected in several passages (Jn 9:41, Ro 14:23, Ja 4:17). The New Testament fundamentally changes the concept of the law from a legal sense to a moral sense. Even under the Old Testament law, God was able to keep a person from sin and taught *the soul that sinneth, it shall die* (Eze 18:20). Scripture states that Zacharias and Elizabeth *were both righteous before God, walking in all the commandments and ordinances of the Lord blameless* (Lu 1:6). It is now even more possible to live a blameless life before God since the Holy Spirit came at Pentecost to fill God's people with His presence and to write the law in a person's mind and heart (He 8:6-13, 10:16). Now the righteousness of the law is *fulfilled in us who walk not after the flesh but after the Spirit* (Ro 8:4). The new, internally written code of God's law entails a change in the meaning of law in the dispensation of grace, which consequently changes the definition of sin. Thus, as John Wesley noted in his sermon on *Christian Perfection,* "We may safely affirm with St. John, that since the gospel was given, '*He that is born of God sinneth not.*'"[29]

The Calvinistic position also recognizes the moral aspect of sin along with the absolute aspect. Often their definitions will emphasize the moral aspect of disobedience but then will shift to the absolute nature of sin and insist all Christians continually sin. They preach that a saved person should live a changed life but also hold that he continues to commit sin. Since all sin is considered equally damning before God, this position struggles to adequately explain the difference between human weaknesses and willful rebellion. Their concept of sin is not firmly built upon Scripture but is predominantly based upon a philosophical presupposition that sin is absolute and any shortcoming of perfection is sin.

Often those who hold to the legal concept of sin will define sin in several different ways, emphasizing the moral aspect then falling back to the absolute definition of sin. The Westminster Catechism, which is the standard guide for English speaking Calvinists, defines sin in what could almost be an Arminian way. It says, "Sin is any want of conformity unto,

---

[29] John Wesley, *Wesley's Standard Sermons* (Salem, OH: Schmul Publishing Co., repr., 1982), 400.

or transgression of, any law of God, given as a rule to the reasonable creature."[30] If the law were understood as the moral law of God fulfilled by love written on the hearts and minds and through walking in the Spirit, Wesleyans would be in complete agreement with this definition. Instead, Calvinists moved a more absolutist direction in their definition and define that law of God as the absolute perfection of God and, therefore, hold that it is impossible to keep the law; thus, they teach that Christians continually sin.

Any attempt to mix the Calvinist and Arminian definitions has not worked. "No hybrid of the two can be created . . . Between Calvinism and Arminianism there is no mutual compatibility. Logic will always force a person to go one way or the other . . .[any hybrid] will be ravaged by the harsh questions of logic and common sense."[31] Any attempt to merge the two will gravitate toward the legal definition. If it is thought that Christians commit sins of ignorance or infirmity, then this belief undermines the Scriptural and logical basis for a sinless life, and it becomes theologically impossible to oppose the commission of any sin. The New Testament has a singular understanding of acts of personal sin and does not describe multiple categories such as sins of infirmity and willful sin; rather the word *sin* is used without modifiers almost all of the time. To add words that are not in the original text such as *habitual, practice*, or *willful* as modifiers to help define different types of sin would be adding to the Word of God.

A major problem for the legal definition of sin is the culpability of babies and those below the age of accountability. Are they committing sin and thus guilty before God? Ulrich Zwingli, the leader of the Swiss Reformation, used a Wesleyan type definition as he dealt with the issue of sin and infants. In reference to young children, he writes, "A defect which of itself is not sinful in the one who has it . . . It also cannot damn him... until out of this defect he does something against the law of God."[32] "An

---

[30] *The Westminister Larger Catechism* (Assembly at Edinburgh, 1648, Sess. 10), question 24, https://prts.edu/wp-content/uploads/2013/09/Larger_Catechism.pdf.
[31] Roger E Olson, *Arminian Theology: Myths and Realities* (Downers Grove, IL: InterVarsity Press, 2006), p. 68.

[32] Ulrich Zwingli, cited by T. A. Noble "The Doctrine of Original Sin in the

act of sin, for Zwingli, is a voluntary transgression of a known law, and he supports this with reference to Romans: 'Knowledge of sin comes through the law' (Ro 3:20), and 'where there is no law, there is no transgression' (Ro 4:15)."[33]

Logically, the legal definition faces a serious problem in understanding sin. Sin demands eternal punishment, and everyone is accountable for his sins. He is guilty in the eyes of God. As the Bible says, *The soul that sinneth, it shall die* (Eze 18:4). Almost all Christians, including Calvinists, would deplore the idea of infant damnation; yet, this is the logical conclusion of the legal definition. According to the legal concept, children have committed sin in ignorance, are guilty for that sin, habitually continue to practice sin, and have never repented and trusted Christ for salvation; therefore, they are guilty before God and would not be allowed entry into heaven (Mt 7:23). The idea of a continual cleansing for those who walk in the light does not apply; babies have never believed in Christ. The answer legal proponents give is that the grace of God automatically forgives babies for sins and takes away the guilt. Logically, this same principle would have to apply to all sins of ignorance or human failure regardless of age or intellectual ability and would include new converts who commit wicked acts in ignorance. The Bible considers them babes in Christ, and they would be treated by God as He would treat other children. Why should this even be considered sin? "Sins of ignorance" would have to be a strange, special class of sins. Sins which are unknowingly committed and are automatically forgiven; Sins for which a person is guilty, but does not know he is guilty; and sins for which he will never held accountable. Why it is even called a sin if it is never treated as a sin? The choice for those who follow the legal definition is clear; it is either infant damnation or a contorted type of sin which does not ever seem to be treated as sin.

The consequences for sin are far too serious for it to be treated

---

Evangelical Reformers":(Summer 2001) *European Explorations in Christian Holiness,* 79.

[33] T. A. Noble "The Doctrine of Original Sin in the Evangelical Reformers:" *Didache*: *European Explorations in Christian Holiness,*" 2000, 79.

flippantly as though everyone constantly does it, including young children below the age of accountability. False doctrine in this area will undermine belief in the awfulness of sin and its destructive, eternal consequences. Scripture emphatically teaches that people must be holy to see God (He 12:14) and that a person's eternal destiny will be based upon the keeping of the law (Ro 2:6-13). One of Christ's final points in the Sermon on the Mount is a warning that, at the final Judgment, Christ will reject those who commit iniquity from entering the kingdom of heaven (Mt 7:23). It is, therefore, of eternal consequence to properly understand what sin and iniquity are and what laws a Christian must keep.

Unacceptable Actions in New Converts

Is it possible that through ignorance a new convert might inadvertently commit some serious offense? While these actions are unacceptable, they are not considered sin unless there is knowledge that it is wrong. These actions fail to meet the basic biblical definition, that sin must be willful and not committed in ignorance. However, Scripture also says that there are a number of actions which a person may not do and still go to heaven (Ga 5:19-21). Therefore, "ignorance" must not be used as an excuse for disobedience to Scripture. When dealing with confusing issues, biblical scholars must carefully follow clear scriptural guidelines. The Bible teaches that everyone who is born of God does not sin, and if a person does sin, he is of the devil (1Jn 3:6:-9). Therefore, according to Scripture, there are only two possible options. Either the action is not considered sin when done in ignorance by a new convert or the action is sin and the person is not born of God. The Wesleyan position, which is based upon Scripture, has always been that an action is not sin unless a person knowingly and willfully violates the law of God.

Perhaps the best answer is to understand that new converts are babes in Christ and consider them as young children under the age of accountability. This seems to be the explanation given in Romans 4:15 and 5:13 which says, *For where no law is, there is no transgression.* If a person is guilty for committing major sins in ignorance, then young children are also guilty of committing sins as well. Are babies and young children condemned for sinning? Whatever position is taken on babies will have to be applied to young converts as well. Eternal death is the consequence of sin. Certainly, children below the age of accountability are neither considered sinners nor are they guilty of committing sin.

God did not give us the answer to every possible scenario that could be imagined. Scripture would then become a book of technical details too bulky for simple comprehension. God is a just and a loving God who will always do the right thing. We can truth him with questions which do not seem to have direct answers. Regardless, we must be Scriptural. The Bible never excuses sin in the life of a Christian.

Failure to Comprehend the New Covenant

F. G. Smith notes that most of the confusion comes from a failure to understand the distinctions in covenants. He writes, "A proper understanding of the difference between the Old Covenant and the New will forever settle the question of the present relation of God's people to sin."[34] No passages from the Old Testament should be used to define sin in the New Testament. Scripture clearly teaches that Christians today are under a New Covenant and not under the Old Covenant (He 8:6-10). No Christian today tries to keep all the details of the Old Covenant with Israel; yet, many insist on going to the Old Covenant God gave to the Jews for their definition of sin. Usually Old Testament passages are given to support the claim that everyone sins. For example, at the dedication of the Temple Solomon prayed, *For there is no man which sinneth not* (1Ki 8:46, 2Ch 6:36). These passages along with a number of others do strongly imply the impossibility of living a life without sin in the Old Testament. However, these statements were written to those of the Old Testament dispensation. Many of the people were illiterate at the time of Solomon. Nevertheless, some saints under the Old Testament covenant were considered perfect, just, or blameless according to the law (Ge 6:9, Job 1:1, Lu 1:6, etc.). By the time of Christ, it certainly

---

[34] F.G. Smith, *What the Bible Teaches,* condensed ed. (Anderson, IN: Warner Press, 1955), 57.

seems that the Jewish people had a confidence in their ability to understand and keep the Old Testament law, and there are those who considered themselves blameless (Php 3:6).

Everything changes in the New Testament. Sin becomes a choice to disobey the New Testament Law as one is led by the Spirit since *if ye be led of the Spirit, ye are not under the law* (Ga 5:18). Love is emphasized as the cornerstone of the law by both Christ and Paul for *he that loveth another hath fulfilled the law* (Mt 22:35-40, Ro 13:8). Keeping the law, which emphasized obedience to that which was written on stone in the Old Testament, was changed to now living in obedience to the New Covenant law as guided by the Holy Spirit and based upon a love for God and others. This transition from one dispensation to the next makes it obsolete to go to the Old Testament for any verse which shows the inability of man to live without sinning. According to Wesley, "Doubtless thus it was in the days of Solomon; yea, and from Solomon to Christ there was then no man that sinned not. But whatever was the case of those under the law, we may safely affirm, with St. John, that, since the gospel was given, 'he that is born of God sinneth not. The privileges of Christians are in nowise to be measured by what the Old Testament records concerning those who were under the Jewish dispensation; seeing the fulness of time is now come, the Holy Ghost is now given.[35]

In the Old Testament sin was based upon a failure to keep a written code. The Old Testament covenant was specifically a promise to the Jewish people. Under the dispensation of grace, the whole world is now under the New Covenant which has replaced the Old Covenant. The written code has been replaced by God writing His law upon our hearts and minds and by the Holy Spirit who lives and directs our lives (He 8:6-13). The power of the Holy Spirit empowers the believer to have victory over all sin.

The Difference between Sin and Human Failure

Another area of confusion occurs when it is assumed that any failing in a Christian life has to do with sin or sinfulness in the person. Wesleyans have always emphasized that there is growth in maturity following the

---

[35] John Wesley, *The Works of John Wesley*, Third Edition., vol. 11, 375.

experience of holiness. A person may make a wrong decision, but have the right motives. We should not confuse immaturity and sinfulness. To illustrate this concept, consider a child who is sick from a cancerous tumor. Surgery needs to be performed, and the physical corruption needs to be removed. Once the child is cured, he can grow naturally and develop into the person God intended him to be. The same is true spiritually. Once the cancer of sin is removed, a spiritual babe in Christ may then develop normally and become the person God intends him to be. There will still be aspects of a person's life which have been contaminated by one's upbringing, personality, culture, and prejudices. Some have identified these behaviors and attitudes as sinful; however, this goes to the heart of the definition of sin. Is sin a moral issue of disobedience and rebellion against God, or is sin a failure to be perfect? Christians will never be absolutely perfect in the sense of never erring, but Christians can and should live a life of perfect obedience to God.

Ultimately, for the Calvinists, sin includes not only disobedience but also human limitations or human ignorance. This definition is foundational to their theology. With that understanding, it is impossible to live a sinless life. In contrast, the Wesleyan definition believes that obedience to God is the core of sin, and human failure, unless intentional, itself is not sin. Wesley pointed out, "Every voluntary breach of the law of love is sin; and nothing else, if we speak properly. To strain the matter farther is only to make way for Calvinism. There may be then a thousand wandering thoughts, and forgetful intervals, without any breach of love . . . But Calvinists would fain confound these together."[36] The terminology used to define and understand sin lays the foundation for our understanding of God's truth. This is the presupposition that underlies Wesleyan thought and distinguishes it from Calvinism.

---

[36] John Wesley, *The Works of John Wesley*, 3rd ed., vol. 12, 394.

Chapter 9
Keswickian Understanding of Sin

The Reformed doctrine teaches the impossibility of a life without sinning, while the Wesleyan doctrine requires that Christians do not sin. The Keswick doctrine was influenced by both groups and finds its place between them. It states, "We ought not to sin, and we need not sin, but as a matter of fact, we do sin.[1] J. Robertson McQuilkin, a follower of Keswick, suggested "as a working hypothesis a view of sin as both a deliberate violation of God's known will and falling short of God's moral perfection.[2] Keswick taught that sin is divided into two categories: willful sin and other sins. While Keswickians believe that all Christians sin they also teach "that the normal Christian life is one of uniform sustained victory over known sin."[3] In addressing the problem of indwelling sin, "Keswick rejects the Wesleyan view (a complete, instantaneous eradication of the indwelling sin tendency) and the Reformed view (a gradual eradication or mortification never completed until glorification)."[4] These "differences between the Wesleyans and Keswick stem from basic dissimilarities in their definitions of sin. This results in a distinct cleavage of thought with regard to what happens in the heart of the sanctified. Wesleyans maintain that the heart itself is cleansed, while Keswick affirms that the sin nature is only counteracted in the sanctified heart."[5]

---

[1] Charles F. Harford, ed., *The Keswick Convention: Its Message, Its Method, and its Men*, (www.alphaedi.com: Alpha Editions, repr., 2020), 107.
[2] Stanley N. Gundry, ed., *Five Views on Sanctification* (Grand Rapids: Zondervan Publishing House, 1987), 173.
[3] Stanley N. Gundry, ed., *Five Views on Sanctification*, 153.
[4] Andrew David Naselli, "Keswick Theology: A Survey and Analysis of the Doctrine of Sanctification in the Early Keswick Movement," *Detroit Baptist Seminary Journal*, no. 13 (2008): 17–67, https://andynaselli.com/wp-content/uploads/2008_Keswick_theology.
[5] W. Ralph Thompson, "An Appraisal of the Keswick and Wesleyan Contemporary Positions" *Wesleyan Theological Journal*, vol. 01 (Spring 1966): 19.

However, both the Wesleyan view and the Keswickian view have a number of similarities. Both accept an instantaneous experience of salvation and the baptism of the Holy Spirit. Both emphasize the empowerment by faith in Christ to give victory over willful sin. Both groups have helped to lead many people to a deeper life in Christ and have encouraged many people to give their lives for foreign missions.[6]

Beginnings of Keswick

The holiness revival in America that occurred in the mid-1800s was brought across to England by a number of American preachers such as Charles Finney, Asa Mahan and others from Oberlin College. Phoebe Palmer and her husband traveled to England in the 1850s, and later the "British campaigns of the Palmers, [John] Inskip, and William E. Boardman awakened an interest in holiness in England which rivaled that in America."[7] Boardman's book *The Higher Christian Life* was accepted by all denominations in spite of the fact that the Methodist doctrines regarding sanctification had earlier been rejected. Another man who had a major influence was Dwight L. Moody who had been touring England just before the Keswick conventions began. Many of these holiness revivalists were not from the Methodist Church and were more accepted into evangelical groups outside English Methodism.

At the height of this spiritual interest, William Boardman, along with Robert Pearsall and Hannah Whitall Smith, began holding meetings. One could say that "Boardman helped to found the Keswick movement . . . with [Robert] Pearsall and Hannah Whitall Smith."[8] God moved in a conference held at Oxford presided over by Pearsall Smith and "a great wave of blessing seemed to sweep all before it."[9] It was at this conference

---

[6] W. Ralph Thompson, "An Appraisal of the Keswick and Wesleyan Contemporary Positions," 19.
[7] Vinson Synan, *The Holiness–Pentecostal Movement* (Grand Rapids: William B. Eerdmans Publishing Co.,1971), 43.
[8] Thomas Ross, "William Boardman: Higher Life, Keswick, and Faith Cure Pioneer." *Faith Saves*, 2014, https://faithsaves.net/william-boardman/.
[9] Thomas Ross, "Keswick or Higher Life roots of the Pentecostal / Charismatic Movements; Biblical, Baptist, Cessationist Sanctification vs. the Continuationist

that Canon Harford-Battersby, the vicar of Keswick, entered into "the rest of faith."[10] This was followed by a convention at Brighton where 8,000 people met for the "purpose of personal consecration to God."[11]

Battersby and a Quaker friend, Robert Wilson, found themselves so inspired and transformed that they wanted to share their joyful experience with others. . . . and issued invitations to "Union Meetings for the Promotion of Practical Holiness."[12] All of the early leaders "experienced a crisis in which they entered the rest of faith."[13] Tragically, actions of questionable morality by Robert Pearsall Smith thrust him completely out of the ministry and almost destroyed the movement. Yet, in spite of the setback, the Keswick Conference was still held and continued. It became the catalyst and focal point for the emerging Higher Life movement in the United Kingdom. The fall of Smith, however, broke the connection with the American holiness revival and left English Calvinists in charge of the work. They "sought to put all the distance possible between its understanding of the Spirit's work in the deeper-life experience and that of the American holiness movement out of which it was born."[14]

The Keswick movement was one of the most powerful revivalistic forces ever to shake England. "The first great definite step urged is the immediate and final abandonment of every known sin and of every weight that hinders advance. Nothing which is revealed in the Word of God to be evil in God's sight can be indulged with impunity."[15] In addition, some of the main steps the Convention emphasized were

---

Second Blessing," part 3, *Faith Saves,* (2014), https://faithsaves.net/sanctification-baptist-higher-life-3/.

[10] Charles F. Harford, *The Keswick Convention: Its Message, Its Method and Its Men,* 31.

[11] Charles F. Harford, *The Keswick Convention: Its Message, Its Method, and its Men,* 32.

[12] https://www.christianity.com/church/church-history/timeline/1801-1900/the-first-keswick-convention- 11630576.html.

[13] Andrew David Naselli, "Keswick Theology: A Survey and Analysis of the Doctrine of Sanctification in the Early Keswick Movement," 22.

[14] Stanley N. Gundry, ed., *Five Views on Sanctification*, 185.

[15] Charles F. Harford, *The Keswick Convention: Its Message, Its Method, and its Men,* 91.

renunciation of whatever is known or even suspected to be contrary to the will of God.... Obedience now becomes the watchword of the soul.... This prepares for close and constant fellowship with God. . . . The sense of Divine possession of one's entire being–spirit, soul, and body–is the natural outcome of such conditions . . . All this fits for the largest possible service to God and man. God gives to all truly consecrated believers the sceptre of holy influence....This is the last stage of the Victorious Life– the stage of triumphant power over sin, prevailing power in prayer, and witnessing power among men.[16]

With this dedication to God, it is no wonder that Keswick has had an incredible impact upon England. The convention at Keswick, which began in a tent, soon became a world-wide missionary movement. Many of the greatest names in spiritual faith along with a number of noted missionaries and ministers have been identified with the movement. These include people such as Hudson Taylor, Andrew Murray, F.B. Meyer, Amy Carmichael, Dwight L. Moody, A.B. Simpson, Billy Graham, and many others.

Differences from Traditional Calvinism

Keswick does not agree with traditional Calvinistic doctrine. Keswick accepts a twofold definition of personal sin – accepting both the Arminian and the Calvinistic definition. Accordingly, it teaches both victory from willful sin and yet no power to live above all sin. Neither Calvinistic nor Wesleyan doctrine separates sin into two different types. Sin in the New Testament is never broken down into the two distinctions given by Keswick. It is simply called sin. Whatever sin is, it must be applied equally to all behavior. Keswick counters by saying, "Wherein then does the teaching differ from the view that we are sinning every moment, in thought, word and deed? . . . You have not perfection in man, but you have

---

[16] Charles F. Harford, *The Keswick Convention: Its Message, Its Method, and its Men*, 90.

Defending the Biblical Definition 97

a perfect Saviour. Never be afraid of drawing too near perfection, you may be sure there will always be limitations in you."[17] Calvinists see sanctification as a human effort by self-discipline to overcome the nature of sin, while the Keswickian feels "the means of sanctification is appropriating the gift by faith alone—not by effort or struggle."[18]

In spite of the theological difficulties, Keswick theology states that by faith in the indwelling of Christ the believer "is to expect not defeat, but victory. He is boldly, and humbly, to 'claim' the promises of liberty and purity, in a valid and wonderful reality. . . . He is to expect to be here and now, 'more than conqueror, through Him that loveth him. . . . And so he is to expect to be, in an ever truer completeness, 'a vessel sanctified, and meet for the Master's use.'"[19] Keswick teaches, "A total abstinence in Christ's name from admitted sinning, of motive and act, and a true and entire dedication of 'spirit, soul, and body' to the will of God."[20] Keswickians believe that the "normal Christian life is one of uniform sustained victory over known sin."[21]

> Never be afraid of drawing too near perfection. You have not perfection in man, but you have a perfect Saviour.

Keswickian theology teaches the fullness of the Spirit and victory over willful sin that is characteristic of Wesleyan theology but incorporates the concepts and the basic definitions of Reformed theology.[22] Keswick was not intended to be a theological movement; it was a spiritual quest in which its leaders had experienced the life changing transformation of Spirit baptism and desired to share their transformation with others. Accordingly, "Keswick theology is impossible to define authoritatively,

---

[17] Charles F. Harford, *The Keswick Convention: Its Message, Its Method, and its Men*, 107.
[18] Andrew David Naselli, "Keswick Theology: A Survey and Analysis of the Doctrine of Sanctification in the Early Keswick Movement, 32.
[19] Charles F. Harford, *The Keswick Convention: Its Message, Its Method, and its Men*, 70.
[20] Charles F. Harford, *The Keswick Convention: Its Message, Its Method, and its Men*, 71.
[21] Stanley N. Gundry, *Five Views on Sanctification*, 153.
[22] Stanley N. Gundry, *Five Views on Sanctification*, 184.

partly because the convention lacked a doctrinal statement and was an unstructured, non-denominational group of diverse Christians."[23] Instead of being doctrinally focused, the movement was instead concerned about the practical and experiential components of religion. Its founding was to replicate the victory being taught and experienced by those who advocated the Methodist doctrine of holiness without dealing with the theological questions and contradictions that would arise.

Differences from the Holiness Movement

In many ways there is much similarity between the Holiness Movement and Keswick. Both emphasize a total consecration of a person's entire being to God. Both believe in an instantaneous moment of justification and sanctification. Both emphasize victorious Christian living over all known sin. And both show the need for the filling of the Spirit as the source for the empowerment of the Christian life. This similarity is not surprising. Keswick was born out of a holiness revival. Its goal was to bring the glorious doctrine of the second work of grace that delivers from sin and baptizes one with the Holy Spirit into the churches of England.

The theological distinctions between holiness proponents and Keswick arose from the fact that "adherents to the Keswick position are recruited, for the most part, from those churches which accept the Calvinistic definition of sin. . . . Since Calvinism looks upon those human weaknesses which produce a lack of conformity to the perfect will of God (mistakes, lapses of memory, ignorance, etc.) as sin, it is not conceivable that followers of Keswick could think of a perfect cleansing of the individual in this world."[24] The convention states, "Keswick has never sought to raise false hopes, it has never given to any the promise of being sinless here. The presence of sin in the believer deeply deplored and lamented is nevertheless acknowledged in all the words spoken from that platform."[25]

---

[23] Andrew David Naselli, "Keswick Theology: A Survey and Analysis of the Doctrine of Sanctification in the Early Keswick Movement," 28.
[24] W. Ralph Thompson, "An Appraisal of the Keswick and Wesleyan Contemporary Positions," 16.
[25] Charles F. Harford, *The Keswick Convention: Its Message, Its Method, and its Men*, 107.

The fundamental issue is the definition of sin. Should sin be defined as willful disobedience to the known will of God, or is sin any falling short of the glory of God? "Keswick clearly teaches that Christians, by the power of the indwelling Spirit, have the ability to choose consistently not to violate deliberately the known will of God. But . . . if sin is defined to include this falling short unwittingly, Keswick does not teach that a person ever in this life has the ability not to sin."[26] Some have accused Keswick of "teaching perfectionism, the view that it is possible to live without sinning . . . Keswick leaders have consistently, officially, and emphatically denied these allegations."[27] One of the leaders stated, "In God's providence Keswick has been kept from ever formulating, as its authentic message, a dream of 'sinlessness.'"[28]

Keswickian views include three different types of sin. They teach that a person can overcome the sin that is willful rebellion against God but hold that sin as an accidental transgression by missing the mark cannot be overcome in this life. In relationship to the sin nature, Keswick often uses the terminology of self instead of sin or of depravity. They teach that the "old man" in Romans 6 is the former self-life that is crucified. Selfishness is represented "as the fundamental sin."[29] They also believe that the sin nature in the heart cannot be eradicated in this life.[30]

With its theological basis being fundamentally Reformed theology, the doctrine has become acceptable to many theologians who are fundamentally opposed to the holiness concept of complete deliverance from sin. One example is the Augustinian-Dispensational perspective. This doctrine accepts the eternal security belief that a one-time act of faith saves a person permanently, no matter how continual and wicked a person's behavior becomes. Some of their theologians state that they are "in

---

[26] Stanley N. Gundry, *Five Views on Sanctification*, 156-157.
[27] Stanley N. Gundry, *Five Views on Sanctification*, 156.
[28] Charles F. Harford, *The Keswick Convention: Its Message, Its Method, and its Men*, 70.
[29] A. M. Hills, *Scriptural Holiness and Keswick Teaching Compared* (Nicholasville, KY: Schmul Publishing Co., 2020), 116.
[30] Marlin Hotle, *In Search of Sanctification* (Salem, OH: Schmul Publishing Company, Inc., 1991), 43.

harmony with the Keswick approach."³¹

Theological Concepts with Which Wesleyan-Holiness Theology Disagrees.

Keswick teaches that Christians sin. Wesleyan's believe Christians live without sinning.³² Keswickians believe that a person may willfully sin and still remain a Christian while holiness theologians hold that (willful) sin causes a person to lose salvation.³³

Keswick proponents may agree with the cheap, free-grace position of eternal security or they may agree that a person cannot consistently choose to do wrong and have any assurance of salvation.³⁴ Holiness people believe that there is a greater problem than not having assurance; those who sin cannot be considered saved.

Keswick doctrine divides personal sin into two categories – willful sin and falling short of God's moral perfection.³⁵ Holiness people hold that sin is only a choice to disobey God.

Keswick does not believe that the sin nature can be eradicated, but can only be suppressed.³⁶ Holiness people, however, believe in the removal of the sin nature. This is shown by the terminology. Keswick emphasizes the higher life while holiness people teach, in addition, the concept of heart purity.

Keswick also confuses the human self for depravity. They see sin as the selfish nature of a person while holiness proponents see sin as more than a perverted selfishness which needs corrected, but as an evil heart that needs to be cleansed.

While many of the Keswickian followers have emphasized a second crisis, others have taught only the need for the salvation experience to

---

[31] Stanley N. Gundry, *Five Views on Sanctification*, 194 and 237. This is the position of John Walvoord from Dallas Theological Seminary.
[32] Charles F. Harford, *The Keswick Convention: Its Message, Its Method, and its Men*, 70.
[33] Stanley N. Gundry, *Five Views on Sanctification*, 160-161, and 194.
[34] Stanley N. Gundry, *Five Views on Sanctification*, 162.
[35] Stanley N. Gundry, *Five Views on Sanctification*, 173.

become sanctified.[36] Some have confused Christian maturity with heart purity with the emphasis being placed upon maturity rather than a second crisis experience.[37]

Keswick theology holds that people are judicially sanctified when they are saved, which means that God sees them as sanctified through the blood of Christ while their heart and actions are still sinful.[38] Holiness people would reject that form of imputed sanctification without genuine holiness of life being imparted as well.

The doctrine of Keswick is a relatively new doctrine that was never taught historically or theologically before the late 1800s. It is not reasonable to assume that God waited 1800 years to give a new revelation. Wesleyan theology, in contrast, was taught by the Early Church and has existed throughout history.

Adherents of Keswick and Holiness often distinguish their theology by specific terms to represent their perspectives. Keswickian theology calls for believers to go on to 'the deeper life' or 'the higher life.' In contrast, holiness people call for heart purity, for the cleansing of the sin nature from the heart of believers. Keswick and Holiness theologies are fundamentally different because of their view of sin. Wesleyans view sin as a voluntary transgression of the known law of God. Keswick views sin as any attitude or action that falls short of the perfection of God. Wesleyans teach that God can eradicate indwelling sin from the heart of the believer. Keswickians believe that the sin nature cannot be eradicated from the heart; rather it can be counteracted or overpowered. Fundamentally, the difference between Keswick and Wesleyans comes down to the sin definition.

---

[36] Stanley N. Gundry, *Five Views on Sanctification*, 55.
[37] Stanley N. Gundry, *Five Views on Sanctification*, 193.
[38] Stanley N. Gundry, *Five Views on Sanctification*, 55.

Chapter 10
The Relational Definition of Sin

The Holiness Movement faced a new challenge in the 1970s as a new relational theology redefined the doctrine of holiness. It also changed what many Arminian theologians believed regarding the definition of sin. It is difficult to grasp exactly what relational theologians believe since it is related to the postmodern understanding of truth. Their doctrine is focused upon experiences rather than being developed as a logical system.

Much of this system comes from existentialist theologian Mildred Bangs Wynkoop, who wrote the book *A Theology of Love*. In this book she gave an experiential foundation for her existential theology. She argued there was a "credibility gap" between what holiness people professed and "everyday human life."[1] Much of this disconnect may have come from changes occurring within the denomination of which she was a part. Historically, Holiness people were vehemently opposed to all forms of "worldliness;" but after mid-century, many members had a desire to fit in with and become popular with others in the larger church world as well as society as a whole. Wynkoop recognized what she perceived as a double-standard. Her solution was to redefine holiness as only relational rather than transformational. She viewed holiness as a change in the status of one's relationship with God instead of a second work of grace where the heart was purified by the baptism of the Holy Spirit. Her focus was on emotions and feeling and a relationship rather than the transformational removal of the sin nature. Accordingly, with her existential philosophical perspective, she rejected the concept of an actual sin nature. She emphasized that sin was not a spiritual corruption, a non-physical spiritual thing, or a substance to be removed; instead, she saw the sin nature as a warp or bent in our human nature that needed to be straightened. Relational theologians, therefore, strongly argue against a clear instantaneous work of grace, emphasizing instead a gradual straightening of the human personality. Relational theology also rejects the baptism of the Holy Spirit and the purification of the heart by the destruction of the sin nature because it denies any spiritual filthiness or impurity exists in the heart that needs to be cleansed.

This relational concept of sin completely redefined the Protestant understanding of inherited sin as was commonly understood by almost all evangelical scholars up to this time, including Wesley and his followers. Relational advocates question key components of the doctrine of inherited depravity. Although they try to deny it, according to Richard S. Taylor this doctrine "was essentially Pelagian."[1]

In her book on the theology of holiness, relational theologian Diane Leclerc wrote, "There is nothing to suggest that people inevitably sin because of that [Adam's] historical experience."[2] She makes the claim that Adam's fall in the Garden is not necessarily the source of depravity for the human race since "all humanity after them has also fallen by sinning. That is the original sin of Adam and Eve can be found in every person."[3] She stated that the same anxiety that caused Adam to sin is found in each person independently of Adam. This would mean that God created a race in which all people are created to sin.

This redefinition of inherited sin has also affected how Wesleyan scholars who have accepted relational holiness define personal sin as well. According to the relational view, sin is understood as the breaking of a relationship rather than the violation of a law. Wynkoop identified sin as "a rupture of fellowship with God."[4] Relational theology, as defined by theologian H. Ray Dunning, understood sin as an act which violated the relationship between God and man.[5] Al Truesdale, another relational theologian, noted that "sin is first a religious problem . . . It is secondarily

---

[1] Richard S. Taylor, *Counterpoints* (Salem, OH: Schmul Publishing Co., 2005), 50.
[2] Diane Leclerc, *Discovering Christian Holiness* (Kansas City: Beacon Hill Press of Kansas City, 2010), 163.
[3] Diane Leclerc, *Discovering Christian Holiness*, 167.
[4] Mildred Bangs Wynkooop, *A Theology of Love* (Kansas City: Beacon Hill Press, 1972), 156.
[5] H. Ray Dunning, *Grace Faith and Holiness*, (Kansas City: Beacon Hill Press of Kansas City, 1988), 286.

a moral problem."[6] Fundamentally, relational theologians see sin as a "wrong way of being. It is failure to worship God. It is a twisted rupture of our relationship with God."[7] They center every aspect of Christian theology around the concept of love. For them, a misplaced love focused upon self is the major issue. "Sin is love, but love gone astray."[9] Instead of viewing sin from a legal viewpoint where wrong actions are sin or from the moral viewpoint where the motive of disobedience is at the forefront, they view sin as breaking a relationship with God. They view the relationship with God and others as their foundation for Christianity.

The lack of a strong biblical basis in Scripture is a major problem of the relational model. Scripture shows a relationship with God as the goal of God's salvation plan, but Scripture proclaims obedience to God is the foundation upon which that relationship is based. Adam and Eve were created to have perfect fellowship with God, but that fellowship was broken through an act, the sin of disobedience. Obedience to God is constantly demanded as a requirement for a relationship with God. John stated that the basis for having fellowship with God is walking in the light (1 Jn 1:7). Isaiah stated that one's *iniquities have separated between you and your God* (Isa 59:2). Jesus said, *If ye love me, keep my commandments* (Jn 14:15). Paul identified justification as the foundation for being reconciled to God (Ro 5:9-10). John made it clear, *We do know that we know him, if we keep his commandments. He that saith, I know him, and keepeth not his commandments, is a liar* (1 Jo 2:3-4). The relational doctrine wants to begin with the relationship rather than obedience. A relationship with God is quite important, but it occurs as a result of keeping God's commands. Having the presence of the indwelling Spirit of God in His fullness is the ultimate relationship between God and man. This perfect unity between God and man occurs as a person dies to self and strives to completely obey God. The relational philosophy gets it backwards by emphasizing the relationship first while Scripture teaches the relationship is based on obedience.

One difficulty for the relational ideology is the danger of post-modern

---

[6] Al Truesdale, *Sin* (Kansas City: The Foundry Publishing, 2022), 35.
[7] Al Truesdale, *Sin*, 35.

subjectivism. Sin and moral behavior are based entirely upon one's opinion of what determines a person's relationship with God. Accordingly, there are, therefore, no objective standards and no solid guidelines for biblical truth. In fact, among the relational holiness people with their subjective truth and emphasis upon love, there is a rising acceptance of the homosexual lifestyle."[8]

On the other extreme, the legal view of the Calvinists results in a theology which proclaims that no one can live a holy life. Ultimately, whether one sees everything as sin or nothing as sin, the end result is the same; sin does not matter. Either conclusion is damning and is not supported by the Bible. The correct balance is found in an objective standard based upon the guidelines given in the New Testament and upon the character of God; however, these absolutes are filtered subjectively through the law, which is written upon the mind and the heart. It is absolute in the sense that it is God's law which is written upon the heart, but it is subjective in the sense that it is revealed through the leadership and empowerment of the Spirit working upon the mind and heart."[9]

Relational theology views the real problem with sin as its effects upon people. Sin causes destruction, suffering, and separation from God. Their view is that Christ is not angry at sin because God's holiness hates sin, but that "God is angered by sin because of its disintegrating effect on us."[10] Their concept logically threatens the entire reason Christ took our place on the cross. Christ died to pay the penalty for the justice that was due. If there was no recompense due, then God could have simply forgiven sin without the necessity of Christ's death. Relational theology, therefore, no longer needs the cross and identifies the problem with humanity as

---

[8] Thomas Jay Ord and Alexa Ord, ed, *Why the Church of the Nazarene Should Be Fully LGBTQ+ Affirming* (N.p.:SacraSage Press, 2023). This book gives the current developments which are occurring in the Church of the Nazarene. They hold a stand against the practice, but there is currently a debate which is occurring. Most of the writers in the book either have left the denomination because of its stand or were anonymous. Thomas Ord as a Nazarene minister openly espouses this position.

[9] This concept is more fully explained elsewhere in the book. It is biblically based upon Hebrews 8:7-13 and Galatians 5:18-25.

[10] Diane Leclerc, *Discovering Christian Holiness*, 141.

emotional hurt and sadness, not sin.

The relational concept has many variations and is not a logical systematic theology; accordingly, some of its positions are contradictory or are difficult to identify, but the major problem is the subjective nature of the beliefs. It has broken with the traditional understanding of the objective nature of sin and has replaced it with a completely subjective belief. It seems to have some similarity and background in the neo-orthodoxy of the twentieth century with the emphasis of a personal encounter with Christ, a rejection of the inerrancy of Scripture, and a reformulation of vocabulary where objective language becomes only metaphorical.

Relational theology has moved outside the scope of what would be considered orthodox evangelical theology. Relational scholars fail to show the historicity of their doctrine outside of modern liberalism and neo-orthodoxy. The major theological tenets underlying relational theology challenge core concepts of almost every aspect of the doctrines relating to God, Christ, sin, salvation, etc.

Chapter 11
Scriptural Evidences That Christians do not Sin

John Wesley was clear in teaching that Christians do not sin. He said, "I believe even babes in Christ . . . do not commit sin. By sin, I mean, outward sin; and the word commit, I take in its plain, literal meaning."[1] This has been the understanding of the followers of John Wesley. Numerous passages of Scripture clearly assert or imply that the child of God should live a sinless life. Any other interpretation of these passages undermines a straightforward understanding of the Bible. Different approaches have been used by those who do not believe a person can live a sinless life, but all of them have the common denominator of reinterpreting the Word of God from its plain meaning to some abstract theological concept. Often the passage in 1 John 3 is the focus of dealing with the issue of sin, but it is not some isolated text. The Holy Spirit led many of the other biblical authors to teach the same truth. In fact, Scripture is so strong that there is no real alternative if one is going to accept a straightforward interpretation of the Bible. This chapter cites many, but certainly not all, of the passages which teach the same truth.

> The concept that Christians do not sin is at the very core of salvation.

The concept that Christians do not sin is not some abstract theological idea. It is at the very core of salvation. If Christians do not sin, then there are many professing Christians who choose to willfully disobey God that will be lost eternally in hell if they do not confess their sins and renew their born again experience. It is absolutely necessary to have a biblical understanding of the plan of salvation. There is only one way to qualify to enter heaven, and it is the biblical way.

---

[1] John Wesley, *The Works of John Wesley*, Vol. 11, "An Answer to the Rev. Mr. Dodd," (Grand Rapids: Baker Book House, 2007), 451.

The definition of sin is at the crux of the principle that Christians can and must live without sinning. If Scripture teaches that Christians do not sin, then any definition of sin which makes it impossible for a human being to live sin free must be a false definition. There are two major competing definitions. One definition emphasizes unattainable, God-like perfection and, consequently, constant sinfulness through ignorance and human failure. The other definition emphasizes choice and the voluntary aspect of disobeying God, and teaches that the grace of God can deliver from sin. Which definition is the biblical definition? The following passages of Scripture emphasize the possibility of sinlessness, which supports the Wesleyan definition.

1 John 3:4-9 These verses are the foundation of the Wesleyan/moral view of sin. The entire debate is settled if just one of these verses means what it clearly says. This passage gives some of the clearest and best examples of the biblical stance on sin. In 1 John 3:4 the Apostle John will give his definition of sin. *Whosoever committeth sin transgresseth also the law: for sin is the transgression of the law*. Literally, the passage means that sin is lawlessness. This is the same Greek word for sin is used throughout the New Testament. All sin is willful sin, and Christians do not commit any sin. John shows this is the correct understanding of sin and gives its application to the Christian life. The New Testament does not distinguish between different types of sin, nor does it say that Christians commit one type of sin but not another. Sin is simply sin. Scholars who do not accept the simple, straightforward explanation of this passage have tried to reword or change the meaning of the passage, but most will admit that there is no other valid explanation for what John said. He simply meant that Christians do not sin.

1. **1 John 3:5a** *He [Jesus] was manifested to take way our sins.*

   This text teaches that Jesus came to take away our sins. Wesleyans understand this as teaching that Jesus came to bring total deliverance from sin in this life. John Wesley writes that "Christ was manifested [which means] that he came into the world for this very purpose to take away our sins to destroy them all, root and branch, and leave none remaining."[2] The Calvinist or legal definition, which holds that we must sin every day in word, thought, and deed does contradict the very purpose of Jesus coming to earth which was to make us entirely and totally free of all sin.

2. **1 John 3:5b-6** *In him is no sin: Whosoever abideth in him sinneth not: whosoever sinneth hath not seen him, neither known him.*

This text gives the underlying foundation for the sinlessness of believers. Wesleyans hold that since in Christ is no sin, those who are in Christ cannot be sinning. In the same way that Christ did not sin when he was a man, so believers who are in Christ will not sin. Fundamentally, if in Christ is no sin, then a person cannot be committing sin and be in Christ at the same time. The *Expositors Bible Commentary* says, "Taken together, the two sentences in v.5 emphasize the logic that underlies the text at v.6: Jesus has never had anything to do with sin–not then and not now . . . if someone lives in him, then that person does not sin. This is the logical implication of John's earlier remarks, for if Jesus has no sin in himself, those who abide in him will be sinless also."[3] The Calvinistic legal definition of sin does not work in this passage. The Wesleyan/moral concept of deliverance from sin is grounded upon the sinlessness of Christ and a person's abiding in Him. If one rejects the idea that humans can be sinless, the same logic must apply to Jesus in this text. The same Greek tenses are used both for Christ in verse five and for those who are in Him in verse six. A person has no strength of his own to live a sinless life; the ability and moral character to live a sinless life comes only through the power of abiding in Christ.

3. **1 John 3:7-8** *Little children, let no man deceive you: he that doeth righteousness is righteous, even as he is righteous. He that committeth sin is of the devil; for the devil sinneth from the beginning. For this*

---

[2] John Wesley, *Notes on the Bible*, 1 John 3:5, accessed June 27, 2023, http://wesley.nnu.edu/john-wesley/john-wesleys-notes-on-the-bible/notes-on-the-first-epistle-of-st-john/#Chapter+III.

[3] Tremper Longman III and David E. Garland, eds. *The Expositor's Bible Commentary* (Grand Rapids: Zondervan, 2006), 460.

purpose the Son of God was manifested, that he might destroy the works of the devil.

John emphasizes that he is not talking about abstract possibilities. Christians are righteous, just as Jesus is righteous. In contrast to the sinless children of God are the children of the devil who do sin. Adam Clarke writes on this text, "Hear this, also ye who plead for Baal, and cannot bear the thought of that doctrine that states believers are to be saved from all sin in this life! He who committeth sin is a child of the devil and shows that he has still the nature of the devil in him."[4] This text shows that Christians must live a righteous life. Can one be of the devil and a child of God at the same time? Jesus came to destroy the works of the devil. Sin is the predominant work of the devil which Jesus came to destroy.

4. **1 John 3:9** *Whosoever is born of God doth not commit sin; for his seed remaineth in him: and he cannot sin, because he is born of God.*

This passage poses quite a problem for those who believe Christians continue to sin. Wesley stated, "If, therefore, you would prove that the Apostle's words, '*He that is born of God sinneth not,*' are not to be understood according to their plain, natural, obvious meaning, it is from the New Testament you are to bring your proofs, else you will fight as one that beateth the air."[5] The seed of God refuses to coexist with sin. If sin comes in, the Spirit of God leaves. Just as light and dark cannot coexist, neither can sin and holiness. Christians do not sin, and sinners do not have the seed of God in them. Christ and the devil do not live together in the same heart.

5. **Matthew 1:21** *Thou shalt call his name JESUS: for he shall save his people from their sins.*

This passage says that Jesus came to *save his people from their sins*. The very purpose for which Christ came to earth and was born as an infant

---

[4] Adam Clarke, *Clarkes Commentary*, vol. 6, (New York: Abingdon Press, n.d.), 915.
[5] John Wesley, *The Works of John Wesley*, 3rd. ed., vol. 6 (London: Wesleyan Methodist Book Room, 1872), 11.

was expressed to Joseph by the angel. Christ did not come just to forgive people of their sins and leave them in a defiled condition. He came to deliver them from their sins. The death of Christ provided the grace for full deliverance from all sin.

Commentator Albert Barnes wrote, "From their sins. This is the great business of Jesus in coming and dying. It is not to save men IN their sins, but FROM their sins"[6] Adam Clarke commented on this verse, "The perfection of the Gospel system is not that it makes allowances for sin, but that it makes an atonement for it: not that it tolerates sin, but that it destroys it."[7] Matthew Henry said, "Those whom Christ saves he saves from their sins; from the guilt of sin by the merit of his death, from the dominion of sin by the Spirit of his grace."[8] Both Calvinist and Arminian scholars agree that this passage teaches deliverance not only from the guilt but also from sin itself.

6. **John 8:34** *Whosoever committeth sin is the servant of sin.*

Whoever is the servant of sin is obviously not the servant of Christ. This passage makes it clear that committing sin makes one a servant of sin. Why would Jesus make this statement if all Christians committed sin? This would become a moot statement. Jesus is distinguishing between two groups: one which commits sin and one which does not. Christians are the group which does not commit sin.

7. **Romans 6:1-5** *What shall we say then? Shall we continue in sin, that grace may abound? God forbid. How shall we, that are dead to sin, live any longer therein? Know ye not, that so many of us as were baptized into Jesus Christ were baptized into his death? Therefore we are buried with him by baptism into death: that like as Christ was raised up from the dead by the glory of the Father, even so we also*

---

[6] Albert Barnes, *Barnes Notes on the New Testament* (Kregel Publications, 1962), 4. Emphasis his.
[7] Adam Clarke, *Clarke's Commentary,* vol. 5 (New York: Abingdon Press, n.d.), 39.
[8] Matthew Henry, *The Bethany Parallel Commentary on the New Testament, Matthew Henry's Commentary* (Minneapolis: Bethany House Publishers, 1983), 5.

should walk in newness of life. For if we have been planted together in the likeness of his death, we shall be also in the likeness of his resurrection:

Paul thoroughly deals with the issue of sin in the Christian life in the book of Romans. After spending several chapters expounding on the death of Christ providing forgiveness for our sin, Paul turns his attention in chapter six to whether there is sin in the life of a Christian. Since God has given us His grace, Paul asks if it is acceptable to continue living a life of sin. The Apostle then uses the strongest language possible to explain that salvation and sin are mutually incompatible.

In order to properly define sin in the New Testament sense, Romans 6-8 must be taken into consideration. Much of it is dealing with the principle of sin in the heart and is teaching deliverance from the internal corruption as well as the outward sinful behavior. However, the removal of indwelling sin, the root cause of committed sins, also changes the outward behavior. Paul clearly believes that a Christian can and does live a life without sinning. Yet, if a person defines sin as either caused by mistakes, human inability, or ignorance in failing to conform perfectly to the character of God, then it is impossible for anyone on this earth to obtain that degree of "sinlessness." That definition of sin simply is not the viewpoint of Paul as he wrote the book of Romans through the inspiration of the Spirit.

8. **Romans 6:6-8** *Knowing this, that our old man is crucified with him, that the body of sin might be destroyed, that henceforth we should not serve sin. For he that is dead is freed from sin. Now if we be dead with Christ, we believe that we shall also live with him:*

Three times in Romans chapter six the Bible states that Christians are *free from sin* (Ro. 6:7, 18, 22). If a Christian is free from sin, then he does not sin. Paul is not talking about the penalty of sin in this passage, but about the way a person is living at the present time. This passage explains that the underlying cause of sin, the old man, is crucified with Christ in His death. Since the source of sin is destroyed, a person is freed from sin. This passage is not teaching a futuristic promise of sinlessness, but a present day reality by noting that we are currently dead to sin with Christ.

The same thought continues in verses nine through fourteen. After conversion, Paul said that those who were converted were to yield themselves *to righteousness unto holiness* in lifestyle. Did Paul really intend for Christians to live this way or was it an abstract statement? The wording of this passage shows that Christians are expected to live accordingly. In this chapter Paul leaves absolutely no doubt that a person can, through Christ, live a life of victory over all sin.

9. **Romans 6:15** *What then? shall we sin, because we are not under the law, but under grace? God forbid.*

In verse 15 Paul repeats the question, *Shall we sin, because we are not under the law, but under grace* (6:15). There is, however, one very distinct difference between the questions in verse one and verse 15. Paul is now asking, "Are we to make provision for a single act of sin?"[9] Paul then answers in forceful language, *God forbid*. In his commentary, David Reese describes the verse this way:

> In the question stated in verse one, Paul used the present tense, asking if we should continue the practice of sinning. In this question, he uses the aorist subjunctive, making the question mean something like, 'Is it permissible to sin occasionally?' The issue is not the continuation of a sinful life as we lived in the past, but now . . . should we make allowance for occasional sin from time to time . . . The answer is a resounding 'no' in the most robust language of negation available to Paul. It is like saying, 'It would be inconceivable to arrive at such a conclusion.'[10]

---

[9] William Greathouse, *Beacon Bible Commentary* (Kansas City: Beacon Hill Press of Kansas City, 1968), 142.

[10] David G. Reese, *The Mystery of God's Mercy: a Commentary on Paul's Letter to the Romans* (Toccoa Falls, GA:, 2021), 133.

10. Romans 6:16-18, 22 *Know ye not, that to whom ye yield yourselves servants to obey, his servants ye are to whom ye obey whether of sin unto death, or of obedience unto righteousness? But God be thanked, that ye were the servants of sin, but ye have obeyed from the heart that form of doctrine which was delivered you. Being then made free from sin, ye became the servants of righteousness. 6:22 But now being made free from sin, and become servants to God, ye have your fruit unto holiness, and the end everlasting life.*

This passage explains that we were once slaves under the power of sin but have now been delivered and made free. It makes a distinct contrast between a slave to sin who was free from righteousness, and a saved individual who is now free from sin. The old master of sin is pictured as completely gone. Our lives are now shown as entirely given over to God as His slaves. To conclude that a Christian continues to sin at all is in total contrast to the direct statements given in these verses.

It is also quite obvious that Paul is not talking about absolute perfection or even sins of ignorance. He is discussing sin in a moral sense of obedience to God. Paul did not use any descriptive terms to describe a certain type of sin; he considered a Christian free of all sin. Those who hold that there is complete deliverance from sin in the form of inherited depravity have every right to claim these verses, since the passage teaches full deliverance from all sin both in nature and in sinful behavior. Certainly, it is clear that at a minimum this passage is teaching full deliverance from all unclean actions and sinful behavior. Had the apostle wished to clarify that the deliverance from sin only applied to willful sin but not to what are called "sins of ignorance" or "sins of infirmity," he could have done so. The apostle obviously did not consider that these human limitations should be identified as sin.

11. Romans 14:22-23 *Happy is he that condemneth not himself in that thing which he alloweth. And he that doubteth is damned if he eat, because he eateth not of faith: for whatsoever is not of faith is sin.*

This passage says that if a person commits behaviors which he, himself, believes are wrong, he will be damned. Paul then ties the idea of damnation to that of committing sin. He assumes his audience understands that the commission of sin causes a person to be damned, and is emphasizing that this action is a sin; thus, a person would be lost.

12. 2 Corinthians 5:21 *For he hath made him to be sin for us, who knew no sin; that we might be made the righteousness of God in him.*

Just as Christ became sin for us, we are made righteous as He was. The terminology here is not just being declared righteous, but the glorious reality of actually being transformed and made righteous.

13. 1 Timothy 5:20 *Them that sin rebuke before all, that others also may fear.*

If sin is something that all Christians do because of ignorance or human failure, should we be constantly rebuking other people publicly for human failure that they cannot help? It is obvious that the apostle is using the moral definition of deliberate disobedience when he uses the term *sin* in this passage.

14. Titus 2:14 *Who gave himself for us, that he might redeem us from all iniquity.*

The word *redeem* is an Old Testament concept that deals with the institution of slavery. A person who was in debt and could not pay was sold into slavery. A kinsman redeemer had the right to buy back a relative from slavery by paying the debt. The slave was then set free. This is the custom referred to in this verse. Christ, our kinsman Redeemer, has paid the debt and set us free from iniquity just as a slave was freed in the Old Testament when his debt was paid. This passage is not discussing freedom from merely the guilt of sin, but from the power and ownership of sin.

Wesley notes that this text teaches that Jesus gave Himself to redeem us from "the power and the very being, as from the guilt of all our sins."[11] This verse clearly teaches that we can be delivered from all sin in this life.

---

[11] John Wesley, *Notes on the Bible*, Titus 2:14, accessed June 27, 2023, http://wesley.nnu.edu/john-wesley/john-wesleys-notes-on-the-bible/notes-on-st-pauls-epistle-to-titus/.

The Calvinist view or legal definition contradicts Paul's teaching that Jesus redeems a person from all sin.

15. 1 Peter 4:1 *For he that hath suffered in the flesh hath ceased from sin.*

The sufferings of Christ and its application to our lives gives Christians the power to quit sinning. The Greek form of the word *cease* is a perfect indicative tense, indicating that a person ceased from sin in the past, and that cessation has not changed; he is still in the state of being *ceased from sin.* The perfect tense with the indicative mood denotes an action completed in the past which continues unto the present. Normally a biblical author does not use the perfect tense unless he is making a deliberate choice to emphasize the meaning of the tense.[12] This passage provides a powerful argument that Peter also emphasized the sinlessness of the Christian.

Albert Barnes says,

> To "suffer in the flesh" is to die. The expression here has a proverbial aspect, and seems to have meant something like this: "when a man is dead, he will sin no more"; referring of course to the present life. So if a Christian becomes dead in a moral sense—dead to this world, dead by being crucified with Christ—he may be expected to cease from sin. The reasoning is based on the idea that there is such a union between Christ and the believer that His death on the cross secured the death of the believer to the world.[13]

The Jamieson, Fausset, and Brown Commentary says, "The Christian is by faith one with Christ: as then Christ by death is judicially freed from sin; so the Christian who has in the person of Christ died, has no more to

---

[12] This is the basic concept Greek scholars give to the perfect tense in the indicative mood. For a discussion of its usage see Daniel B. Wallace, *Greek Grammar: Beyond the Basics* (Grand Rapids: Zondervan, 1996), 573.

[13] Albert Barnes, *Barnes Notes on the New Testament* (Kregel Publications, 1962), 1427.

do with it judicially, and ought to have no more to do with it actually."[14] These commentaries are not from the Wesleyan theological position, but good biblical scholarship, even when it is not from an Arminian point of view, does recognize the impact of what Scripture teaches in these passages.

16. 1 Corinthians 15:34 *Awake to righteousness, and sin not.*

The Apostle Paul tells the Corinthians not to commit sin. Matthew Henry notes that Paul tells them, "Rouse yourselves, break off your sins by repentance: renounce and forsake every evil way."[15] It must be possible to refrain from sin; otherwise, this could not have been the admonition of the Apostle Paul. Once again, any excuse that allows sin in the Christian's life cannot be defended from the Bible.

17. 1 John 5:18 *We know that whosoever is born of God sinneth not; but he that is begotten of God keepeth himself, and that wicked one toucheth him not.*

It is impossible to get away from the clear meaning of this Scripture. The new birth experience changes a person to enable him to quit sinning. We are new creatures in Christ who have been transformed (2Co 5:17). This verse destroys the idea that a person continually commits "sins" of infirmity and ignorance. It simply says that a person who has the new birth does not sin. The Bible could have added the word *willful* or could have explained that it only meant willful sin, but it does not. Scripture obviously does not consider a human failure to be sin or it would have clarified this in the statement. John declares that a person stops sinning at the time of the new birth.

18. Revelation 1:5 *Unto him that loved us, and washed us from our sins in his own blood.*

---

[14]Robert Jamieson, Andrew Fausset, and David Brown, *The Bethany Parallel Commentary on the New Testament, The Jamieson, Fausset, and Brown Commentary* (Minneapolis: Bethany House Publishers, 1983), 1382.

[15]Matthew Henry, *Matthew Henry's Commentary on the Whole Bible*, vol. VI (New York: Fleming H. Revell Company, nd.), 593.

The Greek text used by most modern translations uses the word for being loosed from sin rather than being washed. Either way it is interpreted, it is the same truth. Our sins are gone. It does not say they are only covered, nor does it say we are only delivered from the penalty of sin. It says we are freed from sins or our sins have been washed away. This passage teaches entire deliverance from sin. The passage does not state that one is delivered from only the guilt of sin; it teaches instead the removal of sin.

19. 1 John 2:1 *My little children, these things write I unto you, that ye sin not. And if any man sin, we have an advocate with the Father, Jesus Christ the righteous.*

The Apostle John explains that he wrote this book so that the readers would not sin. The Greek word here is in the aorist tense, implying one action or event. Thus, John is writing that they should not sin even a single time. John certainly views sin as something a Christian can decide to avoid; accordingly, it must be a choice and within the power of the individual. The admonition is followed by the word *if,* not the word *when.* John is encouraging those who are struggling but is making it clear that life without sinning is possible and necessary! This passage completely destroys the concept that people must sin because of ignorance or human fallibilities. John Wesley notes on this verse, "All the words, institutions and judgments of God are leveled against sin, either that it may not be committed, or that it may be abolished."[16]

20. John 5:14 and John 8:11 *Jesus . . . said to him, lo, thou art made whole: sin no more.*

This is the story of the man by the pool of Bethesda who was healed. Jesus commanded the man to cease his sinning. John also relates the story of the woman who had been caught in adultery that was taken to Jesus. Jesus said, *Go and sin no more.* Specifically, Jesus commanded them both

---

[16] John Wesley: *Wesley Notes on the New Testament*; Comment on 1 John 2:1, accessed June 27, 2023, http://wesley.nnu.edu/john-wesley/john-wesleys-notes-on-the-bible/notes-on-the-first-epistle-of-st-john/.

to keep the Law, since breaking the Law was sin. Neither person objected that it was impossible to *sin no more*. Christ warned the healed man that if he did sin again, something even worse would come upon him. Christ taught and those around Him understood that a life without sin was possible.

21. 2 John 1:9 *Whosoever transgresseth, and abideth not in the doctrine of Christ, hath not God.*

Two requirements are given which are necessary for people to have God in their lives. One cannot transgress and one must believe that Christ has come in the flesh. Transgression is another term for sin in the New Testament and is given usually in the context of violating the law. Christians do not transgress the law according to this passage. When a person knows that an action is forbidden by God and yet continues to do it anyway, he cannot claim to be a Christian. He does not know God according to this passage. This little book was given as a warning against losing what one has in Christ. Tragically, many in the church today are throwing away not only their reward but also their salvation by their deliberate choice to transgress the law which God has written upon the heart.

22. Matthew 7:23 *Then will I profess unto them, I never knew you: depart from me, ye that work iniquity.*

The word iniquity, which means to violate the law, is a synonym for sin. Scripture states in 1 John 3:4 that sin is a violation of the law. It is quite clear that at the Judgment, Christ will order those who violate the law to depart. This is the criteria for entry to heaven: A person who keeps the law will be allowed in, but one who commits iniquity is not a follower of God and is not going to heaven. Heaven is unobtainable to those who are living in rebellion to God's law or refusing to come under the authority of the law. In this dispensation it is the New Covenant of grace that Christians must keep. It is God's law written upon the hearts and minds of His people. In that sense the law is subjective, but it is also objective since it is God's law and not man's ideas which are written upon the minds, the seat of knowledge, and the hearts, the seat of the will.

23. Matthew 13:41-43 *The Son of man shall send forth his angels, and they shall gather out of his kingdom all things that offend, and them which do iniquity; And shall cast them into a furnace of fire: there shall be wailing and gnashing of teeth.*

This is the story known as the Parable of the Wheat and Tares. Both the good seed and the tares were allowed to grow together until the time of the harvest. At that time the master burned the tares and gathered the good seed into his barn. When Jesus relayed the parable to his disciples, He stated that at the end of the world, those who commit iniquity will be punished. In contrast, the righteous will go into the kingdom of heaven. Obviously, behavior and obedience to God are the determining factors in people's eternal destiny.

24. 1 Corinthians 6:9 *The unrighteous shall not inherit the kingdom of God.*

Heaven is a holy place, prepared only for those who are righteous. Sin is defined in 1 John 5:17 as *all unrighteousness is sin.* Accordingly, being righteous is not sinning and being unrighteous is being sinful. This Scripture makes it clear that those who are not righteous will not go to heaven. The Bible

> No one who breaks Christ's commands is a Christian or knows God.

teaches that the righteous go into life eternal and those who are unrighteous will go away into everlasting punishment *(Mt 25:46).* Is it possible to be righteous? 1 John 1:9 states that God promises to *cleanse us from all unrighteousness.* The Apostle John also uses the word *righteous* to define who is a Christian. *If ye know that he is righteous, ye know that every one that doeth righteousness is born of him* (I Jo 2:29). Righteousness or living without sinning is the way to distinguish who is of God. *In this the children of God are manifest, and the children of the devil: whosoever doeth not righteousness is not of God* (1Jn. 3:10).

25. 1 John 2:3-4 *And hereby we do know that we know him, if we keep his commandments. He that saith, I know him, and keepeth not his commandments, is a liar, and the truth is not in him.*

Obviously, obedience in keeping God's commands is directly related to committing sin, since sin is rebellion to the law. This passage teaches that if a person knows Christ, he will keep the commands of Christ and not violate His law. This is the way to distinguish who is a Christian and who is not. This Scripture calls a person a liar if he professes to be a Christian but does not keep God's commands. These passages are dealing with the commands of the New Testament; yet, the principle for this comes out of the Old Testament, as well. To fail to keep the law to which one is accountable means one does not know God. We are not directly under the legalistic code of the Old Testament; instead, a Christian is under the law of Christ and the law of love (Ro 8:2; 13:8; 1Co 9:21).

26. Matthew 19:16-17 *Master, what good thing shall I do, that I may have eternal life? And he said unto him . . . if thou wilt enter into life, keep the commandments.*

Jesus, also, emphasized obedience to the law which a person had been given. When asked how to obtain eternal life, the response Jesus gave was to keep the commandments.

27. 1 John 5:3-4 *For this is the love of God, that we keep his commandments: and his commandments are not grievous. For whatsoever is born of God overcometh the world.*

A genuine love for God is shown by one's actions. Since love for God and others is the central concept of Christianity, it is evident that a refusal to love God by willfully breaking His commands is evidence that one does not have the love of God in his heart. Obviously, a failure from ignorance does not indicate a lack of love but a lack of maturity. If a person commits sin, it is evidence that he is not an overcomer, but under the control of the sinful world. Christians overcome the sin of the world and keep God's commands. 1 John 5:3 says, *For this is the love of God, that we keep his commandments.* Those who do not keep God's commands are sinners and not overcomers; furthermore, overcomers cannot be sinners, or they have not overcome. The language in the original is very strong and "there is little way to make a stronger statement in Greek than this. The child of God stands as conqueror. Thus, John is affirming that the spiritual rebirth of a believer is what provides victory over a world standing in opposition to God."[17]

28. Revelation 21:8 *But the fearful, and unbelieving, and the abominable, and murderers, and whoremongers, and sorcerers, and idolaters, and all liars, shall have their part in the lake which burneth with fire and brimstone: which is the second death.*

Scripture will list a number of things which a person cannot do and still inherit eternal life or if he does these things he will go to the Lake of Fire. A major difference between the Calvinistic and the Wesleyan views on sin is the Calvinistic belief that those who commit sin will still go to heaven while the Wesleyans believe a Christian quits sin. These passages give straightforward instruction: these actions will keep you out of heaven. These passages support the Wesleyan but not the Calvinistic beliefs. The authors of the Bible were not trying to give complete lists, but to give examples of types of actions which are not allowed in heaven.

29. Ephesians 5:5 *For this ye know, that no whoremonger, nor unclean person, nor covetous man, who is an idolater, hath any inheritance in the kingdom of Christ and of God.*

30. Galatians 5:19-21 *Now the works of the flesh are manifest, which are these; Adultery, fornication, uncleanness, lasciviousness, Idolatry, witchcraft, hatred, variance, emulations, wrath, strife, seditions, heresies, Envyings, murders, drunkenness, revellings, and such like: of the which I tell you before, as I have also told you in time past, that they which do such things shall not inherit the kingdom of God.*

31. 1 Corinthians 9:9-10 *Know ye not that the unrighteous shall not inherit the kingdom of God? Be not deceived: neither fornicators, nor idolaters, nor adulterers, nor effeminate, nor abusers of themselves*

---

[17] Gary W. Derickson, *First, Second, and Third John*, ed. H. Wayne House, W. Hall Harris III, and Andrew W. Pitts, *Evangelical Exegetical Commentary* (Bellingham, WA: Lexham Press, 2012), 502.

with mankind, Nor thieves, nor covetous, nor drunkards, nor revilers, nor extortioners, shall inherit the kingdom of God.

32. Ephesians 5:27 *That he might present it to himself a glorious church, not having spot, or wrinkle, or any such thing; but that it should be holy and without blemish.*

This passage points out Jesus gave Himself so that His church can be entirely pure and holy, totally without any spiritual fault. Wesley notes that this passage teaches that God will present His church as "not having [any] spot of impurity from any sin."[18] Christ is expecting a people who are without any impurity, without any moral fault, without any spiritual blemish. Since sin is a spiritual blemish or impurity, this text is clearly teaching that one can be free from sin in this life. Calvinist theology, founded upon the legal definition of sin, depicts even Christians as full of spiritual blemishes and spots and wrinkles. The Calvinistic legal definition, therefore, directly contradicts the Apostle Paul who taught that while we may not be physically perfect, we can be spiritually without blemish.

33. Philippians 2:15 *That ye may be blameless and harmless, the sons of God, without rebuke, in the midst of a crooked and perverse nation, among whom ye shine as lights in the world.*

God's people are to be blameless in the crooked and perverse world in which they live. Scripture repeatedly admonishes Christians to be blameless. Obviously, a blameless person does nothing for which he could be considered guilty. Sin makes a person guilty before God; therefore, a blameless person must be a person without sin. The leaders of the church were to be blameless (1Ti 3:2, 3:10, 5:7, Tit 1:6-7). At the return of Christ, His people will be blameless (1Co 1:8, 1Th 5:23, 2 Pe 3:14). Jude also uses a similar word when he proclaims that God is able to present His people faultless before God. While everyone makes mistakes, Scripture

---

[18] John Wesley: *Wesley's Notes on the New Testament*; Comment on Ephesians 5:27, accessed June 27, 2023, http://wesley.nnu.edu/john-wesley/john-wesleys-notes-on-the-bible/notes-on-st-pauls-epistle-to-the-ephesians/#Chapter+V.

teaches a moral completeness which is identified as being faultless (Jude 1:24).

Old Testament

While the Old Testament does teach that there were sins of ignorance mainly regarding to the ceremonial aspects of the Law, there are also a number of passages which teach that it was possible to keep the Old Testament Law. It certainly seems that at the time of Christ, the Jewish people had a confidence that they were living up to the requirements of the Law which God demanded. The idea that the purpose of the Law was to teach people the impossibility of keeping the requirements which God demanded does not seem to be evidenced by the New Testament or by the culture of the time. For example, Zacharias and Elizabeth were both *righteous before God, walking in all the commandments and ordinances of the Lord blameless* (Lu 1:6). When the rich, young ruler came to Christ and asked what he needed to do to inherit eternal life, Christ responded that he needed to keep the commandments. The reply of the young man was that he had kept them from his youth up (Mt 19:16-22). Paul stated that he was *touching the righteousness which is in the law, blameless* (Php 3:6).

34. Exodus 32:33 *And the LORD said unto Moses, Whosoever hath sinned against me, him will I blot out of my book.*

God is talking about the intentional, deliberate sin of idolatry committed by Israel's worship of the golden calf. God does erase names out of the book of life. This verse shows that God erases names for an intentional act of rebellion against His commands. This concept is carried across into the New Testament when at the final Judgment *whosoever was not found written in the book of life was cast into the lake of fire* (Re 20:15). If a person's name being in the book of life is dependent upon living a life of obedience to God, it is critically important that a person is making every effort necessary to keep it there. Many professing Christians today do not meet God's criteria for entrance to heaven.

Defending the Biblical Definition

35. Ezekiel 18:4 and 18:20 *The soul that sinneth, it shall die.*

These verses both make a simple statement that those who sin, die. The Old Testament clearly taught that if a person sins, he dies. It is also obvious from this truth that this is only referring to sins over which a person has control, not the aspect of humanity in which a person cannot be humanly perfect as God is perfect. There will always be errors due to ignorance, inability, or just simply being human. These should not be called sin. This passage teaches that it is possible for a person to live without sinning or there would have been no purpose for this statement by Ezekiel.

36. Ps 119:1-3 *Blessed are the undefiled in the way, who walk in the law of the LORD. Blessed are they that keep his testimonies, and that seek him with the whole heart. They also do no iniquity: they walk in his ways.*

Is it possible to live an undefiled life? Is it possible to live without doing iniquity or breaking the law? These passages are dealing with a current lifestyle, not whether a person has ever sinned in the past. Many Scriptures teach that everyone has committed sin, but it is possible to quit sinning and from that point forward live an undefiled life without iniquity. Absolutely, the power of sin can be broken and a person can live a transformed life. This passage is quite clear that a person can be undefiled, keep God's testimonies (law), and live without breaking His law.

Christ came to fulfill the Old Covenant by providing the ultimate sacrifice for which that covenant was a symbol. He then replaced that covenant with the New Covenant of grace in which the Holy Spirit now possesses the hearts and minds of His followers. It is clear that there was deliverance from sin available in the Old Testament. In the New Testament, an even greater promise of victory over sin is given by the filling of the Holy Spirit, Who empowers His people to fulfill all righteousness.

> The definition of sin is the foundation for completely different concepts of salvation.

The biblical basis of the Wesleyan doctrine rests upon a solid scriptural foundation. The Scriptures referenced in this chapter are not a complete list, but do give biblical evidence for the Wesleyan definition of sin as well as the possibility and the necessity of life without sinning. A misunderstanding of the definition of sin has led to a number of misconceptions of Scripture and of the Wesleyan doctrine. These are not merely definitions of little importance, but they lie at the core of opposing systems of theological beliefs. These doctrinal positions give two differing approaches to salvation and biblical understanding. Often those from the Reformed tradition are unfamiliar with the Wesleyan doctrinal system; however, it is a straightforward, biblical interpretation. If a person accepts that Scripture was meant to be easily read and understood by the common man without having to reinterpret it through a theological preconception, then all Christians can and must live without sin, as is taught by Scripture.

Chapter 12
Historical Understanding of the Doctrine of Sin

Sin is best defined as disobedience to the law of God. In order to appropriately understand the correct definition of sin, a person must be able to define the term *law*. This seems simple, but it is much more complex than it sounds. God has dealt with mankind in different ways under different dispensations or time periods. It would be inappropriate to legalistically apply the Old Testament Law to a person living in the New Testament dispensation of grace. The real question each person faces is what are God's expectations for me today?

In the Garden of Eden

Adam and Eve were completely and perfectly without sin in the Garden. They had no knowledge of good or evil as we would understand it, but they were in perfect communion with God. They had been given only one commandment: Do not eat of the Tree of Knowledge of Good and Evil. Adam and Eve had a certain level and type of perfection, but it would have been far short of absolute perfection. For example, they wore no clothing and had no awareness it was wrong until after eating the forbidden fruit. Their actions were not wrong since there was no comprehension of evil; God did not consider it sin. They were in no way violating the law which God had established for them. The sin of Adam and Eve was to intentionally and deliberately disobey.

Before the Law

During the time between the fall of Adam and the giving of the Mosaic Law, there was still an understanding of good and evil. Each person was expected to keep the law that God demanded in their time period. Man had the natural law and his conscience. God also personally appeared to men and women during this time. With the long life span of this era, the expectations of God were easily passed along orally from generation to generation. The Patriarchs, Job, and Moses all show a comprehension of God's requirements before the law was given on Mt. Sinai. Even prophets such as Baalim, who was not of the nation of Israel, show a comprehension of their duty to obey God's law. The Early Church scholar Tertullian stated, "In short, before the Law of Moses, written in stone-tables, I contend that there was a law unwritten, which was habitually understood naturally, and by the fathers was habitually kept. For whence was Noah found righteous, if in his case the righteousness of a natural law had not preceded?"[1]

Under the Old Testament Covenant of the Law

God chose a special group of people upon which to display his grace, the Children of Israel. To those chosen ones he made a special covenant. God listed out His expectations in a written code. If they kept this code, i.e., the Law, they would be blessed; but if they disobeyed the Law, they would be cursed. This Law was given to a group of mainly illiterate slaves that God delivered from Egypt. A phonetic alphabet had not yet been invented, and writing was only in the process of being developed. Most likely Moses wrote the Law originally in Egyptian hieroglyphics, which has a pictographic alphabet rather than letters. It would entail the memorization of perhaps thousands of pictographs in order to be able to read. One of the twelve tribes of Israel was designated to learn the Law and teach it to the other tribes. Under the covenant established by the Law, sin was the violation of any of the Mosaic laws which had been given by God. This included even a failure through ignorance. A much lesser penalty was imposed for these "sins of ignorance," but they were still considered sin and needed atonement.

The phonetic alphabet was first developed before 1000 B.C. in the land of Palestine and was then spread throughout the Mediterranean world

---

[1] Alexander Roberts, James Donaldson, and A. Cleveland Coxe eds. *Ante-Nicene Fathers*, vol. 3. (Buffalo, NY: Christian Literature Publishing Co., 1885.) Revised and edited for New Advent by Kevin Knight.
<http://www.newadvent.org/fathers/0308.htm>.

by the Phoenicians. It is thought by some that the alphabet was first developed by the Hebrews.[2] With the advent of a more widespread ability to read, the Psalms and the prophets show a greater expectation that keeping the law was a possibility. Psalm 119 indicates an ability to understand and keep God's requirements.

Gentiles outside the Jewish Law

Those who were not of the Israelite race were not included in the special covenant made between God and Israel. Gentiles were still under the same application of the moral code as were all people since the Fall. In Romans Paul addressed the issue, stating, *When the Gentiles, which have not the law, do by nature the things contained in the law, these, having not the law, are a law unto themselves: Which shew the work of the law written in their hearts, their conscience also bearing witness, and their thoughts the mean while accusing or else excusing one another* (Ro 2:14-15). Although a very prejudiced Jew, Peter was shown by God that the Gentiles were also accepted by God if they met His requirements. Peter then said, *Of a truth I perceive that God is no respecter of persons: But in every nation he that feareth him, and worketh righteousness, is accepted with him* (Acts 10:34-35).These passages show that salvation was available to the Gentiles as well as the Jews. Gentiles were under the law of their consciences and required to fear God and live righteously. The prophet Micah specified the requirements of God that applied to both Jew and Gentile as *to do justly, and to love mercy, and to walk humbly with thy God* (Micah 6:8).

Under the New Testament Covenant of Grace

The New Testament clearly states that a Christian is no longer under the Old Testament Law. The Old Testament Law was given only as a temporary measure because of the wickedness of man. With the coming of Jesus Christ and His transforming power, the written code was changed to being filled with and being led of the Spirit. If you *be led of the Spirit, ye*

---

[2] For more information on the alphabet see: Douglas Petrovich, *The World's Oldest Alphabet* (Jerusalem: Carta Jerusalem, 2016), vi. and https://rosenhebrewschool.com/articles/paleo-hebrew-alphabet/.

are not under the law (Ga. 5:18). The Mosaic Law was illustrated by Paul as a schoolmaster who taught what was right and demanded obedience. It is also pictured as a tutor training a child until he became an adult. Once a person was no longer a child, he would comprehend that true salvation is found in faith and faithfulness to Jesus Christ and be held accountable for this knowledge (Ga. 3:19-25, Ga. 4:1-6). The Mosaic Law was given only for the Israelites, but this new dispensation of grace has given to all humanity the same glorious promise of becoming truly righteous through the blood of Christ. All who have accepted the faith of Christ *are the children of Abraham*, (Ga. 3:7)

The book of Hebrews teaches that the Old Covenant has been replaced by a New Covenant. Hebrews says, *Behold, the days come, saith the Lord, when I will make a new covenant with the house of Israel and with the house of Judah* (Heb. 8:8). Establishing this New Covenant, God said, *I will put my laws into their mind, and write them in their hearts* (Heb 8:10). The head is the location of a person's thought capacity, and the heart is the seat of the will. Accordingly, if God's law is placed in the mind, it is impossible to break the law without knowledge; and since the law is written in the heart, the law cannot be broken without the involvement of the will. Therefore, any transgression of the law must be a choice to disobey God along with a conscious violation of what God has commanded. Accordingly, sins of ignorance do not exist under the dispensation of grace.

Throughout the New Testament, the definition of sin is clearly associated with knowledge. Sin is defined as doing something which a person believes is wrong, even though the action in itself is not against the law (Ro. 14:23). Scripture says that he *that knoweth to do good, and doeth it not, to him it is sin* (Jas 4:17). Once again, knowledge is involved in defining sin. To refuse to do what God tells one to do as defined in His word or through God's personal revelation becomes sin. Another New Testament definition is *sin is the transgression of the law* (1Jo 3:4). This passage literally means that sin is lawlessness. Scholars say that the word *lawless* is not an inadvertent breaking of a law, but a rebellion and a refusal to come under the authority of the law. Accordingly, this definition makes sin both a willful and a knowledgeable act.

Early Church Understanding of Sin

Scholars who have studied the early Church have come to the same consensus that from the beginning the church took the position that sin was always a voluntary act; a person sinned by his or her own free choice.. This is true of those outside the Wesleyan tradition as well as those who follow John Wesley. In his book, *The Teaching of the Church Fathers,* John Willis summarizes the Early Church's doctrine, saying that they taught that "there can be no sin unless there first be free consent, for all sin has a voluntary aspect."[3] In his textbook on the doctrine of sin, David L. Smith, a Baptist theologian, explains, "The second-century apologists were unanimous in proclaiming that sin is a willful act of each individual."[4] Steve Copland, a contemporary theologian explains that "Early Church writers always posit sin as a personal choice, a deliberate act of disobedience."[5] Reformed theologian Herman Bavinck said, "Going back to the early church . . . Sin is knowingly breaking God's command and flows from a heart that rebels against God."[6] An article by William S. Babcock in *The Encyclopedia of Early Christianity* stated, "Early Christianity insisted that sin is not inflicted or imposed on human beings apart from or contrary to their own inclinations. At stake here was the specifically moral character of sin: if persons cannot avoid sinning, they cannot be held (morally) responsible for sin."[7]

> Scholars agree that the Wesleyan definition of sin is the historic belief of the Early Church.

---

[3] John Randolph Willis, , ed. *The Teachings of the Church Fathers* (San Francisco: Ignatius Press, 2002), 233.
[4] David L. Smith, *With Willful Intent: A Theology of Sin* (Eugene, OR: Wipf and Stock Publishers, 2003), 18.
[5] Steve Copland, *An Introduction to Practical Systematic Theology* (N.p.: Smashwords, 2021), Kindle Edition.
[5] Herman Bavinck, *Reformed Dogmatics: Sin and Salvation in Theology: Reclaiming the Doctrine of the Early Church,* Kindle Ed., (352).
[6] Herman Bavinck, *Reformed Dogmatics: Sin and Salvation in Christ*, vol. 3. https://www.scribd.com/read/267768284/Reformed-Dogmatics-Volume-3-Sin-and-Salvation-in-Christ.
[7] Everett Ferguson, ed. *Encyclopedia of Early Christianity*. (Routledge, 2013), 1061.

In *The Emergence of the Catholic Tradition,* Jaroslav Pelikan pictures a conflict between the Gnostic systems from Greek tradition and the Christian religion. Gnostics believed that sin was inevitable and that man did not have a free will. The orthodox Christian response was to deny that sin was inevitable and to insist that God "sets before man good and evil, life and death. . . . This could not be if man were not free, endowed with a will capable of obedience and resistance."[8] In discussing the beliefs of the early church, Anglican Gerald Bray reported, "Sin was a personal act of disobedience against God that broke the relationship he had given to his creatures. . . . Jews and Christians both agreed that sin, like evil was not inherent in the created order but was the result of a rebellion against God."[9] In summarizing the doctrine of sin in the early church Bray wrote,

> They (Christians) did not agree with their Gentile contemporaries that sin and evil resided in matter, nor did they accept the Pharisaical idea that sin was essentially breaking the law. So where was sin to be found, if it was so powerful and all-pervasive? Their answer was that sin was a spiritual rebellion against God. . . . One might almost say that whereas pagans believed that human beings were divine spirits/souls trapped in evil material bodies, Christians believed the opposite—that rebellious human spirits were living in naturally good bodies that had been perverted by their spiritual rebellion.[10]

John Wesley certainly did not go outside of traditional Christian theology in developing his definition of sin. Rather, the Calvinistic definition is an aberration of orthodox theology, and Wesley brought a correction to a doctrinal fallacy. In developing his theology, Wesley studied the beliefs of early church leaders. When questioned regarding his

---

[8] Gerald Bray, *God has Spoken: A History of Christian Theology* (United States: Crossway, 2014), 510.
[9] Gerald Bray, *God has Spoken: A History of Christian Theology*, 128.
[10] Gerald Bray, *God has Spoken: A History of Christian Theology*, 371.

definition of sin, Wesley responded, "But is 'a voluntary transgression of a known law' a proper definition of sin?'. . . It is a definition which has passed uncensored in the church for at least fifteen hundred years."[11]

Holiness scholars have followed the tradition of Wesley by also going back to the Early Church in defending their understanding of sin. According to Paul Bassett, at the time when the Shepherd of Hermas was written (pre-A.D. 150), it was "a widely held opinion that the baptized can live without sin."[12] The early church even held that if a person did sin after baptism, he could no longer find forgiveness. They believed that "the baptized Christian can live without sin and forfeits all hope of salvation if he does sin."[13] This underscored the belief that sinlessness was not only possible, but also required.

Reformed theology, as established by John Calvin, broke the consensus with the Early Church on the definition of sin. Calvin admitted his disagreement with St. Jerome regarding whether a person could keep the law, proclaiming, "What was the opinion of Jerome, I regard not . . . I assert also that no man, who shall exist in future, will reach the standard on true perfection, unless released from the burden of the body."[14] It is quite clear from this statement that he disregarded the teaching of the Early Church on this issue. Calvin also misunderstood the concept of moral perfection as it is taught in the Scriptures and by the Early Church. His misunderstandings have since led to the confusion in defining sin in the Reformed churches.

Statements by Early Church Leaders

From the beginning, repeated statements represent the Early Church definition of sin; however, it is not a major theme of their discussions, since there was little debate on the issue. Everyone understood that Christians lived a life of obedience to the commands of God to the best of their knowledge. In the Early Church a Christian was expected to live without sinning, but sin was defined as a voluntary act of the will in defiance to God. The following are some of the statements made by key people in the Early Church. Dates given are approximate.

---

[11] John Wesley, *The Works of John Wesley*, 3rd ed., vol. 12 (London: Wesleyan Methodist Book Room, 1872), 239.

Shepherd of Hermas: (A.D. 100-150) "So long as he is ignorant . . . he does not sin."[12]

Justin Martyr: (A.D. 150) "We maintain one acts rightly or sins by his own free choice."[13]

Tatian: (A.D. 150) "The just man can be deservedly praised for his virtuous deeds, since in the exercise of his free choice he refrained from transgressing the will of God."[14]

Clement of Alexandria: (A.D. 195) "Sin, then, is voluntary on my part."[15]

Origen (A.D. 250) was one of the most brilliant scholars in the Early Church and one of the most prolific writers. In his homily on Luke 1:6, he discusses whether a life above sin is possible. Here is an excerpt in his own words:

> People who want to offer an excuse for their sins claim that no one is without sin. They appeal to the testimony of the Book of Job, where Scripture says, "No one is clean from filth, not even if his life upon the earth has been only one day long. His months can be numbered."¹ But they only mouth the words of this verse and are wholly ignorant of its meaning. We shall answer them briefly. "To be without sin" has two meanings in Scripture. One is

---

[12] Pope Clement I et al., *The Apostolic Fathers*, ed. Kirsopp Lake, vol. 2, The Loeb Classical Library (Cambridge MA; London: Harvard University Press, 1912–1913), 79.

[13] Justin Martyr, *The Second Apology, Chapter 7. The world preserved for the sake of Christians. Man's responsibility*, https://www.newadvent.org/fathers/0127.htm.

[14] Tatian *Address to the Greeks,* Chapter 7, https://www.logoslibrary.org/tatian/address/07.html.

[15] David W. Bercot, ed., "Man, Doctrine Of," *A Dictionary of Early Christian Beliefs: A Reference Guide to More than 700 Topics Discussed by the Early Church Fathers* (Peabody, MA: Hendrickson Publishers, 1998), 414.

never to have sinned at all; the other is to have ceased sinning.[16]

Cyril of Jerusalem: (A.D. 350) "Fearful thing is sin, and the sorest disease of the soul is transgression, secretly cutting its sinews, and becoming also the cause of eternal fire; an evil of a man's own choosing, an offspring of the will. For that we sin of our own free will the Prophet says plainly."[17]

Methodius: (A.D. 300) [God] "gave to every individual the sense of free will . . . For our will is made to choose either to sin or not to sin."[18]

Ambrose of Milan: (A.D. 375) "Sins rest in one's own power."[19] He also said, "No state is so blessed as that wherein one is free from sin."[20]

Augustine: (A.D. 400) "He who sins not voluntarily, sins not at all."[21]

Council of Carthage: (A.D. 419) "Likewise it seemed good, that

---

[16] Joseph T. Lienhard. "Homily 2.: Luke 1.6." *Homilies on Luke, 10–13*, (Catholic University of America Press, 1996), accessed June 12, 2023, https://doi.org/10.2307/j.ctt32b0dn.8.
[17] Cyril of Jerusalem, "The Catechetical Lectures of S. Cyril, Archbishop of Jerusalem," *S. Cyril of Jerusalem, S. Gregory Nazianzen,* ed. Philip Schaff and Henry Wace, trans. R. W. Church and Edwin Hamilton Gifford, vol. 7, A Select Library of the Nicene and Post-Nicene Fathers of the Christian Church, Second Series (New York: Christian Literature Company, 1894), 8.
[18] Archelaus, "The Acts of the Disputation with the Heresiarch Manes," *Fathers of the Third Century: Gregory Thaumaturgus, Dionysius the Great, Julius Africanus, Anatolius and Minor Writers, Methodius, Arnobius,* ed. Alexander Roberts, James Donaldson, and A. Cleveland Coxe, trans. S. D. F. Salmond, vol. 6, *The Ante-Nicene Fathers* (Buffalo, NY: Christian Literature Company, 1886), 204.
[19] Ambrose of Milan, "On the Duties of the Clergy," in *St. Ambrose: Select Works and Letters,* ed. Philip Schaff and Henry Wace, trans. H. de Romestin, E. de Romestin, and H. T. F. Duckworth, vol. 10, *A Select Library of the Nicene and Post-Nicene Fathers of the Christian Church,* Second Series (New York: Christian Literature Company, 1896), 47.
[20] Ambrose of Milan, "On the Duties of the Clergy," 45.
[21] Augustine, *Against the Epistle of Manichaeus,* trans. Richard Stothert, A. D., 397, https://ccel.org/ccel/schaff/npnf104/npnf104.iv.viii.i.html.

whoever should say that the grace of God, by which a man is justified through Jesus Christ our Lord, avails only for the remission of past sins, and not for assistance against committing sins in the future, let him be anathema." The explanatory note and the context states, "That the grace of God not only gives remission of sins, but also affords aid that we sin no more."[22]

The same doctrine continued throughout the Middle Ages. The noted Roman Catholic theologians agree with the doctrine of sinlessness as taught by the early church. The best known of these is Thomas Aquinas (A.D. 1250) who said, "The first cause of sin is in the will, which commands all voluntary acts, in which alone is sin to be found."[23]

Early Church on the Necessity of Living without Sinning

Throughout the Early Church there has been a consensus that sin is a voluntary act of disobedience to God. In addition, the church taught that the grace of God empowered a person with the ability to live a life without sinning in obedience to God. Dates given are approximate.

Ignatius of Antioch: (A.D. 110) "No one who professes faith sins."[24] "Keep God in remembrance, and thou shalt never sin."[25]

Justin Martyr: (A.D. 150) "But there is no other [way] than this: to become acquainted with Christ, to be washed in the fountain spoken of by Isaiah for the remission of sins, and for the rest, to live sinless lives."[26]

---

[22] Henry Percival, trans. *Nicene and Post-Nicene Fathers*, Second Series, Vol. 14. Ed. Philip Schaff and Henry Wace. (Buffalo, NY: Christian Literature Publishing Co., 1900.) A. D. 419, ed. for New Advent by Kevin Knight.
<http://www.newadvent.org/fathers/3816.htm>. Council of Carthage, "Canon 111."
[23] Thomas Aquinas, *Summa Theologica*, accessed February 6, 2023, https://www.ccel.org/ccel/aquinas/summa.FS_Q71_A6.html.
[24] Ignatius, The Epistle of Ignatius to the Ephesians, ch.14, https://www.newadvent.org/fathers/0104.htm .
[25] Ignatius, *Epistle to the Tarsians*, ch. 7, https://www.newadvent.org/fathers/0114.htm .
[26] Justin Martyr, *Dialogue with Trypho*, ch. 44,

Athenagoras: (A.D. 150) describes Christians as "pure from all wrongdoing," [and] "those who are persuaded that nothing will escape the scrutiny of God . . . are not likely to commit even the slightest sin."[27]

Tertullian: (A.D. 200) "We are not baptized that we may cease to sin, but because we have already ceased."[28]

Origen: (A.D. 200) "Insofar as we commit sins, we have not yet put off the generation of the devil, even if we are thought to believe in Jesus. Everyone who is not of the devil does not commit sin."[29]

Didymus the Blind: (A.D. 350) "A person will not sin as long as he walks according to the way of righteousness. If he turns aside from that he will sin, and indeed those who do sin have turned away from their Creator. The ability not to sin is guaranteed by the presence of God's seed in us. This seed is either his power or the spirit of adoption, which cannot sin."[30]

Didymus the Blind: (A.D. 350) "The person who dwells in virtue and true doctrine does not sin....The one who remains in Christ, who is his righteousness and sanctification, does not sin. For how can someone act unrighteously when he is in the company of righteousness, and how can he be content to place corruption alongside holiness? Therefore, anyone who sins is outside Christ and has no part or fellowship in him." [31]

---

https://www.newadvent.org/fathers/01283.htm ch. 44.
[27] R. Newton Flew. *The Idea of Perfection in Christian Theology* (Eugene, OR: Wipf and Stock Publishers, 2005). 135.
[28] King, Lord Peter. *An Inquiry Into the Constitution, Discipline, Unity, and Worship of the Primitive Church: That Flourished Within the First Three Hundred Years After Christ* (Lane & Scott, 1851). 101.
[29] Bray, Gerald L., and Thomas C. Oden, eds., *Ancient Christian Commentary on Scripture, James, 1-2 Peter, 1-3 John, Jude* (Downers Grove, IL: InterVarsity Press, 2014), 198.
[30] Gerald L Bray., and Thomas C. Oden, eds., *Ancient Christian Commentary on Scripture, James, 1-2 Peter, 1-3 John, Jude*. 199.
[31] Gerald L. Bray, and Thomas C. Oden, eds., *Ancient Christian Commentary on Scripture , James, 1-2 Peter, 1-3 John, Jude*. 197.

Ambrose: (A.D. 375) "No state is so blessed as that wherein one is free from sin."[32]

Jerome: (A.D. 400) "If we sin and the devil enter through the gate of sin, Christ will immediately withdraw."[33]

John Chrysostom: (A.D. 400) "Committing sin and making room for the devil amount to one and the same thing sin."[34] "Yet it is possible even for one with a mortal body not to sin."[35]

Augustine: (A.D. 400) "A man can be sinless, but only by the help of grace."[36]

Apostolic Constitutions: (A.D. 300) "He who sins after his baptism, unless he repents and forsakes his sins, will be condemned to Gehenna[hell]".[37]

415 Council of Diospolis: "Man, by God's aid and grace, can be without sin"[38]

---

[32] Ambrose, *On the Duties of the Clergy*, ch. 3, https://www.newadvent.org/fathers/34012.htm.
[33] Jerome, *Against Joviniaus,* 3.2, https://www.newadvent.org/fathers/30092.htm.
[34] Bray, Gerald L., and Thomas C. Oden, eds., *Ancient Christian Commentary on Scripture, James, 1-2 Peter, 1-3 John, Jude*, 199.
[35] John Chryosotom, *Homily 11, On Romans*, http://www.newadvent.org/fathers/210211.htm .
[36] *The Complete Works of the Church Fathers*: A total of 64 authors, and over 2,500 works of the Early Christian Church (Kindle Locations 116398-116399). Amazon.com. Kindle Edition.
[37] David W. Bercot, ed., "Salvation," *A Dictionary of Early Christian Beliefs: A Reference Guide to More than 700 Topics Discussed by the Early Church Fathers*, 590.
[38] G. F. Wiggers, *An Historical Presentation of Augustinism and Pelagianism:From the Original Sources* (Kindle Locations 2383-2384). Kindle Edition.

Severus of Antioch: (A.D. 500) "Insofar as someone who is born of God retains the grace of his new birth he cannot sin in the way he behaves. And the reason for this is that God's seed dwells in him."[39]

Andreas: (A.D. 500's) "As often as we sin we are born of the Devil."[40]

The 418 Synod of Africa council: "The grace of God not only give remission of sins, but also affords aid that we sin no more. Likewise, it seemed good, that whoever should say that the grace of God, by which a man is justified through Jesus Christ our Lord, avails only for the remission of past sins, and not for assistance against committing sins in the future, let him be anathema."[41]

---

[39] Bray, Gerald L., and Thomas C. Oden, eds., *Ancient Christian Commentary on Scripture, James, 1-2 Peter, 1-3 John, Jude*, 200.
[40] Bray, Gerald L., and Thomas C. Oden, eds., *Ancient Christian Commentary on Scripture, James, 1-2 Peter, 1-3 John, Jude*, 199.
[41] Council of Carthage, http://www.newadvent.org/fathers/3816.htm.

Chapter 13
The Concept of Sin from Wesley to the Present

The Theology of Wesley on Sin

John Wesley viewed sin from several aspects; there is a personal choice to commit sin and there is the principle of sin in the heart. Wesley recognized human limitations, but he did not consider *sin* the proper term for them. "This third class of sins, 'improperly so-called,' are those defects that remain with the sanctified who no longer have the remains of the inbred sin. They are not 'condemned for sins of infirmity,' nor for 'involuntary failings' nor for anything that they cannot help."[1] Wesley held that a Christian did not commit willful sin and could be delivered from inbred sin. Wesley did not consider it proper to call the failures due to human limitations, infirmities, and ignorance, sin.

Wesley viewed sin as a moral issue in which a choice was made to break God's law. He wrote, "Nothing is sin, strictly speaking, but a voluntary transgression of a known law of God. Therefore, every voluntary breach of the law of love is sin; and nothing else if we speak properly. To strain the matter farther is only to make way for Calvinism."[2] Wesley also responded, "But is 'a voluntary transgression of a known law' a proper definition of sin?' . . . It is a definition which has passed uncensored in the church for at least fifteen hundred years."[3] He was also quite clear that Christians did not sin. It was stated thus in the Methodist Conference minutes, "If a believer sins, he thereby forfeits his pardon. Neither is it possible he should have justifying faith again, without previously

---

[1] Leo George Cox, *John Wesley's Concept of Sin* (Salem, OH: Schmul Publishing Company, 2002), 78.
[2] John Wesley, *The Works of John Wesley*, 3rd ed., vol. 12 (London: Wesleyan Methodist Book Room, 1872), 394.
[3] John Wesley, *The Works of John Wesley*, 239.

repenting."⁴ In his sermon on *Christian Perfection*, Wesley said that "even babes in Christ are in such a sense perfect, or born of God, as, first, not to commit sin."⁵

Wesley dealt in depth with the concept of deliverance from sin in his sermons, and sometimes misunderstandings have arisen from the teachings of Wesley. For example in his sermon, *On Sin in Believers*, it could be assumed from the title that believers still commit sin. This is not what Wesley meant at all. He is describing the sin nature in the heart. As he states, "The usurper is dethroned. He remains indeed where he once reigned; but remains in chains."⁶ A believer still has a sinful heart, but is not committing willful sin. Wesley, however, further taught that God "is able to save you from all the sin that still remains in your heart. He is able to save you from all the sin that cleaves to all your words and actions."⁷ In defining an action of personal sin, Wesley strongly held that believers do not commit sin as a voluntary act of disobedience; yet he recognizes that a believer has a sinful heart until he is sanctified. He is also emphatic that repentance is necessary for actions which come from that corrupted heart.

John Fletcher was a contemporary of John Wesley who worked in conjunction with John Wesley. His writings were approved and published by Wesley. Fletcher stated, "If I am not mistaken, it evidently follows from these plain words of Christ, (1.) That he taught a personal perfection, and an evangelically sinless perfection, too. (2.) That this perfection consists in not breaking, by willful commission, the least of the commandments."⁸ John Fletcher wrote, "An infirmity is a breach of Adam's law of paradisiacal [absolute] perfection, which our covenant God does not require of us now . . . an infirmity is free from guile, and has its

---

⁴ *Minutes of the 1744 Conference*, ed. John Bennet, https://archive.org/details/johnbenets00unknuoft/page/8/mode/2up.
⁵ John Wesley, *Sermons, on Several Occasions* (Oak Harbor, WA: Logos Research Systems, Inc., 1999).
⁶ John Wesley, *Wesley's 52 Standard Sermons*, (Salem, OH: Schmul Publishing Co., repr., 1982), 125.
⁷ John Wesley, *Wesley's 52 Standard Sermons*, 134.
⁸ John William Fletcher, *The Works of the Reverend John Fletcher*, vol. 2 (New York: B. Waugh and T. Mason, 1833), 596.

root in our animal frame: but a sin is attended with guile, and has its root in our moral frame. . . . A sin flows from the avoidable and perverse choice of our own will."[9] Fletcher taught that believers are under the law of Christ and not under the Adamic law of perfection. Thus, infirmities or incorrect, ignorant actions may be failures in relation to absolute physical perfection, but they are not sins because under the New Covenant, one is now under the law of Christ.[10]

Methodist Doctrine in the Early 1800s

The Methodists who came to America brought with them the theology of John Wesley based upon Wesley's *Standard Sermons*, Wesley's *Notes upon the Bible*, The *Discipline*, and the *Minutes of their Conferences*.[11] Wesley's co-worker John Fletcher's book, *Checks to Antinomianism*, also had a major influence. There were few outside influences theologically upon the American Methodist denomination for the first fifty years of its independent existence, and in 1808, the American Methodist General Conference voted that "The General Conference shall not revoke, alter, or change our articles of religion."[12]

Adam Clarke (1762-1832) was one of the next major theological influences on American Methodism after the founding of the denomination. He wrote Clarke's *Commentary on the Bible*. Clarke viewed any sin as "against the Divine authority; and he who has committed one transgression is guilty of death; and by his one deliberate act dissolves, as far as he can, the sacred connection."[13] He explains, "Christ was manifested to take away our sins, to destroy the works of the devil; and as His blood cleanseth from all sin and unrighteousness, is it not

---

[9] John William Fletcher, *The works of the Reverend John Fletcher*, 605-606.
[10] John William Fletcher, *The works of the Reverend John Fletcher*, 605-606.
[11] *Thomas C. Oden, Doctrinal Standards in the Wesleyan Tradition* (Grand Rapids: Francis Asbury Press of Zondervan Publishing House, 1988), 66.
[12] Thomas, Oden, *Doctrinal Standards in the Wesleyan Tradition*, 56.
[13] Adam Clarke, *The Holy Bible with a Commentary and Critical Notes*, new ed., vol. 6, (Bellingham, WA: Faithlife Corporation, 2014), 810.

Defending the Biblical Definition 143

evident that God means that believers in Christ shall be saved from all sin? . . . And if he who is born of God does not commit sin, then he must be cleansed from all sin."[14] Clarke asked, "Who is a child of the devil? *He that commits sin.* Who is a child of God? *He that works righteousness.* By this text we shall stand or fall before God, whatever our particular *creed* may say to the contrary."[15]

Richard Watson (1781-1833) wrote the *Theological Institutes,* which became the systematic theology that was used in the Methodist course of study throughout most of the nineteenth century.[16] Watson explains that sin is "the transgression of the law by a voluntary agent"[17] and that this rule is "laid down by God himself."[18] Watson further expounds: " 'Sin is the transgression of the law;' and in no other light is it represented in Scripture, when eternal death is threatened as its penalty, than as the act of a rational being sinning against a law known or knowable, and as an act avoidable, and not forced or necessary."[19] Watson's assertion that sin is voluntary and that man has an ability to fulfill the law of God is an important part of any understanding of sin.

Methodist Theology of the Late 1800s

The second half of the 1800s saw the rise of a number of Methodist theologians who wrote systematic theologies. However, Methodist theologians still held true to the core definition regarding sin which was in

---

[14] Adam Clarke and Samuel Dunn, *Christian Theology,* (Salem, OH: Convention Book Store), repr.,1967.
[15] Adam Clarke, Clarke, A. (2014). *The Holy Bible with a Commentary and Critical Notes*, new ed., vol. 6, 915.
[16] *The Theologians of Methodism,* (Salem OH: Schmul Publishing Co., repr., 1992), 65.
[17] Richard Watson, *Theological Institutes: Or, a View of the Evidences, Doctrines, Morals, and Institutions of Christianity* (Nashville, TN: E. Stevenson; F. A. Owen, Agents, 1857), 581.
[18] Richard Watson, *Theological Institutes: Or, a View of the Evidences, Doctrines, Morals, and Institutions of Christianity*, 581.
[19] Richard Watson, *Theological Institutes: Or, a View of the Evidences, Doctrines, Morals, and Institutions of Christianity*, 580.

their heritage. A number of these key theologians were Thomas Ralston, Benjamin Field, Miner Raymond, William Burt Pope, John Miley, R. S. Foster, and Samuel Wakefield, among others. All of these were quite clear that sin is a moral choice to disobey God.

Thomas Ralston (1806-1891) was the first American Methodist to write a systematic theology. His theology was well-known and widely used. He clearly believed in living a life which avoided all sin, saying, "Sin, to be personal and actual, so as to deserve punishment, must be avoidable."[11] Ralston's theology presented sin as a willful act of disobedience.

Samuel Wakefield (1799-1895) wrote a systematic theology that was used as part of the course of study for the Methodist church. He explains "We are free to choose either good or evil, and not impelled in our moral actions by any law of absolute necessity."[20] Wakefield viewed sin as a voluntary offense by a moral being with the capacity to do right or wrong.[21] Wakefield described sin not only as a free moral choice of disobedience, but also something that is incompatible with the Christian life.

Miner Raymond (1811-1897) was very emphatic that regeneration "is salvation from the reigning power of sin."[22] Raymond also stated that this salvation from the reign of sin "excludes natural, unavoidable, imperfections in constitutional or inherited character, and all sins of ignorance—all those cases of non-conformity to law, which arise from errors of judgment and other natural and necessary imperfections inseparable from man's condition in this, his earthly life."[23]

---

[20] Samuel Wakefield, *A Complete System of Christian Theology: A Concise, Comprehensive, and Systematic View of the Evidences, Doctrines, Morals and Institutions of Christianity* (WORDsearch, 2000), 317.

[21] Samuel Wakefield, *A Complete System of Christian Theology: A Concise, Comprehensive, and Systematic View of the Evidences, Doctrines, Morals and Institutions of Christianity*, 293.

[22] Miner Raymond, *Systematic Theology*, vol. 2 (Cincinnati; New York: Hitchcock & Walden; Nelson and Phillips, 1877), 355.

[23] Miner Raymond, *Systematic Theology*, 355.

William Burt Pope (1822-1903) is probably best known for his three-volume work, *A Compendium of Christian Theology*. Pope believed, "Scripture presents a sinless state as actually attained in this life."[24] He emphasized moral responsibility for sin. He states, "Sin is active lawlessness or wilful transgression."[25] "Every act of sin is the expression of the heart's consent to some solicitation."[26] He further explains that in Scripture, sin usually manifests itself "as disobedience to the Divine will."[27] Pope is quoted for saying, "Sin is the voluntary separation of the soul from God."[28] This definition not only emphasizes personal culpability, but also the results of sin—being separated from God. Pope strongly and clearly differentiates sin from human limitations.

John Miley (1813-1895) is widely known for his two-volume systematic theology and his book, *The Atonement in Christ*. When defining sin, he greatly emphasized personal responsibility and explained, "There can be no true definition of sin which omits a responsible personal agency."[29] He further explained that when a person sins, it "could arise only as their solicitations were unduly entertained or followed into some voluntary infraction of the law of probation."[30] His fundamental definition of sin reads: "Sin is disobedience to a law of God, conditioned on free moral agency and opportunity of knowing the law....Omit any specified

---

[24] William Burt Pope, *A Compendium of Christian Theology: Being Analytical Outlines of a Course of Theological Study, Biblical, Dogmatic, Historical, Volumes 1-3*, vol. 3 (London: Beveridge and Co., 1879), 49.

[25] William Burt Pope, *A Compendium of Christian Theology: Being Analytical Outlines of a Course of Theological Study, Biblical, Dogmatic, Historical, Volumes 1-3*, vol. 2, 30–31.

[26] William Burt Pope, *A Compendium of Christian Theology: Being Analytical Outlines of a Course of Theological Study, Biblical, Dogmatic, Historical, Volumes 1-3*, vol. 2, 69.

[27] William Burt Pope, *A Higher Catechism of Theology* (London: T. Woolmer, 1885), 115.

[28] William Burt Pope, *A Compendium of Christian Theology: Being Analytical Outlines of a Course of Theological Study; Biblical, Dogmatic, Historical, Volumes 1-3*, vol. 2, 30.

[29] John Miley, *Systematic Theology*, vol. 1, (New York: Hunt & Eaton, 1892), 527.

[30] John Miley, *Systematic Theology*, 435.

element, or admit any contrary element, and there can be no true definition of sin."[31] Miley also viewed a Christian as someone who was delivered from sin, and did not commit sin.[32] Miley felt that sin must, by logical necessity, be an avoidable act for which each person is individually responsible and one that Christians do not commit.

R. S. Foster (1820-1903) was a professor of systematic theology and later president at Drew Theological Seminary, as well as bishop of the Methodist Episcopal Church for 30 years. Foster attacked the concept that one can sin without having the capacity to do otherwise. He taught that for an act to be a sin, there must have been the reasonable capacity to do otherwise, and knowledge of the wrongness of the act. He explained, "The sin act consists in the willful disobedience of the moral law."[33] Foster was emphatic that it is possible to live without sinning and stated, "You can live this minute without sin! Is it not so? Do it, then. Never mind what is before you. Do not sin now. When each successive minute comes, do likewise. If you will do this, you will not sin at all."[34]

S. J. Gamertsfelder (1851-1925) is known as the dominant theological influence in the Evangelical United Brethren Church (a German Methodist church), and his systematic theology was widely read. Gamertsfelder's writings again placed a strong emphasis on human ability and free will, as opposed to Calvinism. He held that "Every moral being must judge concrete acts whether they are right or wrong. The ability to form such a judgment constitutes man a moral being."[35]

Holiness Writers and Theologians

Early holiness writers and theologians from the late nineteenth and

---

[31] John Miley, *Systematic Theology,* 529.
[32] John Miley, *Systematic Theology,* 332.
[33] Leslie D. Wilcox, *Profiles in Wesleyan Theology*, vol. 1, 3 vols. (Salem, OH: Schmul Pub., 1983), 269.
[34] R. S. Foster, *Christian Purity* (digital edition) From http://wesley.nnu.edu/wesleyctr/books/0401-0500/HDM0497.pdf.
[35] Solomon J. Gamertsfelder, *Systematic Theology* (Harrisburg, PA: Evangelical Pub. House, 1952), 50.

early twentieth centuries maintained the same doctrine of sin. Their theology allowed no acceptance of any sin at all in the life of a Christian.

Daniel Steele (1824-1914) is probably the leading theologian of the early Holiness Movement. He was very clear on the subject of sin. Steele explained, "Every voluntary violation of the known law of God is a realization of sin in its completeness."[36] Steele continued: "There is no sin where perfect love reigns. This may consist with innumerable defects, infirmities, and theoretical and practical errors. To a superficial observer these may look like sins, but a deeper inspection shows that they lack the essential characteristic, namely, the voluntary element."[37] In addressing whether it is possible to remain a Christian while sinning, Steele said, "It follows that every sin sunders the soul from God and makes communion with him and sonship or assimilation to him impossible."[38]

Samuel Logan Brengle (1860-1936) is probably the most widely read Holiness author since the days of John Wesley. Brengle explained, "Indeed, sin is nothing less than lawlessness—a huge selfishness—that amounts to moral and spiritual anarchy."[39] He also wrote, "Regeneration is salvation from the voluntary commission of sin."[40] A key component stressed in Brengle's writings is the possibility of freedom from ALL sin. "The Bible tells us that Holiness is perfect deliverance from sin. 'The Blood cleanseth us from ALL sin.' Not one bit of sin is left, for the old man is crucified, 'that the body of sin might be destroyed, that henceforth we should not serve sin,' for 'we are free from sin.'"[41]

---

[36] Daniel Steele, *Half-Hours with St. John's Epistles* (Boston; Chicago: Christian Witness Company, 1901), 69.
[37] Daniel Steele, *Milestone Papers* digital edition) from: http://wesley.nnu.edu/wesleyctr/books/0101-0200/HDM0161.pdf.
[38] Daniel Steele, *Half-Hours with St. John's Epistles*, 25.
[39] S. L. Brengle, *The Guest of the Soul* (digital edition) from https://onlinechristianlibrary.com/wp-content/uploads/2019/05/the-guest-of-the-soul.pdf.
[40] S. L. Brengle, *Heart-Talks on Holiness* (Atlanta, GA: Chicago, IL; New York, NY; San Francisco, CA: The Salvation Army, 1949), 54.
[41] S. L. Brengle, *Helps to Holiness*, Special Edition. (London; Glasgow: Salvationist Publishing and Supplies, Ltd., n.d.), 11.

J. A. Wood (1828-1905) was one of the most influential voices in the early American Holiness movement. His most notable work was his book *Perfect Love*; it has been called the "textbook of the nineteenth century Holiness Movement."[42] Wood stated, "Can a state of justification be retained while sin is committed? It can not. . . . The commission of sin negates the justified state, and any professing Christian who lives in the commission of sin is a sinner and not a saint. . . . The lowest type of a Christian sinneth not, and is not condemned. The minimum of salvation is salvation from sinning."[43] His fundamental definition of sin is summed up as "Sin is 'the transgression of the law,' and involves moral action, either by voluntary omission, or willful commission, and it always incurs guilt."[44]

W. B. Godbey (1833-1920) was a fiery preacher and scholar from the early American Holiness Movement. He is listed on God's Bible School and College's "Hall of Fame" and was a highly influential evangelist.[45] Godbey translated the New Testament, wrote a commentary on the New Testament, and authored numerous books. Godbey's statements on sin are some of the most colorful and vehement that one will find anywhere. In response to the question of Christians committing sin, he is emphatic, "Of course you cease to commit sin when you are converted."[46] Commenting on 1 John 3:9, Godbey states, "The advocates of sinning religion wage an exterminating war against sanctification on the hypothesis that none can live without committing sin. See how blindly they utterly unchristainize themselves, because it does not take sanctification to stop all sinning, but you see from this verse that regeneration settles the question of committing sin."[47]

---

[42] Wallace Thornton, *Radical Richteousness*, (Schmul Publishing: Salem, OH, 1998), 67.
[43] J. A. Wood *Perfect Love* (digital edition) from http://wesley.nnu.edu/wesleyctr/books/0101-0200/HDM0181.pdf.
[44] J. A. Wood *Perfect Love*
[45] https://www.gbs.edu/alumni/hall-of-fame/.
[46] W. B. Godbey, *Holiness or Hell* (digital edition) from http://media.sabda.org/alkitab-6/wh2-hdm/hdm0394.pdf.
[47] W. B. Godbey, *Commentary on the New Testament,* (digital edition) from

Albert Gray (1886-1969) was a leading theological voice for the Church of God (Anderson). He said, "Sin, as generally used in the New Testament, means a voluntary violation of a known law of God."[48] He reiterates, "Sin is a voluntary act."[49] Gray strongly held to the possibility and the necessity of abstaining from sin. He explained, "One can no longer be counted righteous who has sinned against God."[50] To quote Gray, "Sin must be voluntary in order to be blameworthy,"[51] and "those born of God no longer live in sin."[52] Gray further expounded that, "God does not condone in His children what He condemns in others. 'He that doeth sin is of the devil' (I John 3:8). God has not given special privilege to commit sin to those who profess His name."[53]

Oswald Chambers (1874–1917) had a close connection with God's Bible School, including teaching there briefly. He exhorted,

> Whosoever is born of God doth not commit sin," (1 John 3:9). Do I seek to stop sinning or have I stopped sinning? To be born of God means that I have the supernatural power of God to stop sinning. In the Bible it is never—Should a Christian sin? The Bible puts it emphatically—A Christian must not sin. The effective working of the new birth life in us is that we do not commit sin, not merely that we have the power not to sin, but that we have stopped sinning. 1 John 3:9 does not mean that we cannot sin; it means that if we obey the life of God in us, we need not sin.[54]

---

http://wesley.nnu.edu/wesleyctr/books/0601-0700/HDM0643.pdf .

[48] Albert F. Gray, *Christian Theology* (James L. Fleming, 1944; 2005), 222–223.
[49] Albert F. Gray, *Christian Theology,* 223.
[50] Albert F. Gray, *Christian Theology,* 223.
[51] Albert F. Gray, *Christian Theology,* 428.
[52] Albert F. Gray, *Christian Theology*, 275.
[53] Albert F. Gray, *Christian Theology*, 276.
[54] Oswald Chambers, *My Utmost for His Highest: Selections for the Year* (Grand Rapids, MI: Oswald Chambers Publications; Marshall Pickering, 1986), n.p.

A. M. Hills (1848-1935) president of Texas Holiness University, played a key part in the founding of the Holiness Movement. He was one of the first holiness theologians to write a complete systematic theology. Hills forcefully articulated his understanding of sin. "It is nonsense, akin to blasphemy, to teach that a Holy God commands us to be holy, if sin is an unavoidable necessity."[55] His definition of sin was similar to Wesley's; he explained that sin is "willful acts of disobedience to a known law of God,"[56] and that "sin consists in voluntary actions."[57]

A. W. Tozer (1897–1963) did not have a background in the Methodist Church but identified in many ways with the Holiness Movement. His definition of sin fits with traditional holiness theology. He stated,

> Where there is no freedom of choice there can be neither sin nor righteousness, because it is of the nature of both that they be voluntary. However good an act may be, it is not good if it is imposed from without. The act of imposition destroys the moral content of the act and renders it null and void. . . . Sin is the voluntary commission of an act known to be contrary to the will of God. Where there is no moral knowledge or where there is no voluntary choice, the act is not sinful.[58]

H. Orton Wiley (1877-1961) was a preeminent holiness theologian who wrote a three volume systematic theology which became the official theology for the Church of the Nazarene. It is "the most complete systematic theology the Holiness movement has produced, and it is an important marker of that movement's theological expression."[59] "As late

---

[55] A. M. Hills, *Fundamental Christian Theology, vol. 2,* (digital edition) from http://wesley.nnu.edu/wesleyctr/books/2201-2300/HDM2260.pdf.
[56] A. M. Hills, *Fundamental Christian Theology.*
[57] A. M. Hills, *Holiness and Power,* (digital edition) from https://archive.org/details/holinesspowerfor00hill/page/10.
[58] A. W. Tozer, *That Incredible Christian* (Harrisburg, PA: Christian Publications Inc., 1964), 30.
[59] John R. Tyson, "H. Orton Wiley," ed. Walter A. Elwell, *Handbook of*

as 1984, a survey of evangelical Wesleyan theologians identified Wiley's *Christian Theology* as the greatest influence upon their own scholarly development."[60] Wiley stated that "Sin is rebellion against God."[61] He explained. "To call innocent mistakes in judgment, lapses of memory, and a lack of understanding due to weakened human powers sin is to open the floodgates to all kinds of actual sin."[62] "A sharp distinction must be made between sin and infirmity."[63] Wiley went on to say, "The Scriptures as well as the testimony of human experience, takes into account this distinction between sins and infirmities. . . . We may be kept from sin in this life."[64]

Wiley also strongly emphasized the moral freedom of man who has "the power to obey or disobey"[65] as this "is an essential element in a moral being."[66] Wiley viewed sin as incompatible with entering heaven, and he explained, "Nothing unholy ever enters that city—no sin, whether of act or condition."[67] He quoted Wesley's statement, "We all agree and earnestly maintain, 'He that committeth sin is of the devil.' We agree, 'Whosoever is born of God doth not commit sin.'"[68]

W. T. Purkiser (1910-1992) wrote numbers of theological books, and he seemed to especially focus on the role of sin. He examined the two leading definitions of sin: the ethical or moral definition and the legal definition.[69] Purkiser took these definitions and inserted them into a

---

Evangelical Theologians (Grand Rapids: Baker Book House, 1998), 128.
[60] John R. Tyson, "H. Orton Wiley," 116.
[61] Orton Wiley, *Christian Theology*, 363.
[62] Wiley *Epistle to the Hebrews* (digital edition) from http://wesley.nnu.edu/wesleyctr/books/3201-3300/HDM3275.pdf.
[63] Wiley *Epistle to the Hebrews*.
[64] H. Orton Wiley, *Christian Theology*, 508–509.
[65] H. O. Wiley, & P. T. Culbertson, *Introduction to Christian Theology* (Kansas City: Beacon Hill Press of Kansas City, 1946), 162–163.
[66] Wiley, H. O., & Culbertson, P. T., *Introduction to Christian Theology*, 162–163.
[67] H. Orton Wiley, *God has the Answer* (digital edition) from http://wesley.nnu.edu/holiness-classics-library/?rows=30&search=author&search_value=wiley.
[68] H. Orton Wiley, *Christian Theology*.
[69] W. T. Purkiser, *Conflicting Concepts of Holiness* (Kansas City: Beacon Hill

number of New Testament references which used the word *sin*. He explained, "The ethical...will make good sense in all forty-one references. There are no exceptions. The legal definition will fit and make good sense in only four of this number. It cannot be substituted in any of the remaining thirty-seven without incoherence or self-contradiction."[70] He concluded, "No definition can possibly be accepted as satisfactory which destroys the meaning of 90 percent of the passages in which this specific term occurs."[71] Purkiser's conclusion was, "Sin always involves choice and will."[72] "It is just as impossible to be a 'sinning saint' as it is to be an honest thief, a truthful liar, or a loyal traitor."[73]

Richard S. Taylor (1912-2006) was perhaps best known for his understanding of sin through his book, *A Right Conception of Sin*. Taylor believed that it was essential to a proper understanding of sin to differentiate between infirmities and actual sins. He explained, "By the term 'sin' do we include every mistake in judgment, unknown offense, or other manifestation of human frailty and limitation? Obviously not."[74] According to Taylor, the definition of sin in the Bible depends upon the dispensation. The Old Testament used an absolute legal standard, but the New Testament, under "grace, however, takes into full consideration the circumstances and emotions and motives involved."[75] According to Taylor, it was also crucial. "One single sin is sufficiently serious to bring immediate condemnation and ultimate total apostasy if unrepented of and unforgiven."[76]

Press, 1964).
[70] W. T. Purkiser, *Conflicting Concepts of Holiness,* 49-50.
[71] W. T. Purkiser, *Conflicting Concepts of Holiness*.
[72] W. T. Purkiser *Beliefs that Matter Most*, (digital Edition) from http://wesley.nnu.edu/wesleyctr/books/0301-0400/HDM0393.pdf.
[73] W. T. Purkiser, *Beliefs that Matter Most*.
[74] Richard S. Taylor, *A Right Conception of Sin* (digital Edition) from http://wesley.nnu.edu/wesleyctr/books/0301-0400/HDM0393.pdf.
[75] Richard S. Taylor, *A Right Conception of Sin* (Kansas City: Beacon Hill Press of Kansas City, 1945), 68.
[76] Richard S. Taylor, *A Right Conception of Sin,* 68.

Defending the Biblical Definition 153

Dale Yocum (1919-1987) was a leading Conservative Holiness theologian and educator. He served for a number of years as a professor of theology and president of Kansas City Christian College. Yocum was an author of several theological books and emphasized the distinctions between Calvinistic and Wesleyan beliefs. He differentiated between infirmities, that "may inhere either in the mind or body,"[77] and sin, which "inheres in the moral nature."[78] He also noted that "the Arminians define sin as a willful transgression of a known law of God."[79] Yocum believed with those of the Wesleyan persuasion that the regenerate are "in such a sense perfect as not to commit sin."[80]

Leslie Wilcox (1907-1991) was a longtime professor of theology as well as the academic dean at God's Bible School. He wrote a number of major works, including a systematic theology. The doctrine of sin was very important to Wilcox, who stated that "the question of the definition of sin is one of the most important ones in theology."[81] Wilcox held to Wesley's definition of sin and expounded it this way: "The basic idea of the definition is that the act of sin is a responsible act . . . and done with the consent of his will."[82] He explained further that "the truth back of Wesley's definition lies in the fact that a person knows something is wrong, and willfully transgresses that knowledge."[83] Wilcox pointed out that there must be three different factors involved for an act to be considered responsible.

1. The existence of a standard of right and wrong.

2. Moral evaluation on the basis of the standard that tells him the action is right or wrong.

---

[77] Dale Yocum, *The Holy Way*, (Schmul Publishing Co, Salem, Ohio, 1981) 36-37.
[78] Dale Yocum, *The Holy Way*, 36-37.
[79] Dale Yocum, *Trumpets in Zion* (Hobe Sound Florida: H. S. B. C. Press, n.d.), 24.
[80] Dale Yocum quoting John Wesley, *The Holy Way*, 151.
[81] Leslie D. Wilcox, *Profiles in Wesleyan Theology*, vol. 3, 3 vols. (Salem, OH: Schmul Pub., 1983), 153.
[82] Leslie D. Wilcox, *Profiles in Wesleyan Theology*, vol. 1, 429.
[83] Leslie D. Wilcox, *Profiles in Wesleyan Theology*, vol. 3, 161.

3. Freedom to act.[84]

Wilcox clarified, "Acts of sin are to be carefully distinguished from mistakes, infirmities, and errors in judgment. Some writers, especially those who teach a Calvinistic theology, define sin as any deviation from the absolute perfection of God. . . . We must note at once that this teaching is at variance with the Bible statement which we find in the first Epistle of John."[85] According to Wilcox, "Sins are not the same as infirmities or mistakes."[86] "Wrongs that come from misunderstanding, wrong information, and other human frailties are infirmities or mistakes, but are not sin."[87]

Wilcox did not view sin as compatible with the Christian life. He concluded, "Sin is the breaking of relationship with God, a severance of ourselves from Him. It is an act performed in disregard, independence, or a spirit of antagonism toward God."[88]

Official Doctrinal Statements

The National Holiness Association

In 1948 Harry Jessup wrote a brief summary of Wesleyan-Holiness doctrine for the National Association for the Promotion of Holiness. It was given the official endorsement by that organization as an official designation of their doctrinal teaching. It states:

> We the Holiness people, while declaring the possibility of deliverance from sin, are fully aware of our human frailty with its infirmities and limitations. All these entail humiliation, confession, and regret, but need not bring condemnation. They demand the efficacy of the

---

[84] Leslie D. Wilcox, *Profiles in Wesleyan Theology*, vol. 3, 161-162.
[85] Leslie D. Wilcox, *Be Ye Holy* (Cincinnati Ohio: Revivalist Press., 1977), 40.
[86] Leslie D. Wilcox, *Be Ye Holy*, 44.
[87] Leslie D. Wilcox, *Profiles in Wesleyan Theology*, vol. 3, 163.
[88] Leslie D. Wilcox, *Profiles in Wesleyan Theology*, vol. 3, 164.

atoning blood of the crucified, risen and ascended Redeemer, but they are not accounted to us as sin.[89]

Church of the Nazarene

We believe that actual or personal sin is a voluntary violation of a known law of God by a morally responsible person. It is therefore not to be confused with involuntary and inescapable shortcomings, infirmities, faults, mistakes, failures, or other deviations from a standard of perfect conduct that are the residual effects of the Fall.[90]

Conservative Holiness Movement Statement

H.E. Schmul was one of the founders of the InterChurch Holiness Convention. In a message at Hobe Sound Camp Schmul mentioned that Brother Herron, Brother Wilcox, and some others came up with this definition:

An act of sin is any uncoerced word or thought or deed that violates the will of God, performed by an intelligent responsible person within the age of accountability done in defiance of God or not prompted by love to God or desire to please him. Sin, then, is a responsible act. Now that's a definition that came from our theological wunderkind. . . . And that is the essence of sin.[91]

---

[89] Harry Jessop quoted in *We the Holiness People: What We Believe and Teach*. Schmul Publishing (1987 pg. 67).

[90] Dean G. Blevins et al., eds., *Church of the Nazarene: Manual, 2017–2021* (Kansas City, MO: Nazarene Publishing House, 2017), 28. https://2017.manual.nazarene.org/section/church-constitution/.

[91] H.E. Schmuul, "Sin Repentance and faith," recorded Feb. 9, 1987, Hobe Sound Camp:sermon, Minute 23:30) https://feaministries.org/download/h-e-schmul-1987-02-09-sin-repentance-and-faith-2-cor-78-11/. Some have disagreed on the original opinion of S. D. Herron, but this statement after his discussion with Wilcox should verify his final position.

Wesleyan Holiness Association of Churches

> We believe that sin is the willful transgression of the known law of God, and that such sin condemns a soul to eternal punishment unless pardoned by God through repentance, confession, restitution, and believing in Jesus Christ as his personal Savior. This includes all men 'For all have sinned and come short of the glory of God.'[92]

Bible Methodist Church

> We believe that acts of sin are committed by morally responsible persons choosing to do what they know is wrong or choosing not to do what they know is required. These acts of sin are therefore not to be confused with short-comings, infirmities, faults, mistakes, failures, or other such deviations from a standard of perfect conduct which are the residual effects of the Fall.[93]

InterChurch Holiness Convention

"What is sin? John Wesley defined sin as 'a willful transgression against a known law of God.' This means that there must be knowledge of wrongdoing, or of refusing to obey God, before sin is committed. Mistakes are not sin."[94]

Conclusion

A portion of a speech by C. W. Ruth at the 1901 General Convention of holiness people sums up the thoughts of the Wesleyan/Holiness people

---

[92] *Manual of the Wesleyan Holiness Association of Churches.*
[93] https://www.biblemethodist.org/wp-content/uploads/2019/06/2018-Bible-Methodist-Discipline-rev.-2.pdf. 15.
[94] InterChurch Holiness Convention, "Questions and Answers," accessed April 25, 2021, https://ihconvention.com/build-your-faith/questions-answers/.

regarding sin:

> Friends, if a man is not saved from sin, from what is he saved? What is his religion good for? He could do that without a spark of religion! The truth is, the lowest plane on which a man can be saved at all, is deliverance from all outer sin. We are frequently misunderstood and misrepresented here. It is urged that these holiness people are preaching sanctification in order to have people cease from sinning. Good old-fashioned repentance will bring you to the abandonment of sin. A repentance that does not carry with it the abandonment of sin is a farce, a delusion and a humbug. You may sign your name to a creed, join a meeting house, train with the gang, and call it religion, but you don't know the A, B, Cs of religion, unless you know what it is to forsake sin.[95]

Historian Charles Jones concludes that for Holiness people "sin was conscious disobedience to a known law of God."[96] Leslie Wilcox, Dean of God's Bible School, concurred, arguing that "Holiness writers, following Wesleyan theology, defined sin as a willful transgression of a known law."[97] In his overview of the topic, Caleb Black concludes that "the consensus understanding of sin in the Holiness tradition is that sin is an avoidable, voluntary, morally responsible act that those born of God do not commit."[98]

---

[95] S. B. Shaw, *Echoes of the General Holiness Assembly*, (digital edition) from: http://wesley.nnu.edu/wesleyctr/books/0301-0400/HDM0372.pdf.
[96] Charles Jones, *Perfectionist Persuasion* ,(Metuchen, NJ: The Scarecrow Press, Inc., 1974), 32-33.
[97] Leslie D. Wilcox, *Be Ye Holy*, 40.
[98] Caleb Black, *What About Sin* (Middleburg, PA: N.p., 2021), 86.

Chapter 14
Defining the Sin Nature

Mankind is not only sinful in action but also in nature. What is this evil lurking inside of each person? What is it that causes all people by nature to commit evil? Humankind is so corrupted that Scripture says, *There is none righteous, no, not one . . . There is none that doeth good, no, not one . . . For all have sinned, and come short of the glory of God* (Ro 3:10, 12, and 23). The consequences of sin are that all people have come short of obtaining the glory of God. The cause of sin is an inherent disposition to commit evil. In this aspect, sin is twofold: an evil nature from birth and personal, willful disobedience to the will of God.

Sin has been passed down through the descendants of Adam to the entire human race. As the Bible says, *By one man sin entered into the world, and death by sin; and so death passed upon all men, for that all have sinned* (Ro 5:12). In the story of creation, *God created man in his own image,* and *saw everything that he had made, and, behold, it was very good* (Ge 1:27 and 31). Tragically, the biblical account continues to describe the Fall through deliberate disobedience and the corruption of that which had been originally holy and good. When Adam brought forth a son, instead of being in the image of God, this son was *in [Adam's] own likeness, after his image* (Ge 5:3). While Adam retained the image of God, it was no longer a pure, undefiled likeness. It had become corrupted, and this polluted image was then passed on to his descendants.

Man is born naturally rebellious, depraved, and corrupted. Because of this sin nature, man is separated from God and is no longer able to fellowship with Him. The entire being of man, his heart, his will, his conscience, and his mind, is polluted by sin. At its core, original sin is a combination of selfishness, pride, and rebellion. Sin is a corruption of humanity such as a disease, or a rotting infection. Scripture compares inbred sin to leprosy; a good comparison in our culture would be cancer. Paul describes the sin nature in Romans 7:14-24 as an evil entity which has taken control, warring against the desire to do good and bringing a person into the captivity of sin.

Scholars have described sin as a parasite which has attached itself to mankind. It is not an integral part of being human; it is a non-physical evil which has attached itself to the good which God created and has corrupted it. A good example of this is a disease such as leprosy or cancer. Al Truesdale, a recent professor at Nazarene Theological Seminary, gives a good description noting, "Sin is a power that lays hold of man. It is a 'something' a 'reality.'. . . Sin has carved out its own disruptive history, its own parasitic kingdom in God's good creation."[1] The solution to the sin problem is to have the heart circumcised (Ro 2:29), the stony heart taken out (Eze 36:26), the body of sin destroyed (Ro 6:6), and to lay aside the sin (He 12:1). However indwelling sin is described, it must be destroyed and removed for a person to become morally all God wants him to be.

Peter expresses his personal Pentecostal experience as purification. He described what happened at Pentecost and at Cornelius's house as God *purifying their hearts by faith* (Ac 15:9). Peter's focus was upon what happened to the corruption of the heart. The filth was removed. Earlier in Acts, Luke characterized that same Pentecostal experience as being filled with or the receiving of the Holy Spirit (Ac 2:4, Ac 10:44-47). These are distinct terms describing the same experience. Both the cleansing of sin and the baptism of the Spirit happen simultaneously. The carnal heart cannot abide the indwelling presence of the Holy Spirit. When the Spirit comes, indwelling sin must flee. Peter's emphasis on deliverance from corruption and receiving godliness is again evident when he later wrote, *that we might be partakers of the divine nature* (2Pe 1:3-4).

This concept of deliverance from the sin nature is also clearly the doctrine of the Early Church. Clement of Alexandria (A.D. 200) wrote that we are "to put ourselves to death, slaying 'the old man, who is corrupt through lusts' and raising the new man from death . . . by abandoning the passions and becoming free from sin."[2] Marcarius, (A.D. 380s) who strongly influenced the Eastern Church and, also, John Wesley explained,

---

[1] Al Truesdale, *Sin* (Kansas City: The Foundry Publishing, 2022) 64-65.
[2] Clement of Alexandria, *Ante-Nicene Fathers*, vol. 2, The Master Christian Library, Version 5, CD-ROM (Albany, OR: Ages Software, 1997, 1066.

> We have received into ourselves something that is foreign to our nature, namely, the corruption of our passions through the disobedience of the first man, which has strongly taken over in us, as though it were a certain part of our nature by custom and long habit. This must be expelled again by that which is also foreign to our nature, namely, the heavenly gift of the Spirit, and so the original purity must be restored.[3]

Holiness people have always emphasized the purification aspect of the second work of grace; it removes indwelling sin. But what is indwelling sin? The Bible clearly identifies the sin nature as a non-physical entity of spiritual corruption which must be removed. Almost without fail, the writers of the Bible point to the removal of a corrupt, evil entity. Scripture uses a number of examples to describe the solution.

1. The prophet looks ahead to our day and says, *I will take away the stony heart out of your flesh, and I will give you an heart of flesh* (Eze 36:26). Here, the corruption is represented as a stony heart.
2. Paul describes this as the circumcision of the heart (Ro 2:29). This would represent the cutting away of the evil nature.
3. *Our old man is crucified with him, that the body of sin might be destroyed, that henceforth we should not serve sin* (Ro 6:6). Most scholars see the old man as a picture of the sin nature. The nature of sin is described as a body that must be destroyed.
4. Paul describes this nature as a *body of death* bringing him *into captivity to the law of sin which is in my members.* His heart cry was *O wretched man that I am! who shall deliver me from the body of this death?* (Romans 7:23-24). The sin nature is described as the law of sin and a body of death. In the next chapter Paul rejoices that he is *free from the law of sin and death* (Ro 8:2), and that the Spirit gives life to overcome the body of death (Ro 8:10).

---

[3] Marcarius, *Pseudo-Macarius: The Fifty Spiritual Homilies and the Great Letter*, trans. George A. Maloney (New York: Paulist Press, 1992), 53.

5. This sinful nature is identified as the flesh which is opposed to the Spirit. Flesh refers to that part of humanity which has been corrupted and is under the control of sin. Paul admonishes to put to death the deeds of the body and to crucify the flesh (Ro 8:1-13, Ga 5:16-24).
6. The sin nature will also be described as members which need to be mortified [put to death] and Paul exhorts to *put off the old man with his deeds* (Col 3:5, 9).
7. The author of Hebrews warns us against this nature, describing it as a *root of bitterness springing up* (Heb 12:15). This root of sin must be removed!
8. James identifies a person who has the sin nature as having a corrupted mind which needs to be purified (Ja 4:8). He describes them as being double-minded. They have a mind to serve God and a sinful mind that also serves self.

Holiness people have commonly used the word *eradication* to describe the destruction and removal of the sin nature. The word *eradicate* means to root up or pluck up by the root and comes from the Latin Vulgate translation of *eradicabutur*. This word is used in Matthew 15:13 where Jesus said, *Every plant, which my heavenly Father hath not planted, shall be rooted up.* This passage is describing the defilement of the heart and that evil comes from an inner corruption that needs to be rooted up. Hebrews 12:14-15 is a warning to go on to holiness lest any *root of bitterness* spring up. The concept of rooting out the carnal nature is biblical. Early holiness leaders would have been familiar with raising a garden. When weeding a garden, the roots must be removed, or the weeds will quickly return. Merely chopping off the top is simply ineffective. Indwelling sin, likewise, needs rooted out, just like weeds in a garden.

In 1885 the First General Holiness Assembly comprised of members from ten different denominations met in Chicago. They formulated a Declaration of Principles which formally defined the beliefs of the Holiness Movement. Included in this Declaration is their statement on entire sanctification:

> Entire Sanctification . . . is that great work wrought subsequent to regeneration, by the Holy Ghost, upon the

> sole condition of faith . . . such faith being preceded by an act of solemn and complete consecration. This work has these distinct elements:
> (1) The entire extinction of the carnal mind, the total eradication of the birth principle of sin.
> (2) The communication of perfect love to the soul. . . .
> (3) The abiding indwelling of the Holy Ghost.[4]

Spiritual corruption of the heart must be carefully distinguished from normal human physical appetites. Temptation is not sin. Even Christ was tempted *like as we are* (Heb 4:15). Temptations may also come from bad habits developed before salvation, wrong thinking patterns, or the culture in which a person lives.

Misunderstanding about the second work of grace (sanctification) and the third work of grace (glorification) leads to much confusion. God will deal with the fallen physical nature when a person is glorified. Temptation comes from normal, natural desires which in the right place and time are not sinful; the sin nature is the evil corruption of the unsanctified heart. The corruption of the heart must also be distinguished from the non-moral effects of the Fall such as pain, weakness, infirmities, and mistakes. Sometimes improper actions or mistakes may come from living in a morally corrupted world. The evil culture or background may cause wrong views or psychological damage and patterns of thinking that are harmful as a result of abuse or trauma. Some of these can be subconscious self-defense mechanisms that have warped one's thoughts or actions. In sanctification, God eradicates the underlying, destructive, evil entity that demands its own way in opposition to God, but God does not immediately undo all of the consequences of the Fall. When a person allows God to remove this core problem and consecrates himself to God, it is then by faith that inbred sin is destroyed and a person becomes filled with the Spirit. Subsequently, God continues working to correct the unintended flaws in a person's life.

---

[4] *Guide to Holiness* 76 (1885): 27-28. Quoted in Randy Maddox, "Reconnecting the Means to the End: A Wesleyan Prescription for the Holiness Movement." *Wesleyan Theological Journal*. 33 no. 2 (1998): 29–66.

The cleansing of the corrupt heart also must not be confused with growth in grace. Scripture compared the sin nature to a body of death. This could be thought of as an infection within a person. A certain lady had a diseased spleen which eventually died and began to rot. She soon became deathly ill, and the problem was discovered at the hospital. Surgery was performed, and the rotting "body" was removed. It was either removal of the source of the infection or death. Thankfully, the problem was discovered in time, and the lady survived. Leprosy is pictured in the Bible as a type of carnal infection. The removal of the disease—the infection of sin—is completely different from spiritual growth. God desires to purify a person from the corruption. Only then is one able to grow and develop normally. The removal of the sin principle helps one thrive spiritually and deal with other issues of life in a godly manner. This growth process will continue throughout the rest of life.

Chapter 15
The Definition of Sin Affects all Theology

The doctrine of sin is perhaps the key foundational doctrine of Scripture. Richard S. Taylor stated that "the doctrines relating to sin form the center around which we build our entire theological system. . . . When our concept of sin is off-center our theology will become distorted."[1] The way a person reads and understands Scripture depends upon a predetermined theological perspective. Doctrines of biblical interpretation, salvation, the atonement, predestination, sanctification, and eternal judgment all base their foundation upon the definition of sin. Taylor is correct when he writes, "One who does not have correct views of sin is not apt to have correct views of any other fundamental question."[2]

How the Doctrine of Sin Affects Biblical Interpretation

Doctrinally, there are four bases for truth from which theology is derived. These are often called the Wesleyan Quadrilateral. The primary source of truth is Scripture. When God has made a definitive statement in His Word regarding anything, whether it be salvation, history, or science, etc., it is established truth. If there is a conflict between Scripture and any other source, the Bible must take priority and the other sources be regarded as incorrect. Three resources help to verify, broaden and systematize our understanding of truth. Scripture, therefore, is interpreted using the tools of reason, historical tradition, and experience. God is orderly and His truth can be systematized into a coherent theology. Logical contradictions in any Biblical system of doctrine must be resolved since two contradictory

---

[1] Richard S. Taylor, *A Right Conception of Sin*, rev. ed. (Salem, OH: Schmul Publishing Co., 2002) 12-13.
[2] Richard S. Taylor, *A Right Conception of Sin*, 13.

Defending the Biblical Definition

statements cannot both be true. Another guide for assessing veracity is historical tradition. We stand upon the shoulders of the theological giants of the past. Any new doctrine which does not have historical precedent is likely wrong. God did not wait 2000 years to reveal critical truth which had somehow been missed by all the great saints of the past. The third criterion is experience and the subjective interaction of an individual with God. It was a personal encounter with God that transformed Paul, Saint Francis, John Wesley and multitudes of other people both past and present. Truth works in the real world, and makes a personal difference in people's lives. A theology which has no transformational power or is experientially not true cannot be correct. However, if experience conflicts with Scripture, it is Scripture that is right and lives need to be adjusted to match Scripture. Just because a belief system does not match one's life experiences does not mean the doctrine is incorrect. It may be the individual that is wrong and needs changed, not the theology. All people are warped by personal experiences, upbringing, culture, and personality. These issues influence one's theological understanding. All of these need to be correctly aligned with God's Word.

Throughout history there has always been much debate about the correct way of interpreting the Bible. In the Early Church the conflict was between the allegorical view and the literal view. Recently the controversy has been over the inspiration of Scripture: Is it always accurate and completely inspired by the Holy Spirit, or was it written by men who gave their own views of how to know God? Another current debate is between a cultural only understanding of Scripture in contrast to those who believe that the New Testament was written for all people of all time.

The dispute over the cultural relativity of the New Testament is especially evident in what is commonly known among conservatives as standards. For example, when Scripture gives instructions regarding hair length for men and women (1Co 11:4-16), adornment (1Ti 2:9-10, 1Pe 3:3), or the proper role of women there is disagreement over whether those passages are to be directly applied to our lives today or only to the Greco-Roman culture. Other concepts at issue are homosexual marriage and transgender rights. According to the culturally relative position, only when the culture of the ancient world is understood can the principles of that day be applied to our day. If a direct application of Scripture was only to the first century culture, then the commands of the New Testament become obscure and unclear. Since the church is currently under the dispensation to which the New Testament was written, it is still directly applicable today. This is historically the normative position for evangelical Christians.

In the debate over the definition of sin, there is a strong tendency to interpret Scripture to support a preferred doctrine rather than as accurately as possible. Do we take what the Bible says at face value or do we twist Scripture to fit our opinions? Donald Metz states that "a wrong concept of sin misinterprets the Bible."[3] This sometimes occurs in the translation of the text of Scripture. In other places, while the text has not been altered, the interpretation has been changed to match a favored theology. For example, instead of taking Romans 6:18 and 6:22 literally when it says that a person is *made free from sin*, they reinterpret it to mean that one is free only from the guilt of sin. The text directly states *free from sin* not free from the guilt of sin. The context of Romans six is not discussing guilt; it is proclaiming freedom from the power of sin so that a person can be delivered from the dominion of sin, both in practice and heart. False doctrines about sin have led to the manipulation of the plain, straightforward text of the Bible.

The Satisfaction Theory of the Atonement

Almost all professing Christians recognize that the death of Christ has provided salvation. They recognize that Christ's blood and His blood alone is a sufficient remedy for sin. This basic principle, called the satisfaction theory of the atonement, has been misconstrued to claim that Christ's righteousness has been imputed to Christians who are still unrighteous but are viewed as righteous by God. It is the equivalent of a snowstorm upon the city dump; it looks clean and white to the eye, but underneath, all is rotten filthiness. Calvinists feel that God sees the believer as clean and white through Christ while underneath the filth and corruption still

---

[3] Donald Metz: *Studies in Biblical Holiness*, Kansas City: Beacon Hill Press, 1971), 73.

remains. Wesleyans hold that Christ's righteousness is imparted as well as imputed.

The Calvinistic understanding of the satisfaction theory logically leads to predestination. If Christ has paid the price for all sins, then His blood has sufficient merit to provide forgiveness and salvation no matter what sins or how many sins are committed. If a person is one of the elect, he will then be saved because he has been chosen by God. The elect will trust God for salvation and will persevere in salvation until death. Calvinists believe that since not all people will be saved, Christ only died for the elect and not for everyone in the world.

One modern modification of the Calvinistic doctrine is free-grace theology which maintains that God has provided salvation for all people, allowing anyone the freedom to choose salvation. However, it teaches that once a person has chosen to be born into God's family, he will always be part of it and can never be eternally lost, even if he loses his trust in Christ or chooses a wicked lifestyle. The basis for this theory is the misconception that even Christians sin in "word, thought, and deed" every day. Since Christ has already paid the price for all sins, this ideology contends that a person can never be found guilty before God. This adaptation makes a number of assumptions which are neither logical nor biblical. Scripture teaches that sin causes spiritual death which separates a person from God. God has given mankind their entire lives to determine their destiny. Initial salvation does not remove a person's free will. Only *he that endureth to the end shall be saved* (Mt 10:22, Re 2:10, Heb 10:38-39).

There is much truth in a correct satisfaction doctrine which emphasizes the necessity of punishment for sin, but the Calvinistic restructuring falls short by not clearly teaching that the holiness of God will not co-exist with sin. Not only must the penalty for sin be paid, but also the practice of sin must be discontinued for a person to enter the city of God (Re 21:27). A second error of the free-grace position is the unfairness presented by allowing wicked, morally despicable people who were once saved into heaven, while sending other, perhaps far more morally upright, people to hell.

The Legal Definition Denies Heart Purity

The distortion of doctrine regarding the definition of sin completely changes the concept of sanctification.[4] If a person cannot be completely delivered from the practice of sin, it also must be true that a person cannot be completely delivered from the cause of sin, the indwelling evil nature within the heart. Instead of a radical transformation by the power of God, sanctification becomes a process of works through self-discipline. This process of sanctification continues throughout a person's life with the final victory over the sinful nature only achievable at physical death. Holiness proponents focus upon the reception of a pure heart while the focus for Calvinists has been upon the outward actions. Thus, Calvinists and Holiness people have two different definitions of sanctification. Calvinists believe it is changing behavior in the process of endeavoring to achieve God-like perfection while holiness people view it as heart purity. Holiness people believe entire sanctification occurs when God does a transformational work by filling the heart with the Holy Spirit and cleansing the heart of sin. This is followed by continual growth in grace as a person becomes more Christlike. Confusing these two definitions leads to misunderstanding and misrepresenting the other group.

Among the Calvinists, Keswickian theology accepted a second work, the baptism of the Spirit, which enabled one to suppress evil and live a victorious life over willful sin but not human infirmities. A Keswickian view of the second work of grace emphasizes consecration and the filling of the Spirit but minimizes the aspect of purification and an instantaneous transformation. Rather, Keswickians contend that holiness is continual consecration and a continual cleansing of sin. They preach a gradual loss of self-centeredness rather than a radical, instantaneous transformation in which God purifies the heart. Since they insist that human imperfections are sin, they find it impossible for Christian perfection to be achieved in this life. The Keswickian approach has components of both Holiness and Calvinism and is a middle position. This position has been rejected by most Calvinistic proponents as well as by most holiness people.

---

[4] Donald Metz: *Studies in Biblical Holiness*, 73.

The Legal Definition Makes God the Creator of Sin and Denies the Incarnation

Is it sinful to be human? God created human beings. Did He, therefore, create the sin? If sin is anything less than the perfection of God, then all created beings fall short of that perfection and all are sinful. Neither angels nor people in heaven will have the perfection of God and would thus be eternally sinful. All Christians would reject the idea that God is the creator of sin; it was caused by the Fall. Most Wesleyans hold each individual guilty only for his own personal sin, while most Calvinists regard everyone as guilty at birth merely for belonging to the sinful human race. God created humanity with human limitations, fallibilities, and a lack of omniscience. The Gnostic heresy identified sin with the material world; to be human was to be sinful because a person had a physical body. Since the body was already sinful, they claimed it did not matter what one did, and salvation could only be found in a special knowledge. Similarly, Calvinists declare a person is sinful because he is human and thus not perfect. Calvinists believe that salvation is only found through an imputed righteousness that labels a person righteous while he actually continues to be wicked. Modern Calvinism is a new twist on an old doctrine.

Jesus Christ was fully human, but was in all points tempted like as we are, yet without sin (He 2:14-18, 4:15). Since He was fully human as we are, and since we know He did not sin, then we know that we, too, though mere humans, can live without sinning. Logically, Calvinists must either deny the humanity of Christ or call Him sinful. Both are absolutely unacceptable. Calvinism cannot explain this conundrum with their definition of sin. The Early Church/Methodist definition of sin resolves the problem. Just as Christ lived a holy life and was not sinful, He has made provision to give His followers the divine nature enabling each one to live a holy life and not sin (2Pe. 1:4).

Jesus chose not to disobey and rebel against the Father, and likewise, those who have been born of God can live a life of obedience to God. Jesus set a high standard for all of His disciples to follow. Hebrews 2:14-18 plainly states that Jesus was completely flesh and blood and no different than humanity. He became part of the seed of Abraham and *in all things it behooved him to be made like unto his brethren.* Just as people are tempted, Christ also suffered and was tempted; accordingly, Jesus is able to empathize with and encourage all who are tempted. Richard S. Taylor concludes, "the testimony of the incarnation forever exonerates human nature of the charge of intrinsic sinfulness. . . . Jesus became man not only to redeem human nature, but to exemplify it. . . . The desires of the body and mind . . . are not in themselves sinful."[5] One can either believe in the legal definition of sin or the incarnation, but one cannot logically believe both.

---

[5] Richard S. Taylor, *God, Man & Salvation* (Kansas City: Beacon Hill Press, 1977), 266-267.

Chapter 16
Philosophical and Theological Fallacies

There are two major definitions of sin facing the evangelical religious world today. The Calvinistic definition says that sin is a failure to completely come up to the absolute perfection of God. It considers sin as absolute and even labels things done in ignorance or through human infirmities or failures as sin.

The other definition is predominantly thought of as Arminian, Methodist, or Wesleyan, but was also accepted by the Early Church. It seems to be the majority view of the broader scope of Christianity if one includes Catholics, Anglicans, and most Pentecostals. There is a consensus among them that sin is an act of intentional disobedience to God rather than a failure to be perfect.

The Wrong Definition Makes Christ Sinful and Destroys the Doctrine of the Incarnation

The ancient heresy of Gnosticism identified Christ as a spirit being and not flesh and blood. Logically, Calvinism, which identifies sin with being human, must deal with the same difficulty. It is impossible for any man to achieve the ideal of being as perfect as God. All people are fallible. Humans make mistakes, are emotional, fail, and have faults. Sometimes these flaws are due to lack of knowledge, and sometimes they are the result of human limitations. Jesus Christ was fully human and fully God, but as a human, He would have had the limitations of all humanity.

Scripture is insistent that Christ, as a human, had infirmities and temptations just like us. Hebrews 4:15 states, *For we have not an high priest which cannot be touched with the feeling of our infirmities; but was in all points tempted like as we are.* A later verse implies that Jesus was also ignorant in some ways as we are and was *"compassed with infirmity"* (Heb 5:2). If Christ had been a perfect God-like super-human, it would have been evident to all of those around Him. Angelic, Adamic, or divine perfection would have been obvious. Jesus acted as a normal boy at age twelve when he failed to travel back to Nazareth with his parents; this action seemed to be a failure on Jesus's part. It was not intentional disobedience, however, and thus, not sin. The brothers of Christ did not believe that He was the Messiah until after the resurrection (Mt 13: 53-58, Jn 7:5). The disciples and those of society around Christ did not recognize His divinity until He rose from the dead. Christ seemed to be a normal human being with normal limitations.

When, just after his baptism, Jesus was led by the Spirit into the wilderness to be tempted of the devil, He must have had normal human desires as we have, or He could not have been tempted. When He was tempted to turn the stones into bread, He faced the battle of physical desires. These are not wrong desires, but they were not God's plan for Him at that time. Jesus was tempted to take the easy way out by casting Himself off the pinnacle of the Temple. By the use of miraculous power, He could have established His divinity, but He refused. Jesus was also tempted in the garden just before His arrest. He asked God to allow Him not to have to die, but He willingly submitted to the will of the Father. These all are pictures of a normal human under temptation. Christ simply chose obedience in the midst of temptation. Through the grace given to us by Christ's death, Christians today, likewise, are able to obey God in all temptations.

Scripture is very clear that Jesus never sinned; the Bible says, He *was in all points tempted like as we are, yet without sin* (Heb. 4:15). If sin is inextricably tied to the limitations of humanity, then Jesus Christ would have had to have sinned, or He would not have been truly human. In contrast, if Jesus Christ were a special form of humanity which is impossible for other people to attain on this earth, then he did not truly identify with us. Yet, Scripture says that He was *tempted in all points like as we are*. Jesus was human just like us; He became hungry, and He had emotions. However, He chose not to disobey His Father in heaven; thus, He was without sin.

The truth that sin is a moral choice of a willful act of disobedience

Defending the Biblical Definition

changes the whole focus away from human flaws to human deliberation and voluntary decisions. Jesus Christ was capable of being fully human and not sinning, verifying that sin is not an intrinsic element of being human. If it is possible for Christ as a human to live a life of victory over sin, then it is possible for other people, through grace and the empowerment of the Spirit, to live a life without sinning as well.

The Calvinistic definition fails a test of simple logic when applied to the incarnation of Christ. The conclusions are heretical.

Calvinistic Syllogism
Premise: All humans make mistakes and have flaws.
Premise: Sin is anything short of the absolute perfection of God (including mistakes and human errors).
Premise: Jesus was fully man.
Conclusion: Therefore, Jesus sinned.

Calvinistic Syllogism-2
Premise: All humans make mistakes and have flaws.
Premise: Sin is anything short of the absolute perfection of God (including mistakes and human errors).
Premise: Jesus did not sin.
Conclusion: Therefore, Jesus was not a man.

Wesleyan Syllogism
Premise: All humans make mistakes and have flaws .
Premise: Sin is **only** disobedience to God, **not** mistakes and human errors.
Premise: Jesus was always perfectly obedient to God.
Premise: Jesus was fully man.
Conclusion: Therefore, Jesus was fully man and did not sin.

This helps to depict one of the core problems of the Calvinistic definition of sin. Logically, the choice is between believing in the incarnation or in believing the Calvinistic definition of sin.

The Wrong Definition Makes People Guilty for Being Human Rather Than for Being Disobedient

God created us as human beings. In this, we had no choice. If sinlessness is beyond human capabilities, then all people sin continually and constantly. However, the Bible is very clear that Adam and Eve sinned by deliberate disobedience, not by mere existence. Calvinism is a modern variation of Gnosticism. This mixture of Greek philosophy and Christianity taught that the spirit world was good while the physical world was evil. This basic tenet is rephrased in our theological circles today. The concept of imputed righteousness teaches that people on earth are evil because of human limitations yet our spirits are righteous because of imputed righteousness. This leads to the supposition that evil actions do not matter as long as a person has "a relationship" with Christ; this "relationship" supposedly makes the sins that are being committed irrelevant. This teaching is similar to the Gnostic thought that people constantly commit evil in the flesh while their spirits are holy and good.

Perhaps an example that has been popularly used will effectively illustrate the difference. A father takes his young child into the garden, and the child helps his father plant rows of corn. After planting the seeds, the father also has his child help pull up all the weeds in the garden. A few weeks later there are beautiful, straight rows of corn. The father is proud of the garden, especially since his child helped him. One day while playing outside, the child notices all the plants coming up in the garden. Since his father previously had him pull up all the plants which were coming up, the child promptly pulls up all the corn plants. When his father comes home, he is met by an excited little boy who leads him to the garden and proudly shows him how effectively he has pulled up all the "weeds."

Is this sin? The actions are the same as if in anger the child had gone into the garden and destroyed all the corn plants, yet the motive was quite different. The Calvinist or legal definition calls it sin and cannot effectively distinguish between mistakes and deliberate rebellion. The Wesleyan definition would call it a human failure due to ignorance, but not a sin. How would our heavenly Father view this action? God is concerned about the heart and the moral intent. Growth in grace can teach a person how to better please our heavenly Father. But disobedience and rebellion is biblically what offends God and keeps people from heaven.

The Wrong Definition Makes God the Author of Sin

The Gnostic view that the physical body is sinful led to a view of the Jehovah God of the Old Testament as an evil being. This is an automatic corollary of their belief regarding sin. The Bible totally disagrees. God is a holy God, and He created a holy and good world; yet, in this world, sin, suffering, and evil dominate. Christians vehemently oppose any doctrine that would make God the author of sin; it is a heresy. However, the humanistic world views the existence of evil and suffering as evidence for the non-existence of God. Perhaps this is their most powerful and oft-repeated argument against a belief in God. An incorrect definition of sin is a major presupposition for the humanists who see God as the author of sin and evil. This misconception of sin may be one of the major reasons for the rise of agnosticism and the rejection of God in our world today. Logically, a Calvinistic or legal definition of sin would mean the humanists were correct and God would be evil.

This false definition of sin which separates sin from morality and places the existence of evil in normal human limitations makes it much more difficult to defend God's goodness and holiness. The fall of Adam is not a good argument for the Calvinist. God, of course, knew ahead of time that those He created would fall. To create a race of people who were automatically sinful through no personal fault of their own would certainly seem like God was the creator of evil. If sin, however, is rooted in the will, then sin is the result of a personal decision by each individual to do that which is wrong. Scripture teaches that the blame for the nature of sin falls upon Adam as the head of the human race. Adam made a moral choice to disobey God. The logical premise, then, is that people sin by similarly choosing to disobey and rebel against that which they know is right. This is also the teaching of Scripture.

It does not make logical sense that God would bring mankind into the world and give him laws which he is incapable of knowing as well as unable to keep. This would make God the author of evil. If a teacher gave a surprise exam for which there was no warning and no preparatory material, it would be the fault of the teacher if the students failed the test. Calvinists teach that God has created a scenario in which the true cause of sin is not in human choice, but in the creative act of God.

The Wrong Definition Makes Sin Irrelevant and of No Consequence

All sin separates from God. As the Bible says, *the soul that sinneth, it shall die* (Eze 18:4). If a person has no alternative but to sin, then calling human mistakes sin makes genuine rebellion much less serious. The Calvinistic, legal definition teaches that "Christians" are constantly and compulsively sinning. Then what difference would one more sin make? After all, if all people are already totally dirty and filthy, what's a little more filth; it doesn't really change anything. If sin was truly unavoidable, it would lead to an attitude of "sin boldly" and often.[1] If there is no difference in behavior between a "Christian" and a "non-Christian," "Christians" can freely sin just as much as anyone and still go to heaven. According to this free-grace ideology, if a "Christian" is too wicked, God might punish him by causing him to have an early death, taking him on home to heaven! This horrendous, unbiblical characterization of Christianity is commonly being promoted in our world. The Calvinistic, legal definition of sin logically leads directly to this heresy.

The old-time Calvinists argued that if a person was saved, Christ living in him would cause him to live a holy life. If a person's life was evil, then he had never become a new creature in Christ. Practically, this is the same as the Wesleyan doctrine of backsliding. Both a person who has never been saved and one who is backslidden will need salvation. Likewise, the evidence for a lack of salvation is identical. A Christian's life will bear good fruit. Old-time Calvinists struggled with an assurance

---

[1] Martin Luther quoted by Ryan Reeves "Did Luther Really Tell Us to 'Love God and Sin Boldly'?" This is not a statement of Luther's doctrine but is a quote taken from Martin Luther in a personal letter to Melanchthon in 1521 from Wartburg castle, and the quote has been taken out of context. It was actually an attack against Catholicism rather than an excuse to sin. He did not preach or teach this concept to lay people. https://www.thegospelcoalition.org/article/did-luther-really-tell-us-to-love-god-and-sin-boldly/.

that they had been saved. There were those who lived godly lives for years who then fell away into deep wickedness and died without repenting. According to a Calvinist, this was evidence that they had never been saved. History records that the old-time Calvinist was incredibly insecure about his chances of heaven.

The legal definition of sin teaches a salvation that saves people in their sins not from their sins (Mt 1:21). A salvation that does not deliver from sin would make the death of Christ a "stupendous failure." Christ came to deliver us from our sins. If we are still bound in sin, then God failed in the greatest act of His Godhead. However, Christ did **NOT** fail. As Scripture says, *Thou shalt call his name JESUS: for he shall save his people from their sins* (Mt 1:21).

The Wrong Definition Makes Salvation a Covering of Sin Rather Than a Cleansing from Sin

The legal definition of sin also forces one to accept an atonement theory that does not deliver from sin. This is the idea that Christ's death only covers up sin rather than cleansing sin and purifying the human vessel. Adherents of this theory believe that it is impossible to be truly righteousness while on this earth. Wesleyan theology, in contrast, victoriously proclaims that not only is the righteousness of Christ imputed, it is also imparted—namely a person is actually made righteous. According to the Calvinistic application of their atonement theory, once the blood of Christ has paid for all one's sins, including future sins, it would be impossible for a person to be punished for any sins. Therefore, it cannot matter how a person lives subsequent to justification, for his sins have already been forgiven and covered up. This doctrine excuses deliberate, blatant, godless behavior in the lives of supposed "Christians," for it regards behavior as irrelevant to salvation; all that matters is whether a person says he once believed.

John Calvin and those who strictly followed his doctrine would disagree very strongly with the "sinning religion" idea commonly accepted today. Convinced that if a person was converted, he was changed and lived a holy life, Calvin yet believed a person did still sin. This is not logical, but it was his opinion. As a result, traditional Calvinists teach a limited atonement. According to them, Christ only died for the elect, and only those who are personally chosen by God can be saved. Those chosen then live a holy life as evidence of their election, while those who are not of the elect are damned to hell. The Arminian doctrine of the Wesleyans strongly disagrees and teaches that all men can be saved (Jn. 1:7-9, 3:16, Rom. 5:18, 10:11-13, etc.).

The Wrong Definition Logically Ends in Predestination or Universalism

One erroneous premise postulates that if Christ died for the whole world, then everyone will automatically be saved since their penalty has already been paid. An equally erroneous counter premise contends that Christ only died for those He chose for salvation and not for the whole world. The Penal Satisfaction Theory proposes that Christ took the penalty for sin and satisfied the justice demanded by God. When Calvinistic ideology of imputed righteousness is added, the theory logically ends either in predestination or universalism. This theory submits that if Christ died only for a limited number of people, then predestination is right; but if He died for the whole world, then everyone will be saved and universalism would be correct. Universalism, a belief that everyone will be saved, developed from the logical outcome of Calvinistic doctrine in early American history and is the practical belief of the modern, liberal church world. The rationale that all people will be saved cannot be true since the Bible teaches that some people will be cast into the Lake of Fire and will go into everlasting punishment (Rev. 20:15 and Mt. 25:46). Yet universalism is the logical conclusion of the unbiblical theory of imputed righteousness which allows sinners to go to heaven.

The only other reasonable alternative is the Wesleyan/Arminian position in which free will determines salvation. If salvation is available only to those who choose to believe and obey God, there is no reason to insist that free will ends with a born again experience. Biblically, a person is given a lifetime of free-will decisions to obey God which determines his eternal destination. Wesleyans agree with much of the Penal Satisfaction Theory, but feel that it is incomplete. It is true that Christ died on the cross to take our place and that He became sin for us that we might have His righteousness born in us (2 Co. 5:21). God demands righteousness in our lives for entry to heaven; accordingly, God not only must pay the price for sin in the atonement, but also empower a Christian to live the required sin-free life. Sin is incompatible with God's holiness and will not be allowed in heaven or be tolerated by God in eternity.

The Wrong Definition Allows Evil People in Heaven

If salvation is only a covering up of sin and people who are wicked and sinful still go to heaven, then heaven will be full of evil people who have deliberately chosen not to serve God and are at war with God. Is God going to retract their free will and force them to serve Him? Is salvation a choice, or is it an imposition by the sovereignty of God? Do people truly have free will? This is the basic issue between those who believe in a one-time justification experience that lasts for all eternity and those who believe that a person must maintain righteousness of life to enter heaven. God has given us the free will to obey God, and an obedient life is the evidence that a person has made the choice to be a Christian.

The free-grace interpretation of the apostates in Hebrews 6:6 is a travesty of biblical hermeneutics. The implausible explanation that former Christians who now would crucify Christ again if they had the opportunity will be in heaven because salvation cannot be lost is preposterous.[2] This would mean total apostates will be in heaven!

It would be unholy and unjust for God to allow a blatant sinner into heaven who had been saved as a child but then rejected God and lived an evil life. According to free grace Calvinism, the sinful go to heaven; accordingly, many, if not most, of those in heaven will be evil people. Heaven would then become evil like this world! This would also mean that the Holiness of God is compatible with evil. Wesleyans object and insist that the Holy Spirit does not live in the heart of one who is evil, nor does God allow wickedness into heaven. These fallacies are certainly not the teaching of Scripture (Mt 13:39-43).

---

[2] John F. Walvoord and Roy B. Zuck, ed. *The Bible Knowledge Commentary* (Wheaton, IL: Victor Books, 1983), 794-795. This is the free-grace ideology and not the position of historic Calvinism.

The erroneous doctrine that, contrary to Scripture, everyone continually sins and that sin does not separate from God presupposes eternal security. Some even preach that a person can trust God as savior but not acknowledge Him as Lord. This doctrine teaches that forgiveness is applied to future sins; therefore, it does not matter if one sins, he will still go to heaven since Jesus has already paid the price for all his sins. It is impossible, logically, to accept that "Christians" continue sinning without accepting all of the doctrine of unconditional, eternal security. The eternal security doctrine is not taught in Scripture, nor does it follow logical conclusions.

The Wrong Definition Would Also Change the Natural Reading of the Word of God

When Scripture says, *whosoever is born of God* **sinneth not**, those who hold to the legal definition say it cannot mean what it says (1Jn. 3:9, 1Jn 5:18). When it says, *He that committeth sin* ***is of the devil***, they say it cannot mean that (I Jn. 3:8). Whenever it says that we are ***free from sin***, they say it cannot mean that, either (Rom. 6:18 and 22). When the Bible says, H*e shall save his people* ***from*** *their sins,* they say it cannot mean that (Mt. 1:21). When the word *saints* is used in the New Testament to identify Christians, they reinterpret the word and give it a different meaning, saying that Christians are only imputed as holy. When Scripture warns repeatedly about backsliding, they say it cannot mean that. (Heb. 2:1-3, 4:1, 6:6 and 10:26-27). The erroneous idea that Christians sin undermines the integrity of the Bible. We must accept biblical truth as it is stated in God's Word or the authority of Scripture will be destroyed. To reject the biblical definition of sin is to undermine the inspiration of Scripture and to deny the truth of the Bible.

Conclusion

The Methodist/Wesleyan/Arminian and the Calvinistic concepts of salvation come from two very different philosophical points of view. Underlying these contrasting philosophies is the definition of sin. Wesleyans understand sin as voluntary disobedience to God, while

Calvinists understand sin as any failure to be perfect like God. Wesleyans believe that obedience is an attainable goal through the grace of God while Calvinists teach that all "Christians" will continually and constantly sin. Calvinists emphasize that sin is missing the mark of the perfection of God. Scripture sets the mark at voluntary obedience to God. For those who have been born again and empowered by the grace of God, this is an obtainable goal.

The contrasting definitions of sin automatically lead to differing concepts of salvation. Wesleyans believe that once a person is born again, he or she will quit sinning. Calvinists believe that born-again "Christians" will continue to sin. Wesleyans hold that a person is cleansed from sin. Calvinists hold that a person's sin is covered by the blood of Christ while he or she continues to sin. Wesleyans insist upon the necessity of a godly life. Some free-grace proponents teach that once a person is saved, he or she may live an extremely wicked and godless life in total rebellion to God but will still go to heaven. This doctrine undermines and excuses sin, and will deceive multitudes into trusting in a false deception for their salvation.

Wesleyan doctrine emphasizes complete victory over all sin while Calvinistic theology denies that genuine victory is possible. The Calvinistic concept of salvation is a life of constant failure to live a sinless life. Scripture, however, is clear that Christ came to *save his people from their sins* (Mt 1:21). In 1 John 3:8, the apostle states that *the Son of God was manifested, that he might destroy the works of the devil.* The work of the devil which Jesus came to destroy is obviously sin. Genuine victory over sin is clearly taught in Scripture.

The wrong definition of sin leads many sincere Christians to a life of despair. They try to live perfect like God, but discover that their humanity makes it impossible. They are then overwhelmed with feelings of guilt for their human failures; yet this is not the teaching of Scripture or the demands of God. God wants a person's love and obedience, *and His commandments are not grievous* (1 Jo 5:3). Those overly sensitive individuals need a proper biblical understanding of God and His love, of sin and God's justice, and of the requirements for entrance to heaven.

The historic position of the church is the definition used by the Wesleyan doctrine. It could also be called the Early Church definition or the standard orthodox definition of the church; but most importantly, it is the biblical definition.

Will heaven be a place of holiness and happiness or will it be a place where sinners bring the same evil which exists on this earth into the presence of God?

A proper definition of sin is one of the key foundations of all theology. For too long this doctrine has been ignored. It is time for an open and honest biblical, historical, and logical discussion regarding the definition of sin. Only then can a proper understanding of salvation and God's requirements for heaven be achieved.

Appendix A
Dealing with Sin in 1 John 3

1John 3:4-10 is one of the key passages that states in no uncertain terms that Christians do not sin and that if they do, they are of the devil. It is worth reiterating the position of John Wesley who stated, "If, therefore, you would prove that the Apostle's words, '*He that is born of God sinneth not,*' are not to be understood according to their plain, natural, obvious meaning, it is from the New Testament you are to bring your proofs, else you will fight as one that beateth the air."[1] Most Calvinists struggle with this passage and attempt different explanations, but often admit that their exegesis is weak. Sometimes they do not give any reasons or may even admit that they have no valid explanation, but it is beyond their comprehension that one could live without committing sin. However, a person should examine the text of Scripture and see exactly what the Bible says.

> *1John 3:4 Whosoever committeth sin transgresseth also the law: for sin is the transgression of the law.*
> *5 And ye know that he was manifested to take away our sins; and in him is no sin.*
> *6 Whosoever abideth in him sinneth not: whosoever sinneth hath not seen him, neither known him.*
> *7 Little children, let no man deceive you: he that doeth righteousness is righteous, even as he is righteous.*
> *8 He that committeth sin is of the devil; for the devil sinneth from the beginning. For this purpose the Son of God was manifested, that he might destroy the works of the devil.*

---

[1] John Wesley, *The Works of John Wesley*, 3d ed., vol. 6 (London: Wesleyan Methodist Book Room, 1872), 11.

> *9 Whosoever is born of God doth not commit sin; for his seed remaineth in him: and he cannot sin, because he is born of God.*
> *10 In this the children of God are manifest, and the children of the devil: whosoever doeth not righteousness is not of God, neither he that loveth not his brother.*

The Apostle John is dealing with the beginnings of the Gnostic heresy which tried to combine aspects of Greek philosophy with Christianity. It identified sin with the human body; the body was sinful since it was part of the physical world, while the mind was good since it was not part of the evil, material world. Salvation to the Gnostic came from the possession of a special knowledge and had little to do with behavior. Some of the teachings of Gnosticism have found their way into Calvinistic theology. Calvinistic theology contends that people are not sinful because of disobedience to God, but because people are not absolutely divinely perfect. The Apostle John is dealing with a similar false doctrine in his day as is reoccurring in theology today. Calvinism of our day has the same logical problems as did Gnosticism over a good God creating an evil world and over how Christ could be fully human and yet be sinless at the same time.

Sometimes one can get lost in the writing of Scripture because of its familiarity and a thoughtless preconception from a previously established theological view. Try to grasp John's understanding of sin and his meaning by writing his definition of sin into the passage in simple, modern English, beginning in verse four. John defines sin carefully in this passage by calling it lawlessness. This does not give the idea of inadvertent failures to keep the law, but it is the picture of one who is in defiance of and rebellion to the law. Since this is a summary of John's definition of sin, place this definition where the word *sin* is used.

1 John 3:4-10 Anyone who commits sin also breaks the law: for sin is willful disobedience and rebellion to the law. And you know that Christ came to take away our sins; and Christ lived in complete obedience to the law. Accordingly, anyone whose life is in Christ also does not disobey or rebel against the law of God. If a person does not live in obedience to the law, that person has never seen Christ and does not know Him. Let no one deceive you: he that does that which is right is righteous just like Christ is righteous. Anyone who disobeys and rebels against the law is of the devil who rebelled from the very beginning. Christ came to this earth in order to destroy the disobedience caused by the actions of the devil. Anyone who has experienced the new birth from God does not disobey or rebel against God; because the life of God is in him and it is impossible for the life of God to remain in one who is rebellious. This is how to tell the difference between the children of God and the children of the devil. The children of God do that which is right in obedience to the law and also have love for their brothers in Christ.

This is the simple straightforward meaning of the passage. There are a number of reasons why this interpretation should be accepted. John carefully defines what he meant by sin as he opened the passage. He does not picture sin as human failure or as an abstract perfection which is impossible for human beings to achieve. Sin is simply pictured as an act of lawlessness. The concept of lawlessness is not an accidental failure to keep the law, but the idea of one who refuses to come under the jurisdiction of the law. "It means rejection of law in its broadest extent, flagrant opposition to God, rather than just breaking specific laws,"[2] thus it is deliberate, knowledgeable, disobedience to God's law. This passage is key to the definition of sin used by Wesley and his followers. Wesleyans do not teach a human perfection, only the sinlessness as given in this passage. Those who define sin from a Calvinistic definition or who believe in sins of ignorance cannot comprehend how it is possible for one to live without sinning. Their misconception and ignorance of the Wesleyan definition of sin is the reason they mock the idea of sinless perfection. Because of the confusion over the words *sinless perfection,* Wesleyans rarely use this terminology, but they do maintain that Christians do not sin. It is only logical that God, with His grace and the power of the Spirit, can enable a person to live a victorious, consistent, sinless life.

One of the methods by which a Calvinist tries to get around the plain

---

[2] Thomas Constable, *Notes on 1 John, 2022* ed. (Sonic Light.com, 2022): https://www.planobiblechapel.org/tcon/notes/html/nt/1john/1john.htm.

wording of the text is to go to the Greek and argue that the text of the Greek allows for some sin but not for a lifestyle of continual or habitual sin. John Wesley deals very harshly with this manipulation of Scripture. He says:

> Nor do I conceive there is any material difference between committing sin, and continuing therein. I tell my neighbour here, "William, you are a child of the devil, for you commit sin; you was drunk yesterday." "No, sir," says the man, "I do not live or continue in sin" (which Mr. Dodd says is the true meaning of the text); I am not drunk continually, but only now and then, once in a fortnight, or once in a month." Now, sir how shall I deal with this man? Shall I tell him he is in the way to heaven or hell? I think he is in the high road to destruction; and that if I tell him otherwise his blood will be upon my head. And all that you say of living, continuing in, serving sin, as different from committing it, and of its not reigning, not having dominion, over him who still frequently commits it, is making so many loopholes whereby any impenitent sinner may escape from all the terrors of the Lord. I dare not therefore give up the plain literal meaning either of St. Paul's or St. Peter's words. He soon adds, "whosoever is born of God doth not commit sin; for his seed remaineth in him: And he cannot sin, because he is born of God." (Verse 9) But some men will say, "True: Whosoever is born of God doth not commit sin *habitually*." *Habitually*! Whence is that? I read it not. It is not written in the Book. God plainly saith, "He doth not commit sin;" and thou addest, *habitually*! Who art thou that mendest the oracles of God? That "addest to the words of this book?" Beware, I beseech thee, lest God "add to thee all the plagues that are written therein!" especially when the comment thou

addest is such as quite swallows up the text.³

At issue is a basic, fundamental understanding of the present tense in the indicative mood in Greek. The present indicative is a simple, present statement of fact which could be a one-time action or a repeated occurrence. According to Bill Mounce, "The present active indicative verb in Greek is basically the same as in English. It describes an action that normally occurs in the present. It can be either a continuous or undefined action."⁴ In his Greek grammar Clayton Croy stated that "the [indicative] present tense in Greek does double duty for two kinds of action: simple and continuing."⁵ In another Greek grammar text Daniel Wallace also notes that "the present tense may be used to make a statement of a general, timeless fact."⁶

A more detailed study of the Greek language backs up the sinlessness of the Christian. The Greek present tense in the indicative mood is used in the key verses of 1 John which teach the sinlessness of the Christian (1Jn 3:6-9, Jn 5:18). Some advocate that the present indicative verb teaches that a person may sin occasionally as long as it is not a habitual practice. This is an abuse of the language. A person cannot use the Greek to teach the opposite of the specific meaning of these passages. The best interpretation of the Greek shows these passages teaching a timeless fact. A better explanation is that these passages in 1 John 3:6-9 and 5:18, teach that the Christian continually does not sin. According to Bill Mounce, "If you want to describe an action that happens in the present, there are not two Greek tenses. [Only one] . . . The translator has to make a decision with present tense verbs. Because English distinguishes between an undefined and a continuous action in the present tense, you have to use one or the other in

---

[3] John Wesley, *The Works of John Wesley,* 3d ed., vol. 11, "An Answer to the Rev. Mr. Dodd," London: Wesleyan Methodist Book Room, 1872) 451-452.
[4] William Mounce, *Basics of Biblical Greek* (Grand Rapids: Zondervan, 2009), 131.
[5] N. Clayton Croy, *A Primer of Biblical Greek* (Grand Rapids: William B. Eerdmans Publishing Company, 1999), 9.
[6] Daniel Wallace, *Greek Grammar Beyond the Basics* (Grand Rapids: Zondervan, 1996), page 523.

translating a Greek present tense verb."[7] A Greek author uses the present indicative to indicate that a Christian does not sin at all as a timeless fact, but the tense could also be emphasizing that a person continually does not commit sin. Any other understanding of these passages comes from an imposition of the theology of the translators or scholars.

John's use of the present indicative in 1 John 3 shows his use of the grammar. His normal usage of a present indicative is to make a timeless statement or a statement that something is true in the present and is also true continuously. The idea that a person could be a Christian and sin occasionally as long as it is not habitual is not found in the context. For example, in verse 3 it states that a person purifies (present indicative) himself even as Christ is (present indicative) pure. The idea is that a person purifies his life in the present and continues to keep himself pure. Christ is pure now and continues to be pure. Certainly, Christ is always pure; He does not have a practice of only being pure most of the time with some exceptions. This passage teaches the same concept in verse 6. In verse 3 a person purifies himself on the basis of the purity of Christ; later verse 6 teaches that a person does not sin based upon the sinlessness of Christ. In verse 4 the present indicative is used for the word *transgression*. This is a timeless statement that sin is any violation of the law. It is true of one evil act, and is also true of the practice of evil. Those who feel that the present indicative only means a habitual practice have a real problem with this verse. For example, God would consider any single act of murder a sin. If sin is only habitually committing evil acts based upon the idea that the present indicative only includes a continual practice, then a single act of murder is not sin; a murderer would not be a sinner unless it was a habitual practice.

When verse 6 uses the present indicative to explain that Christians do not sin, one should use the same interpretation that John has been using for the Greek tense. It should be considered a timeless fact that Christians do not sin at all. If a person is abiding in Christ, he does not even commit one

---

[7] Bill Mounce, "Mondays with Mounce," "Can you not sin," (September 28, 2008), https://www.billmounce.com/monday-with-mounce/can-you-not-sin-1-john-3-6.

sin. Daniel Wallace, a leading Greek scholar, agrees that this passage is a general, timeless fact and says "Gnomic presents most frequently occur with generic subjects (or objects). Further, 'the sense of a generic utterance is usually an absolute statement of what each one does once, and not a statement of the individual's customary or habitual activity.' This certainly fits the pattern."[8]

The wording of verses 5 and 6 also reiterates that Christians do not commit a single act of sin. The text states, *In him [Christ] is no sin. Whosoever abideth in him sinneth not: whosoever sinneth hath not seen him, neither known him (1 Jo 3:5-6).* The sinlessness of the Christian is based upon abiding in the Son of God, Who is also sinless. The same Greek present indicative tense is used for Christ as is used for the Christian. Are we trying to say Christ sinned occasionally but not habitually? Absolutely not! Christ is holy and completely separate from sin; and so will be those who abide in Him. Christ did not sin at all, even once. If a person commits any sin, that person is not abiding in the sinless Christ. The same principal is presented again in *3:9* where it says, *His [Christ's] seed remaineth in him: and he cannot sin, because he is born of God.* As long as Christ is in a person, it is impossible to sin. If a person chooses to sin, Christ's seed will leave. Christ is holy and refuses to live in a corrupted heart willingly defiled by sin. This verse is not indicating that it is impossible for a person to go back into a life of sin. It is saying that when a person deliberately chooses to rebel against God, the seed of God will leave. The holiness of God will have nothing to do with abiding in the same heart as one who is in rebellion to God.

The Expositors Bible Commentary says,

> Taken together, the two sentences in v.5 emphasize the logic that underlies the test at v.6: Jesus has never had anything to do with sin—not then and not now. . . . 'If someone 'lives in him,' then that person does not sin. This is the logical implication of John's earlier remarks, for if Jesus has no sin in himself, those who abide in him will be

---

[8] Daniel Wallace, *Greek Grammar Beyond the Basics*, 525. Wallace quotes Buist, M., *Verbal Aspect in New Testament Greek* (Oxford: Clarendon Press, 1990), 217.

sinless also.' . . . If anyone sins, then that person has not 'seen him or known him.' The idea that such a person has 'not seen him' builds on the language of 1:1-3. . . . John continues the thought of vv. 4–6 with two more tests at vv. 7–8. . . . If someone 'does what is right,' then that person is righteous, just as God is righteous. . . . On the other hand, if anyone 'does sin', then that person is 'of the devil.[9]

    Sakae Kubo, a noted Greek scholar, brings out another difficulty when 1 John 1:8 is compared with 3:9. He states that "If the tense is pressed and one concludes that 3:9 is habitual, then 1:8 must likewise be habitual where a present tense stands."[10] This would mean that if 1 John 3:9 means "he that is born of God doth not habitually sin," then 1 John 1:8 would have to mean *if we say that we do not habitually have sin, we deceive ourselves and the truth is not in us.* They both have a present active indicative verb, and must be translated consistently. 1 John 1:8 would then mean that every person habitually has sin, and 1 John 3:9 would say that no one who is a Christian habitually sins. Hence, the logic would conclude that no one is born of God! Kubo sums it up by saying, "We conclude, then, first of all that the absolute view is more in line with the author's context in 3:9; that the habitual view actually plays havoc with the author's intention and argument."[11]

    The same truth is repeated again in 1 John 5:18 *We know that whosoever is born of God sinneth not.* The Apostle John repeats that the presence of Christ living inside a person does give complete victory over sin. The new birth experience is the beginning of spiritual life with the power of God now working inside an individual. A Christian is a new

---

[9] Tremper Longman III and David E. Garland, eds. *The Expositor's Bible Commentary* (Grand Rapids: Zondervan, 2006), 460.
[10] Sakae Kubo, "I John 3:9: Absolute or Habitual?" (Berrian Springs, MI: Andrews University), 56, accessed July 10, 2023, https://digitalcommons.andrews.edu/cgi/viewcontent.cgi?article=1106&context=auss.
[11] Sakae Kubo, "I John 3:9: Absolute or Habitual?"

Defending the Biblical Definition

creature in Christ Jesus (2Co 5:17). The power of the Holy Spirit is now at work, and anyone who has the power of God inside of him will not sin and will, through God's grace, keep himself from sin.

The idea of Christians committing occasional sin as long as it is not habitual has found its way into a number of modern versions of the Bible, but throughout history this has not been the case. Almost all translations before the last few years have consistently translated 1 John 3:6 as a singular action rather than as continuous action. These hundreds of scholars from a wide-range of theological beliefs have been united in this interpretation, but now all of their scholarship is being challenged. It is not coming from a new understanding of the language, but from a theological bias that softens the consequences of sin in a "Christian's" life.

Bill Mounce, one of the main translators of the English Standard Version (ESV), said,

> All right, we came to this in the ESV, and knew we needed to do something with the passage. This paragraph in John 3 is actually the ESV's most paraphrastic translation in all of the New Testament. We discussed it for a long time, asking, are people going to misunderstand this? If we translate it, 'No one who abides in Him sins', are they going to understand that John's talking about a life of sin, of constant sin, of ongoing sin?" And the answer was, "No, they're not. People will look at that and will come up with doctrines of perfection." We were uncomfortable because we had to be interpretive for about ten verses. We translated, "No one who abides in him keeps on sinning." In other words, a true disciple of Jesus Christ does not live in constant sin. We were convinced that is what it meant. We were convinced that people were going to misunderstand the simple 'sins.'[12]

---

[12] Bill Mounce, Biblical Training .org.
https://www.biblicaltraining.org/library/greek-verbs/greek-tools-for-bible-study/william-mounce.

Later, Mounce said, "I think if I had to do it over again, I would change my vote on 1 John 3:6."[13]

Robert Yarborough, a member of the consulting team for the ESV, objected to the translation saying,

> I don't think it's entirely honest with the tense. So I lost this battle because I was a consultant for the ESV. . . . It commits you to an over interpretation you can't defend in other places. But I think the pastoral fear won out, that if you just say does not sin then it's going to create havoc among people and so they said let's just go with what's true theologically, does not go on sinning, but you can see with your own eyes it doesn't say going on, it just says doesn't sin.[14]

This disclaimer simply does not help explain the passage for a Calvinist. They say that a Christian does not habitually sin, but then admit, "In practice, all Christians do sin—isolated sins, habitual sins, and even continuous, durative sins."[15] Thus this explanation is a complete failure. With the wrong theological definition of sin, all Christians would then sin daily, constantly and habitually. According to this paradigm, Christians continue to sin all the time. This doctrine would change the doctrine of salvation. If occasional sin is permissible, then God does not expect the Christian to be truly righteous and does not hold him guilty for sinning. If one accepts a Calvinistic understanding of imputed righteousness, he must, logically, admit that sin does not separate a person from God; thus, a person's behavior has no impact upon his salvation.

Others might add the words *willful* along with *habitual* to the text of

---

[13] Bill Mounce, "Mondays with Mounce," "Can you not sin."
[14] Robert W. Yarborough, "Lecture 10: The first Epistle of John," (The Masters Seminary), accessed July 10, 2023, minutes 57-58, https://www.youtube.com/watch?v=2vSrO0-esjs&feature=youtu.be.
[15] John Battle, *The Present Indicative in New Testament Exegesis* (Grace Theological Seminary, 1975), 179. https://docest.com/the-present-indicative-in-new-testament-exegesis.

Scripture. It would then read that a person who is saved does not commit habitual, willful sin. The concept of willful sin is what a Wesleyan defends as the proper definition of sin. Wesleyans would agree with using the term *willful*, but since all sin is willful, the word does not need to be added. It would merely be repetitious. The apostles in Scripture made it clear; Christians do not commit any sin! Any use of the word *sin* to describe human ignorance or human limitations is an improper use of the term and just confuses the meaning of sin. God is fundamentally concerned about moral behavior. If our motives are right with God, He is satisfied.

Often sympathy for a struggling new convert has precipitated this redefinition of sin. Christ also cares, but does not excuse sin; He has a much more wondrous solution! He will forgive, restore the sinner, and give him overcoming power (1Jn 2:2, 5:4, 5:18). Often, however, it is sin that is habitual that Calvinists excuse. For example: consider a young man addicted to pornography who struggles with breaking the habit after conversion. It is not only an act of sin but also a habitual sin and a continual practice of sinning. The church should have compassion on those who are struggling with any addictive habit, but God will enable a person to overcome. The blood of Christ is readily available and there is forgiveness for failure, but Scripture does not condone intentional sin. 1 John is very clear that if a person commits sin, he does not abide in Christ (3:6), is of the Devil (3:8), does not have the seed of God in him (3:9), is in darkness (1:6), does not know Christ (2:4), and is not born of God (5:18). However, Scripture does make it clear that Christ is our advocate Who will restore one who has backslidden to salvation (2:2). Sometimes, the problem is misnaming actions as sin. A lack of self-discipline or being tempted is not sin. One should not confuse these with what the Bible calls sin—willful disobedience to the known law of God.

A person who sins is identified with the devil. 1 John 3:8 says, *He that committeth sin is of the devil. . . . For this purpose the Son of God was manifested, that he might destroy the works of the devil.* 1 John 5:18 says, *He that is begotten of God keepeth himself, and that wicked one toucheth him not.* The power and works of the devil are destroyed in the life of a Christian. If the devil still has the power to cause one to sin, it shows that the individual is still a servant of the devil and not of God. Modern

Calvinism has weakened the original concepts of both John Calvin and Martin Luther. Calvin commented thus on this verse:

> There is no life of God and of Christ, where men act perversely and wickedly, but that such are, on the contrary, the slaves of the devil; and . . . subjects them to his government, in order that we may know that there is no middle condition, but that Satan exercises his tyranny where the righteousness of Christ possesses not the primacy. . . . Hence two conclusions are to be drawn, that those in whom sin reigns cannot be reckoned among the members of Christ, and that they can by no means belong to his body; for wherever Christ puts forth his own power, he puts the Devil to flight as well as sin.[16]

Commenting on 1 John 3:9, Luther in his commentary wrote,

> To be born of God, therefore, means to purge out sin. Then sin is impaled on the spit. He cannot sin because he is born of God. Nothing is easier than sinning. But to be born of God and to sin are incompatible. While the birth remains, and so long as the seed of God abides in a person who has been born again, he cannot sin. He can, of course, lose his birth and commit sin; but so long as the seed of God is in us, it does not permit that sin to be with it.[17]

Thomas Constable, a long time professor at Dallas Theological Seminary, sums up the idea among current scholarship and says,

> The 'tense solution' in 1 John 3:9 is in the process of

---

[16] John Calvin, *Calvin's Commentaries*, assessed July 10, 2023, https://biblehub.com/commentaries/calvin/1_john/3.htm.

[17] Martin Luther, *Luther's Works: The Catholic Epistles,* vol. 30, (St Louis, MO: Concordia Publishing House 1967), 273.

imploding in the current literature. It was shrewdly questioned by C. H. Dodd in his commentary in 1946 and dealt a major blow by S. Kubo in an article entitled, '1 John 3:9: Absolute or Habitual?' published in 1969. It has since been given up by the three major critical commentaries published since Kubo's article; namely, I. Howard Marshall (1978), Raymond E. Brown (1982), and Stephen S. Smalley (1984). It seems quite clear that the 'tense solution' as applied to 1 John 3:9 is an idea whose time has come—and gone![18]

Although leading Calvinistic scholars have rejected the tense solution, they still insist that Christians do sin. Explanations are varied, inconsistent, and weak as they grasp at straws to pronounce sin permissible. One view suggests that a person does not sin as long as he is abiding in Christ, suggesting a loss of fellowship but not salvation. However, this passage is dealing with more than being in fellowship with Christ; it is dealing with whether one is a child of the devil or whether one is born of God. Others emphasize two natures, one which is sinful and one which is righteous through Christ. In that sense, they propose a person could be righteous and sinful at the same time. This is clearly not what John is teaching in this passage since he is emphasizing that a holy, sinless life is the evidence of salvation. John says in verse 10 that this is the way to distinguish between the children of God and the children of the devil.

Some people feel that a sinless life is merely the ideal, though, realistically an unattainable goal. Bill Mounce says, "Sometimes a goal can be stated absolutely as a means of encouragement. A coach may tell his beleaguered team, 'We do not lose!' A mother may discipline her daughter, 'Good girls do not do that.' Really? A team never loses? Good girls never fail? Of course not. Sometimes the goal stated in absolute terms becomes the motivation for achieving that goal, no matter how imperfectly."[19] Yet, John is not using the language of an ideal; rather, he is

---

[18] Thomas Constable, *Notes on I John*, (Sonic Light.com, 2023): https://www.planobiblechapel.org/tcon/notes/html/nt/1john/1john.htm.
[19] Bill Mounce, "Mondays with Mounce," "Can you not sin."

speaking of things that are literal and actually true. His words clearly stipulate that a Christian will truly be what he testifies that he is.

Daniel Wallace's explanation of the passage is to assign it to a future eschatological meaning. He says, "Thus, the author states in an absolute manner truths that are not yet true, because he is speaking within the context of eschatological hope."[20] However, it is impossible for a person to be a child of the devil in the present and yet have the eschatological hope of a future with Christ. This passage is clearly addressing the way to identify who is a Christian here and now (3:10).

Although the Calvinists do not have a good explanation for this passage, they completely reject any possibility of sinlessness. Wesleyan theologians agree that no one could ever meet the Calvinist ideal of God-like perfection, but disagree on the meaning of sin. This is why it is so critical to get the definition of sin correct. Only then will this passage, as well as the entire plan of salvation, become clear. When sin is defined properly, it is then possible to live without sinning as this passage specifies. Righteousness in behavior is necessary to fulfill God's requirements.

---

[20] Daniel Wallace, *Greek Grammar Beyond the Basics,* 525.

Appendix B
Answering Calvinist's Objections

Calvinists teach that Christians may sin without losing their salvation and also teach that it is impossible to live without continual sinning. Their conclusions are based upon added assumptions rather than strictly the direct, clear words of Scripture. It can be difficult to follow their line of reasoning unless a person is familiar with their theological presuppositions. While there are many passages in the Bible which directly state that Christians do not sin and others which logically prove this truth, there are **no** verses which plainly state that Christians **do** sin. Nevertheless, Calvinists adamantly hold their position without any solid scriptural basis. Obviously, if all Christians sin, the inability to live holy undermines the Wesleyan definition of sin; however, if a person can live a life without sinning, the Calvinistic definition of sin cannot be correct.

Romans 3:23 *For all have sinned and come short of the glory of God*
Some have tried to define sin as falling short of the glory of God and have used this passage in Romans 3:23 as the basis for their definition. Yet, this passage is not trying to define sin. It is giving the consequences of having sinned: namely, a person has come short of achieving God's glory. This passage means that a person has come short of obtaining heaven, or a person has failed in God's creative purpose for man in glorifying God. Either rephrasing gives the results of sin instead of defining it. Furthermore, the passage goes on to teach that righteousness is now obtained, and sin has been overcome by the righteousness that comes only through Jesus Christ.

James 4:17 *Therefore to him that knoweth to do good, and doeth it not, to him it is sin.*
This verse notes that disobedience to God may come through omission

in doing what is right. Calvinists like to expand knowing to do good to the extreme so that everyone continually falls short. They would say, "It is always possible in the context of doing good to do more; for example, You could have prayed more, or you could have witnessed more." James is not trying to set an impossible standard. In fact, the book of James is always practical and reasonable. Theoretical impossibilities are far from the straightforward methodology of James's writing style.

Jesus addressed this issue in the Parable of the Talents in Matthew 25:14-30. The unprofitable servant was condemned because he did nothing. Even doing a little bit would have been acceptable. It was not great success that was demanded. The master only demanded loaning out the money and receiving interest. This passage in James also teaches the importance of knowledge in committing sin, and Wesleyans use this passage to show that for an action to be sin, knowledge is necessary.

Romans 7:15 - 8:4 *For that which I do I allow not: for what I would, that do I not; but what I hate, that do I. 16 If then I do that which I would not, I consent unto the law that it is good. 17 Now then it is no more I that do it, but sin that dwelleth in me. 18 For I know that in me (that is, in my flesh,) dwelleth no good thing: for to will is present with me; but how to perform that which is good I find not. 19 For the good that I would I do not: but the evil which I would not, that I do. 20 Now if I do that I would not, it is no more I that do it, but sin that dwelleth in me. 21 I find then a law, that, when I would do good, evil is present with me. 22 For I delight in the law of God after the inward man: 23 But I see another law in my members, warring against the law of my mind, and bringing me into captivity to the law of sin which is in my members. 24 O wretched man that I am! who shall deliver me from the body of this death? 25 I thank God through Jesus Christ our Lord. So then with the mind I myself serve the law of God; but with the flesh the law of sin. 8:1 There is therefore now no condemnation to them which are in Christ Jesus, who walk not after the flesh, but after the Spirit. 2 For the law of the Spirit of life in Christ Jesus hath made me free from the law of sin and death. 3 For what the law could not do, in that it was weak through the flesh, God sending his own Son in the likeness of* *sinful flesh, and for sin, condemned sin in the flesh: 4 That the righteousness of the law might be fulfilled in us, who walk not after the flesh, but after the Spirit.*

This passage is one of the most commonly used Scriptures to support the supposed impossibility of living without sinning. Paul described himself as a person under the control of a sinful nature which made it impossible to keep the law of God. Many Calvinists hold this passage to be the best a Christian can expect in this life. However, some Calvinist scholars, along with Wesleyans, disagree and contend that Paul is describing his life before conversion, showing the power of the sin nature operating in his life without God's grace. They note that in this section, verses 15-24, there are no references to Christ, grace, salvation, victory, or the Spirit. It is the story of mankind without God, constantly trying but failing to live right. Douglas Moo, one of the most noted scholars of today, stated that the situation in Romans 7 "is, by definition, one that no Christian can ever experience. As Paul has taught at some length in Romans 6, every believer, united with Christ in death and resurrection has been 'set free from sin' (see 6:6, 14, 18, 22). And Romans 8:2 makes it clear that the Spirit sets every believer free from the law of sin and death."[1] Paul teaches the concept of glorious victory over sin in chapter six and then again in chapter eight. To try to use this passage as a description of the normal life of a Christian would destroy the rest of the entire teaching of Paul in the surrounding chapters.

Paul's description does not end with the last verse of chapter 7. He continues this topic into the next chapter. After describing failure under the law, Paul proceeds to describe the freedom from sin that comes through the Spirit in chapter 8. He says, *For the law of the Spirit of life in Christ Jesus hath made me free from the law of sin and death.* In 7:23 the sin nature is described as the law of sin which has brought us into captivity, but in 8:2 the apostle states that a person is delivered by being made free from the law of sin and death. Furthermore, once delivered from the sin nature, a person is now able to fulfill the righteousness of the law. Understanding the entire context of the passage totally undermines any

---

[1] Douglas J. Moo, *Encountering the Book of Romans* (Grand Rapids: Baker Academic, 2002), 126.

possibility of using this passage to prove that all Christians must sin.

1 John 1:8 along with 1:5-2:4 *This then is the message which we have heard of him, and declare unto you, that God is light, and in him is no darkness at all. 6 If we say that we have fellowship with him, and walk in darkness, we lie, and do not the truth: But if we walk in the light, as he is in the light, we have fellowship one with another, and the blood of Jesus Christ his Son cleanseth us from all sin. 8 If we say that we have no sin, we deceive ourselves, and the truth is not in us. 9 If we confess our sins, he is faithful and just to forgive us our sins, and to cleanse us from all unrighteousness. 10 If we say that we have not sinned, we make him a liar, and his word is not in us. 2:1 My little children, these things write I unto you, that ye sin not. And if any man sin, we have an advocate with the Father, Jesus Christ the righteous:2 And he is the propitiation for our sins: and not for ours only, but also for the sins of the whole world. 3 And hereby we do know that we know him, if we keep his commandments. 4 He that saith, I know him, and keepeth not his commandments, is a liar, and the truth is not in him.*

Perhaps the most common passage which is quoted to allegedly prove Christians sin is 1 John 1:8. Other verses in this context, such as 1:7, 2:1, and 2:3, are also misunderstood. This passage cannot be used in any way to show that a Christian sins; in fact, it is a powerful statement that a person can and must be delivered from all sin. Living a sinless life is one of the key themes of the Apostle John. John opened this passage with an absolute statement that a person cannot mix light and darkness and then closes with another absolute, the requirement of obedience. These set the parameters for the passage.

The cultural context of 1 John aids in a proper understanding of these verses. In this book, John is addressing the Greek philosophy which later resulted in the Gnostic heresy. The Greeks deemed that the body was evil and the spirit was good. A Gnostic could claim that while his body was sinful, he himself was without sin in his spirit. In contrast, this is the meaning of the passage as it would have been understood by the people to which John wrote:

If a person is in the light then there is no darkness at all in him and anyone who professes to have fellowship with Christ and lives in the darkness of sin is a liar. In contrast, those who are in the light have fellowship with other Christians, and Christ will cleanse them from the source of sin, the indwelling sin nature as well as all other aspects of sin. Those who do not believe that they have indwelling sin which needs to be cleansed are deceived and do not have the truth. If we confess our sinful behaviors to Christ, he will forgive us. Christ will then continue to cleanse everything in our lives that is unrighteousness, both committed sins and the sin nature. John says that his goal in writing this book is that people do not sin, but if a person falls back into sin, do not give up! Jesus Christ, our advocate, is there to restore us and not us alone, but everyone in the entire world who comes to Him. The evidence that a person truly knows Christ is whether a person keeps Christ's commands. Anyone who professes to be a Christian and does not keep the commands of Christ is a liar.

John understood that this passage would be subject to misinterpretation; therefore, he opens with the statement that there is no sin, which he describes as darkness, in the life of a Christian. John then closes the passage by noting that Christians will keep Christ's commands; if not, they are not Christians but liars. Sandwiched between these two absolutes, John makes his theological argument, but this is done carefully so that there can be no misinterpretation that John is excusing sin in the life of a Christian. In spite of these safeguards, people have separated verses 8 and 10 from the larger context and distorted the meaning.

We must also keep in mind the context of the entire book. John is dealing with the question of sin. Repeatedly throughout the whole book he keeps emphasizing that Christians do not sin. In almost every chapter John comes back to this key theme that a Christian keeps the commands of God and does not sin. Any statement about sin must be viewed within the larger context of the book as John reiterates the necessity of living a sinless, Christian life.

1 John 1:7 *But if we walk in the light, as he is in the light, we have fellowship one with another, and the blood of Jesus Christ his Son* *cleanseth us from all sin.*

Some have used this verse to teach that people must have a continual cleansing since they are supposedly unavoidably continually committing sin. There are multiple problems with this interpretation: First, this passage is not referring to committed acts of sin; it is discussing the sin nature. John deals with the two works of grace in this passage by first addressing the problem of indwelling sin inherited from Adam and then moves to the sinful acts for which people are guilty. Forgiveness for personal sinful behavior is taught in verse 9, while cleansing from indwelling sin is taught in both verses 7 and 9. This passage teaches the cleansing from all sin, not just some sin. Certainly this statement which says *all* must include the source of sin or all does not mean all. Some have added the word *guilt* to this passage; it does not say that people are cleansed from the guilt of sin; it says that they are cleansed from all sin. This cleansing gives freedom from sin, not freedom from merely the guilt of sin. Cleansing is the removal of corruption rather than only forgiveness of guilt.

The basis for a continual cleansing comes from an improper understanding of the Greek. The passage uses the Greek present indicative in the word *cleanseth*. The present indicative can be used in several ways. It can be used similar to most other uses of the present tense in the English language. It may give a present factual statement which may be a simple fact, a one-time action, or a continual action; its usage must be interpreted from the context. In this passage the context is teaching that a person is free from all sin. To claim that a person must be continually sinning in order to need a continual cleansing is the exact opposite of the simple meaning of the verse. It is an improper usage to take a straightforward statement that a person can be cleansed from all sin to mean that a person must continually sin.

1 John 1:8 *If we say that we have no sin, we deceive ourselves, and the truth is not in us.*

There are a number of problems with using 1 John 1:8 as a proof text to try to show that Christians are committing sin. The passage does not say that Christians are continually committing sin; this is a false assumption from an incorrect theology and not Scripture. Read the text carefully. This Scripture uses the word *have* which means that the sin referred to here is something that people possess, the carnal nature, not something they did. The difference between these two concepts of sin is shown by its contrast with verse ten. People have a sin nature in verse 8, but they have sinned in verse 10. The term in verse 8 is the singular term *sin* which logically refers to the singular entity of the sin nature. The use of the word *cleanse* in verse 7, likewise, identifies that this passage is not discussing acts of sin, but the very nature itself. People are forgiven for a committed act of sin, but are cleansed from a corruption.

Another problem is that the context of the passage around this verse does not corroborate the interpretation that Christians sin. Isolating one verse from its context is breaking all hermeneutical principles. Both the verses before and after totally contradict the erroneous assumption that Christians sin. Scripture repeatedly emphasizes that everyone has a sin nature which can be cleansed by the power of God. When the passage discusses acts of sin in verse 9, the past tense is used, clarifying that all have committed sin in the past, but that it is not necessary to keep sinning in the present.

According to Sakae Kubo, many commentators follow B. F. Wescott in interpreting *hamartia* in 1:8 as sinful principle instead of sinful acts.[2,3] These commentators make the distinction between these two meanings on the basis of verses 8 and 10, the former referring to a sinful principle and the latter to sinful acts. "Thus 'to have sin' is distinguished from 'to sin' as the sinful principle is distinguished from the sinful act itself."[4]

It is likely that John was addressing the Greek concept that to be without sin is to have never sinned at all. All are guilty of committing sin

---

[2] Sakae Kubo gives these examples. David Smith, "The Epistles of John," *The Expositor's Greek Testament* (Grand Rapids, Mich., 1956), V, 172; George Findlay, *Fellowship in the Life Eternal: An Exposition of the Epistles of St. John* (London, 1909), p. 106; A. E. Brooke, *A Critical and Exegetical Commentary on the Johannine Epistles*, "*The International Critical Commentary*," (Edinburgh, 1914), p. 18.

[3] B. F. Westcott, *The Epistles of St. John* (Cambridge, 1892), 22.

[4] Sakae Kubo, *I JOHN 3:9 : ABSOLUTE OR HABITUAL?* (Berrien Springs, MI: Andrews University, n.d.), 51.

at one time or another. The great Early Church scholar Origen stated it this way,

> To be without sin has two meanings in Scripture. One is never to have sinned at all; the other is to have ceased sinning. If they say that the phrase 'to be without sin' describes someone who has never sinned at all, then we agree that no one is without sin. All of us have sinned at some time, even though we might have become virtuous afterward. But, if they take the phrase 'no one is without sin' as denying that anyone, after he has sinned can return to the practice of virtues and never sin again, then their opinion is wrong. For, it can happen that someone who has previously sinned can stop sinning and be said to be w i t h o u t sin.[5]

1 John 2:1-4 *My little children, these things write I unto you, that ye sin not. And if any man sin, we have an advocate with the Father, Jesus Christ the righteous: 2 And he is the propitiation for our sins: and not for ours only, but also for the sins of the whole world. 3 And hereby we do know that we know him, if we keep his commandments. 4 He that saith, I know him, and keepeth not his commandments, is a liar, and the truth is not in him.*

The major problem with trying to use this passage to teach that Christians can sin and still remain saved is that this verse does not say that. In fact, it teaches just the opposite. John's goal in writing the book is to ensure that they do **not** sin, which clearly shows that John believed that living a life without sinning was possible. He then stated that *if any man sin* which proves it was possible not to sin or he would have said when (not if) any man sins. The idea that Christians sin is not even implied at all in the passage.

Verse 1 says bluntly that a person should not sin; but if one does, he

---

[5] Origen. *Homilies on Luke.* (Washington DC: United States: Catholic University of America Press: 2010), 10.

should go to Christ, Who is our advocate. Both the backslider and the whole world are lost unless they come to Christ in repentance and faith. The passage implies that a Christian who commits sin is now back in the condition of the lost world needing salvation. This verse is to give hope to those who have lost their salvation due to sin. Thus, a backslider should not despair, but should go to Christ to find forgiveness and restoration.

John was concerned that this passage might be misunderstood to excuse sin, so the context in the next verses helps to clarify the meaning. John makes it perfectly clear in verses 3 and 4 that anyone who does not keep the commands of God cannot still claim to know Christ; instead, he is a liar and without truth.

1 John 5:16-18 *If any man see his brother sin a sin which is not unto death, he shall ask, and he shall give him life for them that sin not unto death. There is a sin unto death: I do not say that he shall pray for it. All unrighteousness is sin: and there is a sin not unto death. We know that whosoever is born of God sinneth not; but he that is begotten of God keepeth himself, and that wicked one toucheth him not.*

When this passage discusses the sin which is not unto death, it does not state the type of death to which it is referring. There is no reason to believe that there are sins which a person is allowed to commit which do not lead to spiritual death. The context clarifies that one born of God does not sin. The traditional teaching in the Early Church was that this referred to eternal death in that the person has sinned away their day of opportunity and has crossed the deadline. While there is little emphasis regarding this doctrine in our day, the teaching that certain sins were irremissible was taught and debated in the Early Church.[6]

Matthew 5:48 *Be ye therefore perfect, even as your Father which is in heaven is perfect.*

Obviously no one is perfect in the complete and full sense that God is perfect. Only God is completely perfect in aspects such as knowledge and power. Absolute perfection will never be true of any created being,

---

[6] David W. Bercot, ed., *A Dictionary of Early Christian Beliefs* (Peabody, MA: Hendrickson Publishers, 2019), 616-617.

whether human or angelic, either now or even in eternity. "'Perfection' in the Old Testament means 'without moral blemish,' and can be used of upright men such as Noah (Gn 6:9) [and] Job (1:1). . . . Here the context defines it as perfection in love, which seeks the good of all men."[7] It is this aspect of perfect love for others that should be used to understand this passage. The wording in Greek is also in the future tense, stating that a person *will be* perfect rather than a command to do something now which would use the imperative tense. Accordingly, this is not a demand; instead, it is a promise of what God will do! Scripture does use the terminology of perfection about 30 times in the New Testament to teach a moral completion that is available in this life. The Wesleyan doctrine has been quite inaccurately portrayed by others who have called them perfectionists and scoffed at them that "nobody is perfect." Wesley taught perfection in love, but not perfection in action.

Luke 11:4 *And forgive us our sins; for we also forgive every one that is indebted to us. And lead us not into temptation; but deliver us from evil.*

The Lord's Prayer certainly does not teach that Christians sin continually, nor should this be considered a daily prayer for forgiveness. Here are a number of reasons which show that this is not the intent of the passage.

1. If this passage were trying to teach this doctrine, it certainly would have stated this doctrine definitively. This passage does not say Christians sin. It is easy to assume a meaning that fits one's theology and then try to use it as a proof text. A proof text must be clear and straightforward without other possible meanings and should usually be the major point the author is trying to make. This passage totally fails to meet these requirements.
2. Some suggest that this passage implies that Christians should pray every day asking to have their sins forgiven; however, neither this

---

[7] C. Allen Willoughby, *A Critical and Exegetical Commentary on the Gospel according to S. Matthew*, International Critical Commentary (New York: C. Scribner's Sons, 1907), 56.

passage nor elsewhere in Scripture is the Lord's Prayer upheld as a daily prayer. This is a model prayer which covers multiple aspects for all of life, including some which may not be applicable on a daily basis.
3. Arminians hold that Christians should not be constantly sinning because God will help them to live victoriously. Calvinists hold that even future sins have already been forgiven so this prayer would be evidence of a lack of faith in the grace of God. Neither theological system logically could advocate asking for sins to be forgiven each day.
4. The key meaning of the statement *forgive us our sins* is that a person's forgiveness for their own sins is based upon one's forgiveness of others. This truth is clearly taught in Matthew's account where the Lord's Prayer is followed by the statement, *But if ye forgive not men their trespasses, neither will your Father forgive your trespasses* (Mt 6:15). This is elaborated further in the Parable of the Unforgiving Debtor which illustrates that our forgiveness by God is based upon our forgiveness of others (Matthew 18:21-35).
5. The usage of the Greek verbs also indicates the difference. The aorist tense is used for our forgiveness by God. This implies that a simple, one-time action is needed for the forgiveness of our sins. This is contrasted with the use of the present indicative tense for our forgiveness of others. The present indicative may show continual action indicating a need to continually forgive others. The use of contrasting verbs in this passage identifies that once a person's sins have been forgiven, there is no need for continual forgiveness since a person is not continuing to sin. In contrast, there is an ongoing need to forgive others throughout all of life. However, everyone has a constant need to confess human failures both to God and others, asking for God's help and also forgiveness from those we have accidently wronged. However, this passage is not addressing human mistakes which are not considered sins.

Hebrews 12:1 *Let us lay aside every weight, and the sin which doth so easily beset us.*

The argument is made that this was written to Christians; therefore, it is Christians who are to lay aside the sin. It certainly does not state in this passage that Christians are committing sin. Everyone is born with a sin nature and repeatedly the book of Hebrews is advocating for the Hebrew Christians to move to a higher plane of spiritual living (4:1 and 6:1). Here the apostle continues the same argument by advocating laying aside the sin nature.

This passage may also have an application to those who are not Christians. Since this book, along with the other books of the New Testament, was to be read to the whole church, it should be assumed that there would be admonitions directed to those in the church that were not saved. These Hebrew Christians were struggling, and many of them may have been backsliding. The apostle may have been admonishing them to overcome whatever sin it was that was causing them to lose faith in Christ.

A number of other passages can be used as admonitions to go on to holiness as does this passage in Hebrews. While a person may be free from committing acts of sin, he or she may still have the sinful tendencies in the heart. Wesleyans teach complete victory over the nature in a second work of grace, while Calvinists teach that these tendencies need to be suppressed through personal discipline. Many passages in Scripture address overcoming the sin nature. The presence of the sin nature in a Christian should not be confused with sinful actions of rebellion against God. In **2 Corinthians 7:1** Paul admonishes the people to cleanse themselves *from all filthiness of the flesh and spirit, perfecting holiness in the fear of God*. This is clearly a passage which teaches the need to complete the work of holiness which was begun when one was regenerated. Another similar passage is **1 John 3:3** which says, *Every man that hath this hope in him purifieth himself, even as he is pure*. This passage also is referring to the work of sanctification which purifies a polluted heart. This passage does not state that a person was committing sin, but only that further purification was needed.

James 5:16 *Confess your faults (sins) one to another, and pray one for another, that ye may be healed.*

Defending the Biblical Definition

The Greek word, *paraptoma,* translated *faults* in verse 16, is often used in the New Testament as a synonym for sin, but it can be used for shortcomings as well as sin. All people, including Christians, have many shortcomings, but from the biblical definition of sin, these deficiencies are not sins. A similar word, *patio,* is used in James 3:2 which is translated *offend.* This word likewise can mean to make a mistake, to stumble or to fall, and is not referring to sin. Another place where *paraptoma* is used is Galatians 6:1 where it should also be translated fault and not sin. In Galatians 6:1 and in James 5:16 the implication is that the person may have backslidden; otherwise, there would be no reason to be restored or to be spiritually healed. It does not state that these people are Christians in these passages.

Ministers speaking to a church are usually addressing a mixed audience of both Christians and non-Christians. This would have been true for letters written to New Testament churches as well. To assume that this book, or any other biblical book, is only applicable for Christians is an assumption only. Even the best of churches include those who are not saved and need the message of forgiveness of sins.

Many of the modern translations substitute the word *sins* instead of faults in the statement that a person should *confess your faults one to another* (Ja 5:16). This is due to a textual difference in the manuscripts between the Byzantine text and the Greek texts used in much of modern scholarship. The question regarding which is the more accurate Greek text is a completely different issue than the scope of this study. It is clear, however, that this would be a poor passage to try to prove that Christians sin since there is a question over the Greek word in the actual text.

These are the Scriptures that the Calvinists use to defend their theological misconception that God does not deliver from sin in this life. Their conclusions are based upon reading Scripture with their theological presuppositions. None of these passages prove that Christians sin. In contrast, the passages that the Wesleyan position uses are very clear and straightforward definitions of sin or statements that Christians may live victorious, sinless lives.

Calvinists begin with the assumption that it is impossible not to sin and then build a doctrine to fit that premise. It then is expanded to include any failure or flaw so that even those among them who never willfully break God's law are told that they still sin. For them, life is a constant cycle of failure, defeat, and hopeless futility. The Bible proclaims the power of our omnipotent God is sufficient to enable every true believer to live a victorious, holy life of righteousness, more than conquerors, free from sin and Satan! What a mighty and glorious God we serve!

Appendix C
Righteousness is Required for Heaven

The focus is commonly upon the requirements for salvation, but salvation is only a means to an end. The ultimate goal is entrance to heaven and missing hell. A study of the New Testament shows just under one hundred verses which give the requirements for one's eternal destination. Of these, less than ten give faith as a requirement while fifty-six give the requirement of righteousness. Sometimes the idea of being righteous is confused with works of merit. These should never be confused; no one can earn through personal sacrifice any merit toward entry to heaven. However, the terminology of salvation also includes the idea of a radical change in behavior. Scripture equates salvation with conversion, regeneration, justification, and being born again. All people are sinful and guilty before God, and it is impossible for one to save himself. The only hope is for one to fall at the foot of the cross and beg for mercy trusting in Christ for salvation. Through Christ and Christ alone one finds pardon and the power to become a new creature in Christ; however, when Christ forgives, He also changes the behavior of the individual. A person who does not live a transformed life does not meet the requirements for heaven. The following is a list of Scriptures which prove that righteousness is the major requirement for heaven.

Matthew
1. Matt. 3:10 *And now also the ax is laid unto the root of the trees: therefore every tree which bringeth not forth good fruit is hewn down, and cast into the fire.*
2. Matt. 5:8 *Blessed are the pure in heart: for they shall see God.*
3. Matt. 5:20 *For I say unto you, That except your righteousness shall exceed the righteousness of the scribes and Pharisees, ye shall in no case enter into the kingdom of heaven.*
4. Matt. 5:22 *But I say unto you, That whosoever is angry with his*

brother without a cause shall be in danger of the judgment: and whosoever shall say to his brother, Raca, shall be in danger of the council: but whosoever shall say, Thou fool, shall be in danger of hell fire.

5. Matt. 5:29 *And if thy right eye offend thee, pluck it out, and cast it from thee: for it is profitable for thee that one of thy members should perish, and not that thy whole body should be cast into hell.*
6. Matt. 6:15 *But if ye forgive not men their trespasses, neither will your Father forgive your trespasses.*
7. Matt. 7:19 *Every tree that bringeth not forth good fruit is hewn down, and cast into the fire.*
8. Matt. 7:21 *Not every one that saith unto me, Lord, Lord, shall enter into the kingdom of heaven; but he that doeth the will of my Father which is in heaven.*
9. Matt. 7:23 *And then will I profess unto them, I never knew you: depart from me, ye that work iniquity.*
10. Matt. 12:36-37..*But I say unto you, That every idle word that men shall speak, they shall give account thereof in the day of judgment. For by thy words thou shalt be justified, and by thy words thou shalt be condemned.*
11. Matt. 13:41-42 *The Son of man shall send forth his angels, and they shall gather out of his kingdom all things that offend, and them which do iniquity; And shall cast them into a furnace of fire: there shall be wailing and gnashing of teeth.*
12. Matt. 13:49-50 *So shall it be at the end of the world: the angels shall come forth, and sever the wicked from among the just, And shall cast them into the furnace of fire: there shall be wailing and gnashing of teeth.*
13. Matt. 18:8 *Wherefore if thy hand or thy foot offend thee, cut them off, and cast them from thee: it is better for thee to enter into life halt or maimed, rather than having two hands or two feet to be cast into everlasting fire.*
14. Matt. 18:34-35 *And his lord was wroth, and delivered him to the tormentors, till he should pay all that was due unto him. So likewise*

shall my heavenly Father do also unto you, if ye from your hearts forgive not every one his brother their trespasses.
15. Matt. 19:16-17 *And, behold, one came and said unto him, Good Master, what good thing shall I do, that I may have eternal life? And he said unto him, Why callest thou me good? there is none good but one, that is, God: but if thou wilt enter into life, keep the commandments.*
16. Matt. 23:27, 33 *Woe unto you, scribes and Pharisees, hypocrites! for ye are like unto whited sepulchres, which indeed appear beautiful outward, but are within full of dead men's bones, and of all uncleanness. . . Ye serpents, ye generation of vipers, how can ye escape the damnation of hell?*
17. Matt. 24:48-51 *But and if that evil servant shall say in his heart, My lord delayeth his coming; And shall begin to smite his fellowservants, and to eat and drink with the drunken; The lord of that servant. . . shall cut him asunder, and appoint him his portion with the hypocrites: there shall be weeping and gnashing of teeth.*

Mark - Acts
18. Mark 10:17,19 *And when he was gone forth into the way, there came one running, and kneeled to him, and asked him, Good Master, what shall I do that I may inherit eternal life? Thou knowest the commandments, Do not commit adultery, Do not kill, Do not steal, Do not bear false witness, Defraud not, Honour thy father and mother.*
19. Mark 12:38,40 *Beware of the scribes . . . which devour widows' houses, and for a pretence make long prayers: these shall receive greater damnation.*
20. Luke 12:46 *The lord of that servant will come in a day when he looketh not for him, and at an hour when he is not aware, and will cut him in sunder, and will appoint him his portion with the unbelievers.*
21. Luke 13:26-27 *Then shall ye begin to say, We have eaten and drunk in thy presence, and thou hast taught in our streets. But he shall say, I tell you, I know you not whence ye are; depart from me, all ye workers of iniquity.*
22. Luke 16:29-30 *saith unto him, They have Moses and the prophets; let*

them hear them. And he said, Nay, father Abraham: but if one went unto them from the dead, they will repent.
23. Luke 18:18,20 *And a certain ruler asked him, saying, Good Master, what shall I do to inherit eternal life? Thou knowest the commandments, Do not commit adultery, Do not kill, Do not steal, Do not bear false witness, Honour thy father and thy mother.*
24. Luke 20:46-47 *Beware of the scribes, which desire to walk in long robes, and love greetings in the markets, and the highest seats in the synagogues, and the chief rooms at feasts; Which devour widows' houses, and for a show make long prayers: the same shall receive greater damnation.*
25. John 10:27-28 *My sheep hear my voice, and I know them, and they follow me: And I give unto them eternal life;*
26. Acts 17:31 *Because he hath appointed a day, in the which he will judge the world in righteousness by that man whom he hath ordained; whereof he hath given assurance unto all men, in that he hath raised him from the dead.*
27. Acts 24:15 *And have hope toward God, which they themselves also allow, that there shall be a resurrection of the dead, both of the just and unjust.*

Pauline Epistles
28. Rom. 2:5-7 *But after thy hardness and impenitent heart treasurest up unto thyself wrath against the day of wrath and revelation of the righteous judgment of God; Who will render to every man according to his deeds: To them who by patient continuance in well doing seek for glory and honour and immortality, eternal life:*
29. Rom. 2:13-16 *For not the hearers of the law are just before God, but the doers of the law shall be justified. . . . In the day when God shall judge the secrets of men by Jesus Christ according to my gospel.*
30. Rom. 6:22-23 *But now being made free from sin, and become servants to God, ye have your fruit unto holiness, and the end everlasting life. For the wages of sin is death; but the gift of God is eternal life through Jesus Christ our Lord.*

Defending the Biblical Definition   215

31. I Cor. 6:9-10 *Know ye not that the unrighteous shall not inherit the kingdom of God? Be not deceived: neither fornicators, nor idolaters, nor adulterers, nor effeminate, nor abusers of themselves with mankind, Nor thieves, nor covetous, nor drunkards, nor revilers, nor extortioners, shall inherit the kingdom of God.*
32. Gal. 5:19-21 *Now the works of the flesh are manifest, which are these; Adultery, fornication, uncleanness, lasciviousness, Idolatry, witchcraft, hatred, variance, emulations, wrath, strife, seditions, heresies, Envyings, murders, drunkenness, revellings, and such like: of the which I tell you before, as I have also told you in time past, that they which do such things shall not inherit the kingdom of God.*
33. Eph. 5:5 *For this ye know, that no whoremonger, nor unclean person, nor covetous man, who is an idolater, hath any inheritance in the kingdom of Christ and of God.*
34. Phil. 3:17-19 *Brethren, be followers together of me, and mark them which walk so as ye have us for an ensample. (For many walk, of whom I have told you often, and now tell you even weeping, that they are the enemies of the cross of Christ: Whose end is destruction, whose God is their belly, and whose glory is in their shame, who mind earthly things.)*
35. Col. 3:5-6 *Mortify therefore your members which are upon the earth; fornication, uncleanness, inordinate affection, evil concupiscence, and covetousness, which is idolatry: For which things' sake the wrath of God cometh on the children of disobedience:*
36. II Th. 1:8-10 *In flaming fire taking vengeance on them that know not God, and that obey not the gospel of our Lord Jesus Christ: Who shall be punished with everlasting destruction from the presence of the Lord, and from the glory of his power; When he shall come to be glorified in his saints, and to be admired in all them that believe (because our testimony among you was believed) in that day.*

Hebrews and General Epistles
37. Heb. 6:8 *But that which beareth thorns and briers is rejected, and is nigh unto cursing; whose end is to be burned.*
38. Heb.10:26-27 *For if we sin wilfully after that we have received the*

knowledge of the truth, there remaineth no more sacrifice for sins, But a certain fearful looking for of judgment and fiery indignation, which shall devour the adversaries.

39. Heb. 12:14 *Follow peace with all men, and holiness, without which no man shall see the Lord:*
40. Ja. 1:12 *Blessed is the man that endureth temptation: for when he is tried, he shall receive the crown of life, which the Lord hath promised to them that love him.*
41. Ja. 5:9 *Grudge not one against another, brethren, lest ye be condemned: behold, the judge standeth before the door.*
42. I Pet. 4:17-18 *For the time is come that judgment must begin at the house of God: and if it first begin at us, what shall the end be of them that obey not the gospel of God? And if the righteous scarcely be saved, where shall the ungodly and the sinner appear?*
43. II Pet. 2:9 *The Lord knoweth how to deliver the godly out of temptations, and to reserve the unjust unto the day of judgment to be punished:*
44. I John 2:17 *And the world passeth away, and the lust thereof: but he that doeth the will of God abideth for ever.*
45. I John 3:15 *Whosoever hateth his brother is a murderer: and ye know that no murderer hath eternal life abiding in him.*
46. Jude 7 *Even as Sodom and Gomorrha, and the cities about them in like manner, giving themselves over to fornication, and going after strange flesh, are set forth for an example, suffering the vengeance of eternal fire.*
47. Jude 13 *Raging waves of the sea, foaming out their own shame; wandering stars, to whom is reserved the blackness of darkness for ever.*

Revelation

48. 2:5-7 *Remember therefore from whence thou art fallen, and repent, and do the first works; or else I will come unto thee quickly, and will remove thy candlestick out of his place, except thou repent. . . . To him that overcometh will I give to eat of the tree of life, which is in the*

midst of the paradise of God.
49. 2:10 *Be thou faithful unto death, and I will give thee a crown of life.*
50. 3:4-5 *Thou hast a few names even in Sardis which have not defiled their garments; and they shall walk with me in white: for they are worthy. He that overcometh, the same shall be clothed in white raiment; and I will not blot out his name out of the book of life, but I will confess his name before my Father, and before his angels.*
51. 14:12 *Here is the patience of the saints: here are they that keep the commandments of God, and the faith of Jesus.*
52. 21:8 *But the fearful, and unbelieving, and the abominable, and murderers, and whoremongers, and sorcerers, and idolaters, and all liars, shall have their part in the lake which burneth with fire and brimstone: which is the second death.*
53. 21:27 *And there shall in no wise enter into it any thing that defileth, neither whatsoever worketh abomination, or maketh a lie: but they which are written in the Lamb's book of life.*
54. 22:11 *He that is unjust, let him be unjust still: and he which is filthy, let him be filthy still: and he that is righteous, let him be righteous still: and he that is holy, let him be holy still.*
55. 22:14-15 *Blessed are they that do his commandments, that they may have right to the tree of life, and may enter in through the gates into the city. For without are dogs, and sorcerers, and whoremongers, and murderers, and idolaters, and whosoever loveth and maketh a lie.*
56. 22:18-19 *For I testify unto every man that heareth the words of the prophecy of this book, If any man shall add unto these things, God shall add unto him the plagues that are written in this book: And if any man shall take away from the words of the book of this prophecy, God shall take away his part out of the book of life, and out of the holy city, and from the things which are written in this book.*

Bibliography

Aquinas, Thomas *The Summa Theologica of Thomas Aquinas.* Accessed April 7, 2023. https://www.ccel.org/ccel/aquinas/summa.FS_Q74_A2.html.

Archelaus. "The Acts of the Disputation with the Heresiarch Manes," *Fathers of the Third Century: Gregory Thaumaturgus, Dionysius the Great, Julius Africanus, Anatolius and Minor Writers, Methodius, Arnobius,* ed. Alexander Roberts, James Donaldson, and A. Cleveland Coxe, trans. S. D. F. Salmond, Vol. 6, *The Ante-Nicene Fathers.* Buffalo, NY: Christian Literature Company, 1886.

Arminius, James. *The Works of James Arminius.* 1550–1609. N.p.: Library of Alexandria. Kindle edition. Https://a.co/gJELp7Y.

Ambrose of Milan. "On the Duties of the Clergy" in *St. Ambrose: Select Works and Letters,* Edited by Philip Schaff and Henry Wace, Translated by H. de Romestin, E. de Romestin, and H. T. F. Duckworth, Vol. 10, *A Select Library of the Nicene and Post-Nicene Fathers of the Christian Church,* 2nd Series. New York: Christian Literature Company, 1896.

Augustine. *Against the Epistle of Manichaeus.* Translated by Richard Stothert. https://ccel.org/ccel/schaff/npnf104/npnf104.iv.viii.i.html.

Augustine. *Of True Religion.* Chicago: Henry Regenery Company, 1964.

Barnes. Albert. *Barnes Notes on the New Testament.* Grand Rapids: Kregel Publications, 1962.

Barrett, Matthew. ed. *Reformation Theology,* quoted by Maas, Korey D. Wheaton, IL: Crossway, 2017.

Bates, Matthew W., "The external-relational shift in faith (pistis) in New Testament research: Romans 1 as Gospel-allegiance test case." *Currents in Biblical Research* 18, no. 2 (2020): 176-202.

Battle, John. *The Present Indicative in New Testament Exegesis.* N.p.: Grace Theological Seminary, 1975. https://docest.com/the-present-indicative-in-new-testament-exegesis.

Bavinck, Herman. *Reformed Dogmatics: Sin and Salvation in Christ.* Vol. 3. https://www.scribd.com/read/267768284/Reformed-Dogmatics-Volume-3-Sin-and-Salvation-in-Christ.

Bennet, John. ed. *Minutes of the 1744 Conference.* https://archive.org/details/johnbenets00unknuoft/page/8/mode/2up.

Bercot, David W. ed. *A Dictionary of Early Christian Beliefs: A Reference Guide to More than 700 Topics Discussed by the Early Church Fathers.* Peabody, MA: Hendrickson Publishers, 1998.

Black, Caleb. *What About Sin.* Middleburg,PA: N.p. 2021.

Blevins, Dean G. et al. ed. *Church of the Nazarene: Manual, 2017–2021.* Kansas City, MO: Nazarene Publishing House, 2017.

https://2017.manual.nazarene.org/section/church-constitution/.
Bray, Gerald. *God has Spoken: A History of Christian Theology*. United States: Crossway, 2014.
Bray, Gerald L. and Oden, Thomas C. Oden. eds. *James, 1-2 Peter, 1-3 John, Jude*. N.p.: InterVarsity Press, 2014.
Brengle, Samuel L. *Heart-Talks on Holiness*. Atlanta, GA: Chicago, IL; New York, NY; San Francisco, CA: The Salvation Army, 1949.
Brengle, Samuel L. *Helps to Holiness*, Special Ed. London; Glasgow: Salvationist Publishing and Supplies, Ltd., n.d.
Brengle, Samuel L. *The Guest of the Soul*. https://onlinechristianlibrary.com/wp-content/uploads/2019/05/the-guest-of-the-soul.pdf.
Brooke, E. *A Critical and Exegetical Commentary on the Johannine Epistles. The International Critical Commentary*. Edinburgh: N.p. 1914.
Brown, Irwin L. *Further Insights into Holiness*, ed. Kenneth Geiger. Salem, OH: Schmul Publishing Co. Inc., 1990.
Buist, M. *Verbal Aspect in New Testament Greek*. Oxford: Clarendon Press, 1990.
Calvin, John. *Calvin's Commentaries*. Assessed July 10, 2023. https://biblehub.com/commentaries/calvin/1_john/3.htm.
Calvin, John. *Institutes of the Christian Religion*, 1559 ed., Trans. Henry Beverage, Book 3, Chap. 2, Sec. 11. https://ccel.org/ccel/calvin/institutes/institutes.v.iii.html.
Chambers, Oswald. *My Utmost for His Highest: Selections for the Year*. Grand Rapids, MI: Oswald Chambers Publications; Marshall Pickering, 1986.
Chapman, James Blaine. *Holiness Triumphant, and Other Sermons on Holiness*. Kansas City: Beacon Hill Press 1946. https://a.co/2rZc2J1.
Chryosotom, John. *Homily 11, On Romans*. Accessed June 24. http://www.newadvent.org/fathers/210211.htm.
Clarke, Adam and Dunn, Samuel. *Christian Theology*. 2nd ed. Salem, OH: Convention Book Store, 1967.
Clarke, Adam. *Clarkes Commentary*, Vols. I-VI, New York: Abingdon Press, n.d.
Croy, N. Clayton, *A Primer of Biblical Greek*. Grand Rapids: William B. Eerdmans Publishing Company, 1999.
Clement I. et al. *The Apostolic Fathers*. ed. Kirsopp Lake. Vol. 2. *The Loeb Classical Library*. Cambridge MA: Harvard University Press, 1912–1913.
Clement of Alexandria. *Ante-Nicene Fathers*. Vol. 2. *The Master Christian Library*. Version 5. CD-ROM (Albany, OR: Ages Software, 1997.
Constable, Thomas. *Notes on 1 John, 2022* ed. Sonic Light.com, 2022. https://www.planobiblechapel.org/tcon/notes/html/nt/1john/1john.htm.
Copland, Steve. *An Introduction to Practical Systematic Theology: Reclaiming the Doctrine of the Early Church*. N.p.:Smashwords, 2021. Kindle Edition.
Council of Carthage. Accessed July 10, 2023. http://www.newadvent.org/fathers/3816.htm.
Cox, Leo George. *John Wesley's Concept of Sin*. Salem, OH: Schmul Publishing Company, 2002.

Cyril of Jerusalem. "The Catechetical Lectures of S. Cyril, Archbishop of Jerusalem," *S. Cyril of Jerusalem, S. Gregory Nazianzen*, ed. Philip Schaff and Henry Wace, trans. R. W. Church and Edwin Hamilton Gifford, Vol. 7. A *Select Library of the Nicene and Post-Nicene Fathers of the Christian Church*, 2nd. Series. New York: Christian Literature Company, 1894.

Dayton, James R., Jr. *Getting the Reformation Wrong*. Downers Grove, IL: IVP Academic, 2010.

Derickson, Gary W. *First, Second, and Third John*, ed. H. Wayne House, W. Hall Harris III, and Andrew W. Pitts, *Evangelical Exegetical Commentary*. N.p.:Lexham Press, 2012.

Discipline of the Bible Methodist Connection of Churches, N.p.: The General Conference, 2018. https://www.biblemethodist.org/wp-content/uploads/2019/06/2018-Bible-Methodist-Discipline-rev.-2.pdf. 15.

Dunning H. Ray. *Grace, Faith, and Holiness: A Wesleyan Systematic Theology*. Kansas City: Beacon Hill Press of Kansas City, 1988.

Enns, Paul. *The Moody Handbook of Theology*. Chicago: Moody Publishers, 2008.

Ferguson, Everett. ed. *Encyclopedia of early Christianity*. N.p.:Routledge, 2013.

Findlay, George. *Fellowship in the Life Eternal: An Exposition of the Epistles of St. John*. London: Hodder and Stoughton, 1909.

Fletcher, John William. *The Works of the Reverend John Fletcher*, New York: B. Waugh and T. Mason, 1833.

Flew, R. Newton. *The Idea of Perfection in Christian Theology*. Wipf and Stock Publishers, 2005.

Foster, R. S. *Christian Purity*. http://wesley.nnu.edu/wesleyctr/books/0401-0500/HDM0497.

Gamertsfelder, Solomon J. *Systematic Theology*. Harrisburg, PA: Evangelical Pub. House, 1952.

Geisler, Norman, *Systematic Theology*. Minneapolis: Bethany House, 2004.

Godbey, William Baxter, *Commentary on the New Testament*. Cincinnati: Revivalist Office, 1897.

Godbey, W. B. *Holiness or Hell*. http://media.sabda.org/alkitab-6/wh2-hdm/hdm0394.pdf.

Gray, Albert F. *Christian Theology*. N.p.: James L. Fleming, 1944; 2005.

Guide to Holiness 76 (1885): 27-28. Quoted in Randy Maddox, "Reconnecting the Means to the End: A Wesleyan Prescription for the Holiness Movement." *Wesleyan Theological Journal*. 33 no. 2 (1998): 29–66.

Gundry, Stanley N. ed. *Five Views on Sanctification*. Grand Rapids: Zondervan Publishing House, 1987.

Harford, Charles F. ed. *The Keswick Convention: Its Message, Its Method, and its Men*. Reprint, www.alphaedi.com: Alpha Editions, 2020.

Henry, Matthew. *The Bethany Parallel Commentary on the New Testament; Matthew Henry's Commentary.* Minneapolis: Bethany House Publishers, 1983.

Hills, Aaron M. *Fundamental Christian Theology.* http://wesley.nnu.edu/wesleyctr/books/2201-2300/HDM2260.pdf.

Hills, Aaron M. *Holiness and Power.* https://archive.org/details/holinesspowerfor00hill/page/10. Digital.

Hills, Aaron M. *Scriptural Holiness and Keswick Teaching Compared.* Nicholasville, KY: Schmul Publishing Co., 2020.

Hood, Ralph W. Jr., Hill, Peter C., and Williamson, W. Paul. *The Psychology of Religious Fundamentalism.* New York: The Guilford Press, 2005.

Hotle, Marlin. *In Search of Sanctification.* Salem, OH: Schmul Publishing Company, Inc., 1991.

Ignatius. *The Epistle of Ignatius to the Ephesians.* https://www.newadvent.org/fathers/0104.htm .

Ignatius. *Epistle to the Tarsians.* https://www.newadvent.org/fathers/0114.htm.

InterChurch Holiness Convention. *Questions and Answers.* Accessed April 25, 2021. https://ihconvention.com/build-your-faith/questions-answers/.

Jamieson, Robert, Fausset Andrew, and Brown David. *The Bethany Parallel Commentary on the New Testament; The Jamieson, Fausset, and Brown Commentary.* Minneapolis: Bethany House Publishers, 1983.

Jerome. *Against Joviniaus.* https://www.newadvent.org/fathers/30092.htm.

Jones, Charles. *Perfectionist Persuasion.* Metuchen, NJ: The Scarecrow Press, Inc. 1974.

Justin Martyr. *Dialogue with Trypho.* Accessed 8/10/2023. https://www.newadvent.org/fathers/01283.htm.

Justin Martyr. *The Second Apology. The world preserved for the sake of Christians. Man's responsibility.* Accessed 8/10/2023. https://www.newadvent.org/fathers/0127.htm.

King, Peter. *An Inquiry Into the Constitution, Discipline, Unity, and Worship of the Primitive Church: That Flourished Within the First Three Hundred Years After Christ.* N.p.: Lane & Scott, 1851.

Kubo, Sakae. "I John 3:9: Absolute or Habitual?" Berrian Springs, MI: Andrews University. Accessed July 10, 2023. https://digitalcommons.andrews.edu/cgi/viewcontent.cgi?article=1106&context=auss.

Leclerc, Diane. *Discovering Christian Holiness.* Kansas City: Beacon Hill Press of Kansas City, 2010.

Longman, Tremper III and Garland, David E. eds. *The Expositor's Bible Commentary.* Grand Rapids: Zondervan, 2006.

Luther, Martin. *The 95 Thesis,* 1517. Https://www.luther.de/en/95/thesen.html.

Luther, Martin. *Luther's Works: The Catholic Epistles.* St Louis, MO: Concordia Publishing House 1967.

Marcarius, *Pseudo-Macarius: The Fifty Spiritual Homilies and the Great Letter*, Trans. George A. Maloney. New York: Paulist Press, 1992.

McGrath, Alister E. "John Henry Newman's Lectures on Justification: The High Church Misrepresentation of Luther." *Churchman* 97, no. 2 (1983): 112-122.

Metz, Donald. *Studies in Biblical Holiness*. Kansas City: Beacon Hill Press, 1971.

Miley, John. *Systematic Theology*. New York: Hunt & Eaton, 1892.

Moo, Douglas J. *Encountering the Book of Romans*. Grand Rapids: Baker Academic, 2002.

Mounce, William. *Basics of Biblical Greek*. Grand Rapids: Zondervan, 2009.

Mounce, William. Biblical Training .org.
https://www.biblicaltraining.org/library/greek-verbs/greek-tools-for-bible-study/william-mounce.

Mounce, William. "Mondays with Mounce.," "Can you not sin." September 28, 2008, https://www.billmounce.com/monday-with-mounce/can-you-not-sin-1-john-3-6.

Mounce, William. https://www.youtube.com/watch?v=7Ib4UxY7G8w. Youtube video.

Naselli, Andrew David. "Keswick Theology: A Survey and Analysis of the Doctrine of Sanctification in the Early Keswick Movement," *Detroit Baptist Seminary Journal*, no. 13 (2008): 17–67, https://andynaselli.com/wp-content/uploads/2008_Keswick_theology.

Nicholson, Roy S. *True Holiness: The Wesleyan Emphasis*. Salem, OH: Schmul Publishing Co. 2012 Reprint.

Ockenga, Harold J. *The Church of God*. Westwood, NJ: Fleming H. Revell Co., 1956.

Oden,Thomas C. *Doctrinal Standards in the Wesleyan Tradition*. Grand Rapids: Francis Asbury Press of Zondervan Publishing House, 1988.

Oden, Thomas C. *Life in the Spirit: Systematic Theology.* San Francisco: Harper SanFrancisco, 1992.

Olson, Roger E. *Arminian Theology: Myths and Realities*. Downers Grove, IL: InterVarsity Press, 2006.

Ord, Thomas Jay and Ord, Alexa. eds. *Why the Church of the Nazarene Should Be Fully LGBTQ+ Affirming* . N.p.:SacraSage Press, 2023.

Origen. ed. Lienhard, Joseph T.. "Homily 2.: Luke 1.6." *Homilies on Luke, 10–13*. Catholic University of America Press, 1996. Accessed June 12, 2023. https://doi.org/10.2307/j.ctt32b0dn.8.

Ortiz, Jared. *Catholic World Report* (November 25, 2019): https://www.catholicworldreport.com/2019/11/25/Augustine-consolation-after-rape-and –the-reshaping-of-society/.

Percival, Henry trans. *Nicene and Post-Nicene Fathers*, eds. Schaff, Philip and Wace, Henry. Buffalo, NY: Christian Literature Publishing Co., 1900. A. D. 419, ed. for New Advent by Knight, Kevin.
<http://www.newadvent.org/fathers/3816.htm>. Council of Carthage, "Canon

111."
Petrovich, Douglas. *The World's Oldest Alphabet.* Jerusalem: Carta Jerusalem, 2016. https://rosenhebrewschool.com/articles/paleo-hebrew-alphabet/.
Pope, William Burt. *A Compendium of Christian Theology: Being Analytical Outlines of a Course of Theological Study, Biblical, Dogmatic, Historical.* London: Beveridge and Co., 1879.
Pope, William Burt. *A Higher Catechism of Theology.* London: T. Woolmer, 1885.
Purkiser, Westlake Taylor. *Beliefs that Matter Most.* http://wesley.nnu.edu/wesleyctr/books/0301-0400/HDM0393.pdf.
Purkiser, Westlake Taylor. *Conflicting Concepts of Holiness.* Kansas City: Beacon Hill Press, 1964.
Rainbow, Paul A. *The Way of Salvation.* Eugene, Oregon: Wipf &Stock, 2005.
Raymond, Miner. *Systematic Theology.* Cincinnati; New York: Hitchcock & Walden; Nelson and Phillips, 1877.
Reasoner, Vic, *Fundamental Wesleyan Systematic Theology.* Evansville:IN, 2021.
Sanders, Ed Parish. *Paul: The Apostle's Life, Letters, and Thought.* Minneapolis: Fortress Press, 2015.
Roberts, Alexander, James Donaldson, and Cleveland Coxe, eds. *Ante-Nicene Fathers.* Buffalo, NY: Christian Literature Publishing Co., 1885. Revised and edited for New Advent by Knight, Kevin. http://www.newadvent.org/fathers/0308.htm>.
Roberts, Alexander, James Donaldson, and Cleveland Coxe, eds. *Fathers of the Third Century: Tertullian, Part Fourth; Minucius Felix; Commodian; Origen, Parts First and Second.* Vol. 4. The Ante-Nicene Fathers. Buffalo, NY: Christian Literature Company, 1885.
Ross, Thomas, "William Boardman: Higher Life, Keswick, and Faith Cure Pioneer." *Faith Saves,* 2014. https://faithsaves.net/william-boardman/.
Ross, Thomas, "Keswick or Higher Life roots of the Pentecostal / Charismatic Movements; Biblical, Baptist, Cessationist Sanctification vs. the Continuationist Second Blessing." *Faith Saves,* 2014, https://faithsaves.net/sanctification-baptist-higher-life-3/.
Shaw, S. B. *Echoes of the General Holiness Assembly.* http://wesley.nnu.edu/wesleyctr/books/0301-0400/HDM0372.pdf.
Smith, David. "The Epistles of John." *The Expositor's Greek Testament.* Grand Rapids: N.p., 1956.
Smith, David L. *With Willful Intent: A Theology of Sin.* Wipf and Stock Publishers, 2003.
Smith F.G. *What the Bible Teaches.* Condensed ed. Anderson, IN: Warner Press, 1955.
Steele, Daniel. *Love Enthroned.* Accessed July 10, 2023. http://wesley.nnu.edu/wesleyctr/books/1801-1900/HDM1892.pdf.
Steele, Daniel. *Half-Hours with St. John's Epistles.* Boston; Chicago: Christian Witness Company, 1901.

Steele, Daniel. *Milestone Papers.* http://wesley.nnu.edu/wesleyctr/books/0101-0200/HDM0161.pdf.
Synan, Vinson. *The Holiness–Pentecostal Movement.* Grand Rapids: William B. Eerdmans Publishing Co.,1971.
Tatian. *Address to the Greeks.* https://www.logoslibrary.org/tatian/address/07.html.
Taylor, Richard S. *A Right Conception of Sin.* Kansas City: Beacon Hill Press of Kansas City, 1945.
Taylor, Richard S. *A Right Conception of Sin: Revised and Enlarged.* Salem, OH: Schmul Publishing Co., 2002.
Taylor, Richard S. ed. *Beacon Dictionary of Theology.* Kansas City: Beacon Hill Press of Kansas City, 1983.
Taylor, Richard S. *Counterpoint: Dialogue with Drury on the Holiness Movement.* Schmul Publishing Co., 2005.
Taylor, Richard S. *God, Man & Salvation.* Kansas City: Beacon Hill Press, 1977.
The Complete Works of the Church Fathers: A total of 64 authors, and over 2,500 works of the Early Christian Church (Kindle Locations 116398-116399). Amazon.com. Kindle Edition.
The Theologians of Methodism. Reprint. Salem OH: 1992.
Thompson,W. Ralph. "An Appraisal of the Keswick and Wesleyan Contemporary Positions" *Wesleyan Theological Journal*, vol. 01 (Spring 1966).
Thornton,Wallace. *Radical Richteousness.* Schmul Publishing: Salem, OH, 1998.
Tozer A. W. *That Incredible Christian.* Harrisburg, PA: Christian Publications Inc., 1964.
Truesdale, Al. *Sin* . Kansas City: The Foundry Publishing, 2022.
Tyson, John R. "H. Orton Wiley," ed. Walter A. Elwell, *Handbook of Evangelical Theologians.* Grand Rapids: Baker Book House, 1998.
Wakefield, Samuel. *A Complete System of Christian Theology: A Concise, Comprehensive, and Systematic View of the Evidences, Doctrines, Morals and Institutions of Christianity* . N.p.: WORDsearch, 2000.
Wallace, Daniel. *Greek Grammar: Beyond the Basics.* Grand Rapids: Zondervan, 1996.
Wallace, O. C. S. *What Baptists Believe.* 1913, Reprint, Piqua, OH: Calvary Baptist Church, 2000.
Watson, Richard. *Theological Institutes: Or, a View of the Evidences, Doctrines, Morals, and Institutions of Christianity.* Nashville, TN: E. Stevenson; F. A. Owen, Agents, 1857.
Westcott, B. F. *The Epistles of St. John.* Cambridge, 1892.
Wesley, John. *The Basics of the Theology of John Wesley.* Edited by Nicholas Black. Middleburg, PA: N.p. 2021.
Wesley, John. *Notes on the Bible.* Accessed 6-27-2023. http://wesley.nnu.edu/john-wesley/john-wesleys-notes-on-the-bible/notes-on-st-pauls-epistle-to-titus/.

Wesley, John. *Wesley's 52 Standard Sermons.* Reprint, Salem, OH: Schmul Publishing Co., 1982.

Wesley, John, *The Works of John Wesley.* London: Wesleyan Methodist Book room, 1872.

Wesleyan Holiness Association of Churches. *Manual of the Wesleyan Holiness Association of Churches.*

Westminister Larger Catechism. Assembly at Edinburgh, 1648. https://prts.edu/wp-content/uploads/2013/09/Larger_Catechism.pdf.

Wiggers, G. F. *An Historical Presentation of Augustinism and Pelagianism .* From the Original Sources (Kindle Locations 2383-2384). Kindle Edition.

Wilcox Leslie D. *Be Ye Holy.* Cincinnati Ohio: Revivalist Press., 1977.

Wilcox, Leslie D. *Profiles in Wesleyan Theology.* Salem, OH: Schmul Pub., 1983.

Wiley H. Orton. *Christian Theology.* Kansas City: Beacon Hill Press of Kansas City, 1940–1952.

Wiley, H. Orton. *Epistle to the Hebrews.* Accessed July 10, 2023, http://wesley.nnu.edu/wesleyctr/books/3201-3300/HDM3275.pdf.

Wiley, H. Orton. *God has the Answer.* Accessed July 10, 2023, http://wesley.nnu.edu/holiness-classics-library/?rows=30&search=author&search_value=wiley.

Wiley, H. O. & Culbertson, P. T. *Introduction to Christian Theology* (Kansas City: Beacon Hill Press of Kansas City, 1946), 162–163.

Willis, John Randolph. ed. *The Teachings of the Church Fathers.* San Francisco: Ignatius Press, 2002. P. 233.

Willoughby, C. Allen. *A Critical and Exegetical Commentary on the Gospel according to S. Matthew; International Critical Commentary.* New York: C. Scribner's Sons, 1907.

Wishart, David Torrance. ed. *John 11-21 and I John.* Grand Rapids: Eerdmans, 1994.

Wood J. A. *Perfect Love .* Accessed July 10, 2023, http://wesley.nnu.edu/wesleyctr/books/0101-0200/HDM0181.pdf.

Wynkoop, Mildred Bangs. *A Theology of Love.* Kansas City: Beacon Hill Press of Kansas City, 1972.

Wynkoop, Mildred Bangs. *Foundations of Wesleyan Arminian Theology.* Kansas City: Beacon Hill Press, 1967.

Yarborough, Robert W. "Lecture 10: The first Epistle of John.," The Masters Seminary. Accessed July 10, 2023, https://www.youtube.com/watch?v=2vSrO0-esjs&feature=youtu.be.

Yocum, Dale. *The Holy Way.* Schmul Publishing Co, Salem Ohio, 1981.

Yocum, Dale. *Trumpets in Zion.* Hobe Sound Florida: H. S. B. C. Press,N.d..

Index

Adikia, 65
Adam, 2, 11, 12, 41, 44, 69, 70, 82, 103, 104, 127, 141, 158, 174, 175, 202
Age of accountability, 71, 87, 88
Anabaptists, 47
Anglicans, 47, 171
Anomia, 65, 66
Aquinas, Thomas, 7, 136
Ambrose of Milan, 135, 138
Apostolic Constitutions, 138
Arminians, 47, 80, 153, 207
Arminius, James, 33, 34, 59, 78, 81
Athenagoras, 137
Augustine, Saint, 5, 7, 35, 75, 76, 135, 138
Babcock, William S. 131
Backsliding, 38, 39, 49, 52, 57, 133, 145, 148. 152, 154
Baptists, 47, 52, 59, 131
Barnes, Albert, 67, 111, 116
Bassett, Paul, 133
Bates, Matthew W., 25, 37
Battle, John, 192
Bavinck, Herman, 131
Bercot, David W., 138, 205
Bible Knowledge Commentary, 179
Bible Methodist Discipline, 76, 77, 156
Black, Caleb, 157
Boardman, William E., 94
Bray, Gerald E., 132, 137, 138, 139
Brengle, Samuel Logan, 147
Brown, Irwin L., 75
Buist, M, 189
Bunyan, John, 38
Calvin, John, 7, 30, 48, 49, 50, 54, 85, 133, 177, 194
Carmichael, Amy, 96
Chapman, James B., 2
Chambers, Oswald, 149
Church of the Nazarene, 1, 7, 77, 150, 155, 159
Clarke, Adam, 37, 81, 82, 110, 111, 142, 143
Clement of Alexandria, 134, 159
Consciences which are oversensitive, 23, 24
Consequences of sin, 12, 89, 90
Constable, Thomas, 80, 185, 194, 195

Copland, Steve, 131
Council of Carthage, 136
Cox, George Leo, 140
Cyril of Jerusalem, 135
Dayton, James R., 24
Derickson, Gary W., 65, 122
DeYoung, Kevin, 54
Didymus the Blind, 137
Diospolis, Council of, 138
Dunning, H. Ray, 59, 103
Encyclopedia of Early Christianity, 131
Enns, Paul, 62, 85
Eradication, 35, 60, 93, 100, 101, 102, 103, 161, 162
Eternal Security, 2, 3, 4, 23, 28, 54, 55, 56, 57, 99, 100, 179
Evangelical Arminian, 31, 58, 59, 60, 61
Exell, Joseph S., 66
Expositors Bible Commentary, 109, 189, 190
Faults and infirmities, 7, 22, 23, 35, 44, 59, 77, 87, 91, 155, 156, 171, 208, 209
Finney, Charles, 58, 94
First General Holiness Assembly, 161, 162
Fletcher, John 141, 142
Flew, R. Newton, 137
Foster, R.S., 146
Free-grace theology, 31, 53-58, 61, 100, 167, 176, 179, 180
Gamertsfelder, S.J., 146
Geisler, Norman, 8, 75, 85
Godbey, William Baxter, 45, 67, 148
Gray, Albert, 149
Graham, Billy, 96
Greathouse, William, 113
Gundry, Stanley M., 93, 99, 100, 101
Hamartano, 9, 64, 66, 71, 83
Harford-Battersby, Canon, 95
Harford, Charles F., 93, 96, 98, 99
Henry, Matthew, 111, 117
Herron, S.D., 155
Hills, Aaron Merritt, 99, 150
Hodge, Charles, 75
Hodges, Zane, 80
Homosexuals, 38, 61, 105, 165
Hood, Ralph, 5
Hotle, Marlin, 99
Ignatius, 136
Ignorance, 44, 50, 59, 62, 70, 71, 75, 85, 87, 88 89, 128, 130
Impartation of righteousness, 28, 84, 101, 167
Imputation of righteousness, 5, 28, 47, 83, 84, 101, 166, 167
Incarnation, 9, 169, 170-173
Inskip, John, 94
InterChurch Holiness Convention, 77, 156

International Critical Commentary, 206
Jamieson, Robert, Andrew Fausset, and Brown, David, 117
Jerome, 133, 138
John Chrysostom, 138
Jones, Charles, 157
Jones, Martin Lloyd, 54
Justification, 49, 36, 55
Justin Martyr, 134, 136
Keswick, 26, 59, 93-101
King, Lord Peter, 137
Kubo, Sake, 80, 190, 203
law natural, 69, 78, 127-129
Law of Christ, 28, 32, 35, 41, 43, 44, 47, 121, 142
Leclerc, Diane, 60, 103, 105
Luther, Martin, 23, 36, 48, 49, 176, 194
Lutheran, 23, 47, 48, 78
Mahan, Asa, 94
Marcarius 159, 160
McGrath, Alister E. 49
McQuilkin, J. Robertson, 93
Melanchthon, 78
Methodius, 135
Metz, Donald, 1, 166, 168
Meyer, F. B., 96
Miley, John, 145, 146
Moo, Douglas, 199
Moody, Dwight L., 58, 94, 96
Mosaic law, 42, 43, 44, 46, 65, 69, 70, 78, 90, 91
Mounce, William, 80, 188, 191, 195
Murray, Andrew, 96
Naselli, Andrew David, 93, 98
National Holiness Association, 154, 155
Nehemiah, 37
Neo-Calvinism, 51, 52, 61
Neo-Wesleyan, 60, 61
New Covenant, 10, 32, 41, 42, 43, 45, 46, 78, 82, 90, 91, 129, 130
Nicholson, Roy S., 81
Noble, T. A., 88
Obedience, 40
Oberlin College, 94
Oden, Thomas C., 79, 137, 138, 139, 142
Ockenga, Harold J., 63
Olson, Roger E., 87
Ord, Thomas, Jay, 105
Origen, 134, 137, 204
Ortiz, Jared, 76
Palmer, Phoebe 94
Paraptoma, 66

Pelagian doctrine, 33, 103
Pelikan, Jaroslav, 132,
Pentecostals, 59, 171
Petrovich, Douglas, 129
Perfection, 44, 64, 70, 76, 81, 84, 86, 92, 96, 97, 99, 147, 162
Pistis, 37
Pope, William Burt, 145
Postmodern, 4, 102
Predestination, 5, 6, 24, 29, 30, 31, 34, 47, 51, 59, 80, 163, 167, 178
Presbyterian, 47
Pope, William Burt, 80
Puritan, 47
Purkiser, Westlake Taylor, 1, 71, 72, 75, 151, 152
Rainbow, Paul, 55
Ralston, Thomas, 144
Raymond, Minor, 144
Reasoner, Vic, 54
Reese, David G. 113
Relational theology, 59, 60, 61, 102-106
Repentance, 26, 29, 31, 34, 35, 36, 48, 56, 60, 117, 140, 156, 157, 205
Ruth, C.W., 157
Schmul, H.E., 155
Severus of Antioch, 139
Shaw, S.B., 157
Sheldon, D. N., 66
Shephard of Hermas, 134
Simpson, A. B., 96
Sin Original, 62, 92, 93, 100, 102, 158-163
Sinlessness, 11, 17, 40, 50, 56, 63, 80, 82, 86, 100, 107-126, 133, 136-139, 146, 148, 149, 169, 170, 185
Smith, David L., 131
Smith, Hannah Whitall, 94
Smith, Robert Pearsall, 94, 95
Stanley, Charles, 55
Steele, Daniel, 7, 8, 79, 81, 147
Strong, James, 66
Struggling Christians, 20, 21
Synod of Africa Council (418), 139
Tatian, 134
Taylor, Hudson, 96
Taylor, Richard S., 6, 23, 42, 60, 103, 152, 153, 164, 170
Temptation, 3, 20, 21, 22, 38, 53, 162, 171, 172, 206, 216
Tertullian, 128, 137
Testing the definitions, 13, 71
Thompson, Ralph W., 93, 98
Torrey, R. A., 58
Torrance, David Wishart, 49
Truesdale, Al, 103, 104, 159
Victory, 11, 12, 14, 15, 16, 18, 21, 22, 25, 26, 35, 58, 60, 63, 74, 91, 93, 94, 96, 97, 98, 122,

125, 168, 173, 181, 190, 199
Wakefield, Samuel, 144
Wallace, Daniel, 80, 189, 196
Wallace, O. C. S., 52
Walvoord, John, 100
Watson, Richard, 143
Wesleyan Holiness Association of Churches, 156
Wesley, John, 1, 5, 6, 7, 33, 34, 35, 44, 60, 61, 76, 77, 80, 82, 86, 92, 107, 109, 110, 115, 118, 123, 132, 133, 140, 141, 159, 183, 186, 187
Wescott, B.F., 203
Westminister Catechism, 86, 87
Wiggers, G.F., 138
Wilcox, Leslie, 153, 154, 155, 157
Wiley, H. Orton, 37, 82, 150, 151
Willis John Randolph, 131
Wilson, Robert, 95
Wood, J.A., 148
Wynkoop, Mildred Bangs, 59, 60, 81, 102, 103
Yarborough, Robert W., 192
Yocum, Dale, 153
Zwingli, Ulrich, 87, 88

Made in United States
Orlando, FL
21 February 2024